INSULT TO INJURY

Ray Bourhis and Matthew Bourhis

INSULT to INJURY

Insurance, Fraud, and the Big Business of Bad Faith

Second Edition

BRITTANY PRESS

Brittany Press
http://www.brittany-press.com

Printed in the United States of America

Ordering Information
Quantity sales. Special discounts are available on quantity purchases by corporations, associations, and others. For details, contact info@Brittany-Press.com.

Orders by US trade bookstores and wholesalers. Please contact BCH: (800) 431-1579 or visit http://www.bookch.com for details.

Library of Congress Cataloging-in-Publication Data

Names: Bourhis, Ray, author. | Bourhis, Matthew, author.
Title: Insult to injury : insurance , fraud, and the big business of bad faith , second edition / Ray Bourhis and Matthew Bourhis.
Description: Includes bibliographical references and index. | San Francisco, CA: Brittany Press, 2021.
Identifiers: LCCN: 2021910695 | ISBN: 978-1-7367918-0-6
Subjects: LCSH UnumProvident Company (Chattanooga, Tenn.)--Trials, litigation, etc. | Tort liability of insurance companies--United States. | Disability insurance claims--United States. | Bad faith (Law)--United States. | Insurance companies--Corrupt practices--United States. | BISAC BUSINESS & ECONOMICS / Insurance / General
Classification: LCC KF1301.5.I58 B68 2021 | DDC 345.73/0263--dc23

Second Edition

25 24 23 22 21   10 9 8 7 6 5 4 3 2 1

To my parents, Frank and Louise, who taught me a lesson about insurance companies that I will never forget, and to my children, Danielle, Matthew, Bobby, and Andrew, who inspire the best aspects of everything in everyone they meet.

–Ray

To my father and all our clients, for sharing your knowledge and dedication to justice with me. And to Ann Marie Do, without whom I would never be able to carry the baton forward.

–Matthew

CONTENTS

ACKNOWLEDGMENTS

A NUMBER OF VERY TALENTED AND SPECIAL PEOPLE HAVE DEVOTED enormous effort toward going after insurance companies when their drive to increase profits obscures their duty to policyholders and to the general public.

In particular we would like to recognize Sharon Arkin, Amy Bach, Mike Bidart, Alan Casper, Terry Coleman, Frank Darras, Doug DeVries, Ken Friedman, Rick Friedman, Lee Harris, Stan Jacobs, Richard Langerman, Arnie Levinson, Gerry Mannion, Suzanne McCafferty, Jeff Metzger, Phil Pillsbury, Mark Quigley, Jeff Rubin, Bob Scott, Bill Shernoff, Charles Surrano, and Frank Winkles.

We owe a debt of gratitude to many individuals who patiently read through the manuscript and made many thoughtful suggestions and corrections. These include Peter Scheer, Larry Kaplan, Moira Buxbaum, Sheila Murphy Betta, Mary Martin, Ivory Madison, Crissie Dondero, Dr. Liz Ellen LaFollette, Peter Horn, and Danielle Lawless Bourhis.

NOTE TO READERS

THIS BOOK WAS FIRST PUBLISHED IN 2005. AT THAT TIME MY son Matthew was still in high school and I did not have the slightest idea that he would someday go to law school and join me in my insurance litigation practice in San Francisco. Today, I am so honored to be practicing with him, teaching him a few of the ropes I have picked up over the years, and learning from him every day of my life.

The updates in chapter 16 were written by Matthew and involve many cases that have been handled by him and that carry forward the tradition that led me to the work we now both do. Our hope is to contribute toward moving our profession and our system in a direction that helps those it was intended to serve.

Insult to Injury is based on hundreds of hours of deposition and trial testimony and on thousands of pages of documents, memos, and files, as well as on conversations. We have made every effort to present these records and conversations accurately. In order to present a readable narrative of the events, we took minor liberties with the text that did not change the gist of the testimony or content. References are provided in the endnotes to allow interested readers to pursue these subjects in more depth. With the exception of a few instances involving individuals who have been required to sign confidentiality provisions in settlement agreements—in one case involving a doctor who is now deceased and in another involving a patient of Dr. Hangarter's, for example—names used in the text are accurate.

March 2021

JOAN HANGARTER'S NOTE

M Y EXPERIENCE WITH INSURANCE COMPANIES SHOWS HOW OUT of control large corporations are in our society. They have the money, the lawyers, the PR firms, the lobbyists, and the friends in high places to be able to get away with just about whatever they want. The rest of us have just a piece of paper with a promise on it–a promise that can prove worthless if the insurer chooses not to honor it. I hope you find this story useful in fighting your own battles to get your rightful benefits.

Joan Hangarter

INTRODUCTION:
CORPORATE AMERICA

O NE SCHOOL OF THOUGHT HOLDS THAT LAWYERS SHOULD BE ABOVE the fray, maintaining an almost clinical detachment from their cases–that they should be dispassionate. But that is not what we believe. The growing element of corporate America that knowingly sells products that maim and kill, that creates dangerous blackouts through artificial energy crises, that uses fraudulent tactics to steal retirement benefits from employees, that deploys lobbyists to buy votes and neutralize regulators, and that reduces ethical consider-ations to a cost-benefit analysis should not lead to a clinical detach-ment. To the contrary, it should produce a sense of outrage.

Many CEOs believe that their companies' principal responsibil-ity is to the shareholders, that their duty is to make as much money as possible, and that this is simply our system. But you know what? That is not our system. Our system is spelled out in our Constitution, and our Constitution says nothing about profits. The word you find in the Constitution is "people." We are a nation of, by, and for people. Not a nation of, by, and for profits.

Nothing is inherently evil about profits, but they are not supposed to be made by lying, cheating, and defrauding people–by destroying their lives. Unfortunately, the conscience of our nation has shifted in such a way that tends to reward such conduct at the expense of ordi-nary individuals. It is a perverse system that emanates from corporate America and has been defended zealously in every court and lobbied for aggressively with every governmental entity in the country.

As comprehensive as the training is, law school doesn't prepare you for the world of litigation. A savvy insurance company with its battalions of lawyers can run a young practitioner into the ground. Demurs, motions, interrogatories, subpoenas, marathon depositions, double and triple teaming, more motions, continuances–all of these are time-consuming and very expensive. The same insurer that will scrimp to save fifty cents when defending a policyholder in a lawsuit filed against him or her will spend whatever it takes to fight off a bad-faith suit against itself.

∧ ∨ ∧ ∨ ∧

GORDON GEKKO CLAIMED THAT "GREED IS GOOD" AND IT WAS "JUST A part of capitalism."

Back in the sixties it was Ken Lay and Bernie Ebbers, Dennis Koslowski and Frank Quattrone, Andrew Fastow and John Rigas. It seemed like you couldn't pick up a newspaper without reading about some bigwig from a Fortune 500 securities organization, chemical company, investment bank, accounting firm, energy conglomerate, product manufacturer, pharmaceutical corporation, clothing retailer, or defense contractor who had cheated, defrauded, bribed, or stolen every dime he could get his corrupt, greedy hands on.

Today, you can add Ivan Boesky, and Raj Rajaratnam, Bernie Madoff, and Michael Milken. And these guys are just the top layer: the Oscar winners, the best in show, the crookedest of the crooks.

This isn't a little deal anymore. Corporate hotshots aren't stealing thousands and hundreds of thousands of dollars; its millions and hundreds of millions. And they're not stealing from the rich and giving to the poor. They're stealing from the poor and stuffing it into their tailored pockets. Guys are doing thirty to life for a simple bank robbery while the real crooks are going to political fund-raisers and swapping rooster jokes with the leader of the free world. Sometimes it seems as though everybody who's anybody must be doing it, prowling relentlessly for the fast buck.

Given this climate, it shouldn't surprise anyone that an industry as large as insurance–in the United States alone, we spend more than $2,000 for every man, woman, and child per year on premiums–would be ripe for criminal misconduct in the name of profit and greed.

Why are so many corporate role models stealing from their own customers and employees? How do they get away with it? Why do our institutions tolerate it? Can anything be done to stop it?

Read on. Perhaps a story about a company that used to give a "Hungry Vulture Award" (see Exhibit 1) to "deserving employees" can shed a little light on the dismal state of corporate America. Why? Because to paraphrase the most quoted man in the history of folk music, "You don't have to be an ornithologist to know a raptor when you see one."

INSULT TO INJURY

Chapter One

FALSE PROFITS

T HE WOMAN SEATED BEFORE ME HAD PAIN AND SADNESS ETCHED deeply into her face. Her eyes were dark and hollow; her gray-brown hair tired and stiff. The corners of her mouth were fixed in a dry frown. She had the look of a frightened, skittish animal, betrayed and immensely fragile. She appeared on the verge of lunging for the door, poised to make a run for it before uttering a word. Watching her as she fidgeted with the papers on her lap, struggling to maintain her composure, I felt an air of uneasy tension settling in between us.

A few years earlier, Joan Hangarter had everything going for her. She had a successful chiropractic practice; two great kids; a nice house in upscale and comfortable Novato in Marin County, California; a late-model car; and a relationship she saw as solid and lasting. Then one day in 1997, while she was performing a difficult lumbar manipulation on a patient, Joan felt a sudden ripping pain in her right forearm. The pain radiated up the arm to the base of her neck. She thought her condition would improve, but instead it worsened. Months later, following extensive testing, her doctors told her that her injuries were permanent and that she would no longer be able to perform the demanding maneuvers required in her work. She was devastated.

Joan may have made some bad decisions and lousy investments over the years, but there was one choice she had made that she believed would carry her through. Years before she had given in to a "won't take no" insurance saleswoman. "She was very insistent," Joan recalled. "She explained that the policy she was trying to sell me would keep a roof over my head if anything should ever happen that prevented me from continuing in my career.

"'You've studied and built your practice for years,' she told me. 'You have responsibilities. A mortgage. Big monthly expenses. Unexpected things happen in life. What would you do? Retrain? Start all over? Empty out your retirement account? Take some menial job for a fraction of what you're now earning?'

"She knew I was about to become a mother. How could I not protect my baby?"

Joan bought an "own-occupation" disability policy from the Paul Revere Life Insurance Company and, for almost a decade, dutifully paid the $3,000-a-year premium. Following her accident and diagnosis, Paul Revere investigated her claim, reviewed her medical records, and evaluated her condition. It concluded that she was disabled and began paying the monthly benefits.

Paul Revere continued to pay until after the company was swallowed up by its chief competitor, Provident. Suddenly, Joan's benefits were cut off.

I listened to her describe the downhill plunge of her life: how her injuries had prevented her from treating her patients; how she had been forced to sell her practice; how, following the termination of her benefits, she had lost almost everything; how her car had been repossessed and she and her children had been evicted from their home and driven into bankruptcy and onto welfare. I saw a defeated person, a woman who appeared to have little reason to live. But when I asked about her children, Joan's demeanor changed. She transformed into a proud mother, talking about Elana and Anton, their personalities, their hobbies, their school activities.

After talking to her about her history with Provident and about what had happened to her, I knew Joan had a good case. Unfortunately, good cases don't always go the plaintiff's way. I wasn't about to give this woman who had been kicked so hard any inflated hopes.

"If you sue this company," I said, "if you take them on, they will try to crush you any way they can. They have billions of dollars. They will spend whatever it takes to fight you. They will try to destroy you and your case."

I watched her carefully to see if my words were sinking in.

"They will attack you personally. They will call you a fake. They will say you made stupid mistakes and choices in your life and that you are trying to blame them for your problems. They will go after your former employees."

I wasn't making any of this up or exaggerating in the slightest. I had seen this company use just such tactics with other clients we had represented against it.

"They will send investigators to film your every move. They will take your deposition for days at a time. They will subpoena your tax records. They will accuse you of insurance fraud–"

"These are bad people," she interrupted. "They are *really* bad." I heard an intense firmness in her voice as she took responsibility for her faults. "I've made some big mistakes," she said, "but I'm disabled. I can't *be* a chiropractor anymore. They know that's true. They were wrong in cutting me off. If they hadn't done that, we wouldn't have been ruined. We wouldn't have been thrown out of our home. We wouldn't be living on food stamps.

"Yesterday," she said, her eyes welling up, "my son, Anton, was looking at some old photos from the good days. He turned to me and asked, 'Mommy, will we ever be normal again?'

"Mr. Bourhis," Joan said, now sounding more determined than defeated, "I don't care what they do to me. They can't be allowed to get away with this."

∧ ∨ ∧ ∨ ∧

THE CONCEPT OF INSURANCE IS NOTHING NEW. IT DATES BACK TO THE maritime industries of ancient China and Babylonia. The Chinese had a system to lessen the loss of cargo in the treacherous Yangtze River. A group of shipowners threw money into a pot (the birth of premiums) to cover the loss of goods on a single boat.

The Babylonians developed an interesting variation called *bottomry contracts*. Shipowners negotiated loans on their vessels. If the ships didn't make it back to port, the debt was wiped clean. Insuring, in one form or another, against maritime loss carried through to the Greeks, Romans, and Byzantines.

A catastrophic occurrence in London in 1666 made it abundantly apparent that a new type of insurance was needed–for fire. The Great Fire of London raged for four days, destroying more than thirteen thousand buildings and leveling 436 acres. An enterprising gentleman named Nicholas Barbon promptly started a business to protect against future fire loss.

One hundred years later, the always-enterprising Benjamin Franklin founded one of the first fire insurance companies in the United States, the Philadelphia Contributorship, which is still in existence today.

Variations and nuances progressed through the centuries. Otto von Bismarck instituted a social insurance in Germany as an end run against socialism. Its basic tenet was that for the good of all society, the individual must be protected. (Bismarck's creation worked so well that despite the upheavals following the world wars, Germany's national health insurance never stopped functioning.) In the late nineteenth century, disability insurance in its more modern guise made an appearance. With the rise of unions, workers demanded that they no longer be treated as commodities to be used and tossed away. Since employees gave up part of their lives making widgets and what-have-yous, they wanted more than a salary. They wanted peace of mind.

That's what disability insurance is all about. Whereas car insurance protects something that is tangible, disability insurance is a protection for something that is intangible–in case there comes a time when you are no longer able to work because of an injury or illness. Since profits could be made in selling this type of protection, naturally the private sector rushed in.

Insurance companies don't make the real money on premiums. The big returns come from their investments. The 1980s were a decade of double-digit interest rates and bond returns. Businesses that earned their profits by accumulating and investing cash prospered and grew exponentially. There was no better business for this than insurance. And with its high premiums, long-term policies, low marketing costs, and limited risk, there was no better insurance line for this than disability. This was the time to rake it in, the time to corner the market. All you had to do was come up with a seductive benefits package, price premiums aggressively, hire swarms of hungry sales agents, put them on high commission schedules, and stand back. The premium dollars would fly in, the cash would be thrown into the bond market, and profits would soar. If the competition didn't match you, step for step, you would own them before they could walk out the door. The weak and the tentative would fall to the side, and the resolute, the daring, would take over. It was the same old deal. The meek might inherit the earth, but before long, the bold would get it all back and would be disinheriting them.

In 1983, there were dozens of disability insurers in the business but only three heavyweights: Provident Life and Accident Insurance Company of Chattanooga, Tennessee; the Paul Revere Life Insurance Company of Worcester, Massachusetts; and Unum Life Insurance Company of America of Portland, Maine. Whether through loose lips, competitive surveillance, or coincidental stupidity, all three companies came up with similar plans.

Between 1983 and 1989, Provident, Paul Revere, and Unum had nearly a hundred thousand agents plowing the fields from Maine to California and throughout Canada. They were all selling "own-occupation" (own-occ) individual disability insurance. These policies held the enticing promise of payment should the insured become unable to perform the duties of his or her "own occupation."

The pitches were almost identical:

Buy ours; it's noncancelable.

No, buy ours; the premiums can never be raised.

No, buy ours; it will pay benefits for life, not just to age sixty-five.

Wait; we'll throw in annual cost-of-living adjustments to cover inflation.

Each company played on fear. The promotional material contained shocking statistics on the number of people seriously injured every year (see Exhibit 2). This was accompanied by dire warnings about what could happen to someone who can no longer work. Auto accidents, sports injuries, illnesses, diseases–the litany of potential calamities went on and on.

"Don't think it can't happen to you," the sales agents warned. "That's what everybody thinks. Then it happens. And your life is ruined–along with the lives of all of those who are depending on you. But if you buy this policy, it will protect you if you are ever unable to perform your specific job. Your *specific* occupation."

Policy after policy was sold.

Happy projections came into the boardrooms. Double-digit interest rates—so good for insurance companies, so bad for mortgage seekers—would continue into the foreseeable future. Premiums were priced accordingly and *could not be raised*.

Of course, claims would be made on these policies—people would be injured or would develop covered illnesses—but claims payments would be far surpassed by the fat investment revenues.

Profits were just sitting there, waiting to be plucked, like juicy, fat little plums in a vast, glorious orchard that stretched from sea to shining sea—plums worth billions of dollars. As long as the interest rate projections that formed the basis for all of this continued to be correct, the profits would fly along as expected. You would need an army of counters just to keep tabs on the increasing profits.

The problem was the projections were wrong.

∧ ∨ ∧ ∨ ∧

A COPY OF THE MEMO RESTED ON THE POLISHED MAHOGANY COFFEE table next to a confidential analysis of the problem. Not only had the double-digit rates of the 1980s failed to hold up into the 1990s, but they had plummeted to half their 1980s levels. And as the rate predictions went out the window, so too did the claims/investment-profits formula that had provided the basis for the 1980s pricing calculations—calculations that had been used to price every own-occupation policy sold between 1983 and 1989.

Short-term claims—sprains and pains with small payouts and speedy recoveries—were not the problem. It was the high-benefit, long-term claims, claims that would have to be paid year after year, that suddenly posed the threat.

Because Provident had been the most aggressive in its attempts to corner the disability market, it was now facing the greatest exposure for losses. It knew the number of own-occ policies it had sold. It knew the size of the long-term disability benefits that were in place. It knew the extent and duration of the existing claims being paid. It knew the estimates of future claims that would be filed over the lives of the policies in force. It knew the terms of the insurance contracts it had written. It knew it could not make interest rates go up. It knew it was in trouble.

In 1993, Provident was forced to take a $423 million charge, a loss of almost half a billion dollars, caused by having to increase the company's reserves in order to pay existing and projected claims (see Exhibit 3). This, undoubtedly, was just the beginning. If interest rates remained low, losses would continue to grow, which would have a very substantial effect on profits and, worse, on stock prices.

It was amazing, really, the kinds of blunders high-powered corporate executives with degrees from prestigious business schools were capable of making. These wonder boys, handpicked by the Provident board, had screwed up like rank amateurs.

But it wasn't just the senior management. Too many board members were out of touch. And while they were playing golf, attending charity socials, and checking on their portfolios, the barn was burning.

How the interest-rate projections could have been so far off the mark was a mystery. But they were. Why the leadership had thought it was a great idea to sell policies for which premiums could not be raised was equally mysterious. But they did.

Now these own-occ policies were going to cause shareholders a huge, expensive headache. The more shares one held, the bigger the headache. And this company had some very big shareholders. The situation had all the makings of an ugly, severe, and very real problem.

What could the company do? Cut costs? Lay off employees? Slash overhead?

The Provident board did what such boards always do in these situations—it brought in a new CEO.

Enter J. Harold Chandler. To many, Chandler was an odd choice—*very* odd. But whatever had gone on behind closed doors stayed there, and the choice was made.

This isn't to say that Chandler's academic credentials weren't impressive. He had graduated Phi Beta Kappa in 1971 from Wofford College, a small, fairly selective institution in Spartanburg, South Carolina. He earned an MBA from the University of South Carolina and went through the advanced management program at Harvard.

In his early forties, Chandler projected an aura of competence. And while detractors found him aloof, detached, and somewhat arrogant, he packaged himself as an aw-shucks, regular kind of guy. It made little difference. CEOs aren't hired for their common touch. Boards want to turn over the reins to someone who can deliver.

In the case of Provident, the board was looking for someone who could get the company back on the profit-making track. Yet some real head shaking occurred over Chandler's appointment. Beyond owning his own policies, there was little evidence that the man knew anything about insurance. He was, of all things, a banker. He had spent more than twenty years with the Citizens & Southern Corporation, which became NationsBank Corporation, rising to become president of its Mid-Atlantic Banking Group.

Despite his lack of experience in the insurance industry, the handful of powerful individual and institutional stockholders whose shares in the company were worth hundreds of millions of dollars—the investors who really controlled things—anointed Chandler to lead Provident to "Moneyland." To provide him with a powerful incentive to accomplish this goal quickly, in addition to his fat salary, the shareholder bigwigs gave Chandler options to purchase hundreds of thousands of shares of Provident stock at the price of thirty dollars per share. The only catch was that the options would expire in five years. If the stock price rose substantially and rapidly, Chandler's personal take would be in the multimillions of dollars. If, on the other hand, the price stayed flat or went down, his options would be worthless.

Such an arrangement is not uncommon in corporate America. Many argue that awarding stock options is a legitimate way to attract—and keep—top talent. If an executive has stock options and the share price is rising, he or she will be less likely to jump to a competitor. Dot-coms in the 1990s were especially prone to using options as an incentive. How else were they to lure people away from established firms such as Intel or Microsoft?

Also, some argue that the carrot option is useful in getting management to try all that much harder to increase profits and push the stock price skyward. The good of the company becomes the very good of the executive.

But options have their critics, not the least of whom is former Federal Reserve Board chairman Alan Greenspan, who would blame what he called the "infectious greed" of the 1990s partially on stock options. "The . . . spread of shareholding and options among business managers," Greenspan said in 2002 after the Enron debacle, "perversely created incentives to artificially inflate reported earnings in order to keep stock prices high and rising. The incentives they created overcame the good judgment of too many corporate managers." Greenspan could well have added that the problem was a lack of effective countervailing disincentives to serve as financial deterrents against profitable fraudulent activities.

In the case of Enron, top management hid problems in the company through creative accounting in order to exercise options before the stock price plummeted. Twenty-nine insiders walked away with $1.1 billion (with CEO Ken Lay's share being $104 million).

Chandler took over as CEO of Provident within weeks of the company's taking its $423 million charge. So what if he didn't know anything about insurance regulations? Perhaps so much the better.

What Chandler *did* know was what was really important. As a banker, he knew how to count.

∧ ∨ ∧ ∨ ∧

ACROSS THE COUNTRY, JOAN HANGARTER WAS COMPLETELY UNAWARE of the situation in Chattanooga. Even if she had noticed an announcement of Chandler's ascendancy, it would have made no impression on her. She had, after all, purchased her policy from Paul Revere. In any case, she had other concerns to think about.

Joan started the 1990s doing well. Her kids were wonderful. Her fiancé, Bruce Wexler, was ambitious and filled with ideas. At the height of the internet boom, when people were scrambling for ways to exploit the potential of the World Wide Web, Wexler was working on a start-up company that would sell music online while protecting the artists' copyrights. His technology could also be used for webcasts and online concerts. It was a heady time, filled with ahead-of-the-curve, moneymaking possibilities. Joan was right there at Wexler's side. But more importantly, she had her practice.

Health conscious, she looked more like a fitness instructor than a chiropractor. So unless you knew her background, chiropractic would have seemed an unlikely career for her to choose. When she entered the field in the 1980s, it was still viewed as a step off the mainstream by some. After all, the practitioners weren't *real* doctors. They didn't even solve problems by prescribing pills.

Chiropractors believe that many varieties of ill health stem from the spine being misaligned, that roadblocks in the spinal highway keep nerve impulses from reaching their destinations. By manipulating the spine at specific locations, chiropractors can solve or at least ameliorate specific health problems.

Though modern chiropractic began only a century ago, records exist of manipulations being performed as far back as 2560 BC. The legitimacy of the profession received a big boost in 1944 when veterans were allowed to use GI Bill of Rights grants for chiropractic training. In 1972, Congress okayed Medicare payments for chiropractic treatment. Thirty years later, members of the armed forces and veterans were accorded benefits as well.

Today, an estimated thirty-five million people entrust their bodies to approximately seventy thousand chiropractors in the United States. But as late as 1997, most of those practitioners were men–84 percent versus 16 percent women.

Despite all this, there was little question of Joan entering the profession. Naysayers of chiropractic could naysay all they wanted. Joan knew its healing power firsthand. At thirteen, she was diagnosed with scoliosis, curvature of the spine. The traditional treatment was wearing a brace for more than sixteen hours a day until the spine straightened or surgery. The latter was recommended for Joan. Her father opted for a third option. He took her to a chiropractor, who treated her for two years. As a result, no operation was necessary.

The profession also appealed to her because she loved helping people, so Joan put herself through chiropractic school working as a waitress. After passing the state boards, she borrowed $10,000 to start her business and began the long, hard task of building her practice. Working from 6 a.m. to 7 p.m. daily, Joan built a solid referral network from the ground up, one step at a time. She was loved and respected by her many patients–who ranged from children with sports injuries to adults with back problems. Her easy smile and confident proficiency impressed both those she treated and the numerous medical doctors and other professionals who steadily sent their patients to her.

Beyond enjoying the feeling of success that came from the solid growth of Solano Chiropractic, Joan was truly fulfilled by the work she was doing. She was treating people who were in pain, as she had been as a child, and she was making them well. Little else could have provided her with the satisfaction she was getting from what she was doing.

On first analysis, Provident and Chandler were faced with a seemingly unsolvable conundrum. On one hand, there was nothing the company could do about low interest rates, while on the other, it was receiving more and more long-term claims every day.

Whether Chandler was truly ignorant of them or not, there are certain rules governing the insurance industry. One is the implied promise of good faith and fair dealing. This means that an insurance provider cannot unfairly deny a policyholder the peace of mind that he or she pays for when buying a policy.

It is illegal for an insurance company to unreasonably delay, terminate, underpay, or reject a valid claim. Investigations of a claim must be full, fair, and objective. The company's financial interests must never, ever be put above those of the policyholder. The insurer may never conceal benefits—which wouldn't be hard considering that most policies read as if they were written in random Chinese characters. Any ambiguities in coverage must be read in favor of the claimant. All of this means the company has to pay up honestly on *legitimate* claims.

The "legitimate" part is what Provident decided to use to its advantage. After all, the insurer got to decide what a "legitimate" claim was. If the claimant disagreed, he or she could just sue the multibillion dollar company with its battery of in-house lawyers and army of high-priced outside counsel.

∧ ∨ ∧ ∨ ∧

NOT LONG AFTER CHANDLER'S ARRIVAL, RALPH MOHNEY WAS TAPPED to take over Provident's entire claims department. Mohney's background was in accounting and tax. Despite being put in charge of the department, Mohney had never handled a single insurance claim in his life. But he, like Chandler, was a numbers cruncher.

Outside consultants were hired, the situation was analyzed, strategy sessions were conducted, and the problem was examined from every angle. Through it all, one fact was certain. There were two sides of the equation–interest rates and claims. No matter what, one side was in granite–Provident could do absolutely nothing about the low interest rates. The other side, the claims side, was another matter entirely. It was there that changes could be made–bold, aggressive changes.

Starting in 1994 a number of initiatives would be instituted by Chandler and Mohney–initiatives that would put in place new procedures for dealing with claims *and* claimants. These initiatives would change the direction, the very philosophy, of the company.

As a result of the profitability of these initiatives, by 1997 Provident was able to consume its former rival, Paul Revere. By 1999 it would gobble up Unum as well. Through it all, Chandler, Mohney, and their "philosophy" would endure. Endure and thrive.

∧ ∨ ∧ ∨ ∧

UNDER PROVIDENT'S NEW CORPORATE PHILOSOPHY, THE CLAIMS DEPARTment began aggressively searching for reasons *not* to pay claims. Methods would be developed. Strategies would be deployed. Obstructions would be raised, delays instituted, and medical determinations challenged.

This was much to the misfortune of Joan Hangarter and many others who found their lives destroyed and themselves falling down the rabbit hole.

Chapter Two

LICENSED TO STEAL

I T WAS IN MARCH 1997 THAT IT HAPPENED. THOMAS L. SEJAC WAS NO lightweight. At 247 pounds in his bare feet, moving him would have proved a challenge to an NFL lineman.

While you don't need the ability to bench press a Buick to be a chiropractor, power, force, and upper-body strength are required. Manipulations are performed on the pelvic region and on the cervical, thoracic, and lumbar spine. Procedures include a lot of pulling, tugging, twisting, pressing, and bending. A chiropractor can't merely tell patients to position themselves on the treatment table; he or she has to do it. "The procedures are very specific," Joan was to explain later. "It may look like I'm just moving anything, but that's not correct. I've decided on what has to be adjusted, and how. And it's very precise."

Sejac was not an easy man to maneuver on the treatment table. As Joan grappled with Sejac's hips, trying to position his lower back, she felt a jolt in her right arm followed by a sharp pain in her upper spine. She shook her head. She would probably be making an appointment with a chiropractor herself.

When the pain worsened, Joan sought treatments from a fellow practitioner. But she experienced no improvement. Finally she sought relief from Dr. Steven Isono, an orthopedist. The persistent pain was now in her upper arm, forearm, neck, and shoulder. Dr. Isono ordered an MRI (magnetic resonance imaging) scan. It showed that Joan was suffering from cervical disc disease. Subsequent MRIs showed a deteriorating condition.

Despite this, Joan continued working. She didn't want to let her patients down, and she didn't want to lose them. Sometimes she wore a shoulder brace, but the pain persisted. If she was inactive, it was deep and nagging. During manipulations, it would become very sharp and, as Joan described it, stabbing. "Sometimes," she said, "it would feel like muscle was coming off the bone. Like it was ripping. With tremendous amounts of burning in my upper scapula, in my neck."

Joan tried another chiropractor. She went to physical therapy twice a week for two months.

"They worked on my neck and also on my arm," she said. "And it was brutal. They'd go in and rub the arm and stretch it. But it didn't do any good. It got worse."

In June 1997, on the recommendation of her doctors, Joan asked a former employee and fellow chiropractor, Parissa Peymani, to temporarily take over her practice. The doctors hoped Joan's condition would improve if she didn't put significant stress on her injuries.

Rather than improve, Joan's condition worsened.

In July, she filed a disability claim with Paul Revere. She filled out stacks of forms, signed medical and financial releases, and answered a battery of questions from company claims officials.

After a standard investigation, Paul Revere approved the claim. Joan would receive benefit payments of $8,100 a month.

Naturally, Joan was worried about her condition, but she had her safety net, the disability policy. Patricia Meyers, the Paul Revere agent who had sold the policy to Joan, may have been persistent to the point of annoying, but Joan was glad she had listened to her. Without the policy, Joan would have had difficulty taking time off for recuperation.

ᴧ ᴠ ᴧ ᴠ ᴧ

MEANWHILE, THE PAUL REVERE LIFE INSURANCE COMPANY WAS, ITSELF, not in the best of health. The company was founded in the late 1800s by Charles A. Harrington, a math professor at Worcester Polytechnic Institute, and his brother, Frank. Charles Harrington had figured out, by a lot of chicken scratch on a blackboard, how a small insurance company could make a lot of money. The company started out as the Masonic Protective Association—Charles was a founder of Boston's Masonic shrine. The company's name was later changed to the Massachusetts Protective Association and then, finally, to Paul Revere Life Insurance Company.

In the early 1990s, Paul Revere hit the same low-interest wall as Provident. In 1997, when Provident took it over, the agreement was valued at more than a billion dollars.

J. Harold Chandler hailed the move, saying it represented a unique opportunity to bring together two highly focused, successful insurance companies. He felt that the companies were an excellent fit that would significantly enhance their ability to grow revenues and earnings across all product lines and would provide "superior value" to shareholders and customers.

Some Paul Revere policyholders would find the new company's performance to be anything but superior.

Joan was now going to be dealing with Chandler's Provident. In March 1999, Provident called for an independent medical examination (IME, see Exhibit 5) in Joan's case. A doctor of its choosing would evaluate Joan's claim, even though Paul Revere had already done so and had been paying benefits.

The examining doctor in an IME is handpicked by the insurance company; in this case, Provident picked Dr. Aubrey Swartz, an orthopedist. Dr. Swartz was charged with examining Joan, writing a report, and forwarding his conclusions to Provident's claims department. Dr. Swartz said nothing to Joan following the examination, and Joan assumed his report would confirm her injuries and disabilities.

A month later, after consulting with her own doctors, Joan realized her condition was permanent. She would not be recuperating. She would never again be able to return to chiropractic. It made no financial sense to continue to have another doctor treat her patients for a percentage of the fees. This would ultimately result in the loss of both her patients and her business. And so, even though the practice had limited value without Joan's involvement, she had no choice but to sell it.

In April 1999 she negotiated a deal with Dr. Leonard Sugarman for just over $134,000. He wrote a check for $25,000 with the balance to be paid monthly over the next three years.

The money from Sugarman wasn't a fortune, but it was enough to enable Joan to make a deposit on the purchase of the house she and

Bruce Wexler were renting. They could then live on Joan's $8,100-a-month disability payments while Bruce got his business going.

A few weeks later, Joan had a visitor: claims representative Ken Seaman. Provident, Seaman said, after reviewing Dr. Swartz's report, had decided that Joan *could* perform her professional duties after all. Her benefits would be terminated immediately.

Joan was stunned. "There must be some mistake," she protested. "I've tried and tried. There's no way I can do the work."

Seaman was adamant. Joan's benefits were being cut off. Couldn't Provident at least pay some benefits while she learned to do something else? Joan pleaded.

Seaman was firm. The answer was no. There was nothing he could do.

"But I've sold my practice. I have no money. I have two children. Can't you do something?"

Seaman shook his head. The decision had been made.

Joan was to get no reprieve. On May 21, 1999, Provident sent her a termination letter, signed by Joseph Sullivan, a claims representative (see Exhibit 6). Quoting rhyme and verse from the policy, the letter told Joan she wasn't qualified for benefits under either the total disability or the residual (partial) disability provisions. She was not, said the letter, disabled. Provident based its decision, it explained, on the wording of its policy, the facts of her case, and the results of its IME report. Joan had received her last check.

With her safety net yanked from under her, Joan's life spiraled downward. Dr. Sugarman defaulted on his note, Joan and Wexler were evicted from the house they were intending to buy, losing their down-payment, and Joan's personal property—furniture, clothes, everything—had to be put into storage. Then Wexler became physically abusive.

Because Joan was practically broke, her best friend from high school, Madeline Schwarzman, gave Joan some money so she could take shelter at her sister Hildy's house. Joan piled her kids in the car and drove over five hundred miles to Encinitas, California. There she, as she put it, "camped out for weeks with the children" in her sister's tiny house. She tried to perform some part-time chiropractic work, but the pain was excruciating so she couldn't do it. She searched for other job opportunities but was so despondent and frightened that she broke down in tears during an employment agency interview. Then one afternoon while Joan was glancing down at her sister's kitchen table, her eyes caught an article in the *Wall Street Journal* about a law firm that was accusing UnumProvident of fraudulently terminating the disability benefits of its insureds in order to boost profits. Until seeing this article, Joan had no idea that there might be anything she could do to fight Provident's actions. She called, talked to us, withstood a bombardment of tough questions about her medical condition and the facts of her case, and scheduled an appointment.

By this point, Wexler was pleading with Joan to come back. He had an idea: Why not combine his internet experience with Joan's knowledge about chiropractic to form a company that would design and build websites for chiropractors? Joan didn't like the idea, but she was desperate. She returned with her children to Novato, moved into a tiny apartment with Wexler, and went to work on the product. However, with no funding and little equipment, the enterprise was doomed from the start. Beyond this, she found it very difficult to work with Wexler. He was volatile, prone to violent outbursts, and extremely demanding. Their relationship continued to deteriorate until finally, during a tremendous fight on May 31, 2000, Wexler slapped Joan, twisted her arm, and threatened to smash her with a heavy guitar and throw her out the window.

Elana and Anton, terrified, called 911. After investigating the situation, the police arrested Wexler. A restraining order was subsequently issued precluding him from having further contact with Joan. But the damage had been done. Wexler's business idea had been Joan's last hope, and it evaporated like dry ice on a skillet. Joan was forced to file for bankruptcy, she had to apply for food stamps, and a month later her car was repossessed. She became increasingly despondent and was put on Prozac for acute depression. Through it all, Provident refused to budge. It wouldn't pay her a dime.

∧ ∨ ∧ ∨ ∧

YOU MIGHT WONDER HOW INSURANCE COMPANY EXECUTIVES COULD believe they could get away with blithely refusing to live up to their company's policy provisions. What could they be thinking when making such decisions? How could they think they could get away with it?

To answer this question, we need to examine the only three *potential* sources of oversight that exist to curtail any kind of corporate misconduct. These are federal regulatory enforcement, state regulatory enforcement, and private regulatory enforcement.

As far as the insurance industry is concerned, the first option, federal regulatory enforcement, requires only a short discussion—very short. There is *no* federal regulatory enforcement. None. That's because there's nothing to enforce. There are no federal insurance regulations.

People often express surprise about this. How is it possible that the same federal government that oversees communications, banking, manufacturing, pharmaceuticals, energy, securities, interstate commerce, and practically everything else (from the use of dirty words on the radio to the permissible size of mud flaps on tractor-trailers) has not enacted a single antifraud law regulating insurance? Easy—it's all about lobbying.

In 1945, as a result of insurance industry "urging," in concert, undoubtedly, with the usual palm-greasing payoffs that have come to be known as "campaign contributions," Congress enacted the McCarran-Ferguson Act. This act actually prevented the federal government from enacting *any* insurance consumer protections at all. Today, believe it or not, out of the millions of pages of federal statutes, codes, guidelines, requirements, and standards, not a single provision, a single sentence, or a single word regulates insurance practices. As a result, an insurance company can scam policyholders from Maine to California with false coverage promises, outrageous claims denials, and intimidating policy cancellations without the slightest concern that federal authorities might crack down on them. They won't. The only federal involvement with the subject of fraudulent insurance practices is that (to the extent that revenues are not filtered offshore) the government collects a chunk of the illegal profits in the form of taxes. Many argue persuasively that, given the current composition of Congress, if this situation were to change today and the federal government *were* to suddenly become involved in insurance regulation, it would not be good for consumers. Any such regulations would wind up protecting insurance companies instead of safeguarding policyholders.

Well, what about the states? Most states have what are called *unfair insurance practices acts*–legislation making it illegal for insurance companies to

- engage in unreasonable delay
- underpay, terminate, or deny valid claims
- put their financial interests above those of their policyholders
- conceal benefits from claimants
- interpret policy ambiguities against insureds
- use their superior size or wealth to intimidate or undersettle claims
- force policyholders to sue them in order to obtain benefits due

In addition, all states have insurance departments–agencies responsible for enforcing these and other provisions of the state's insurance regulations.

So if all states have enacted insurance laws, what's the problem? The problem is that insurance code standards are the easy part. It's the remedies that complicate matters. There's not a single insurance department in America that has the authority to sue an insurance company on behalf of a cheated claimant. What insurance departments do, as far as claims practices are concerned, is to investigate whether insurers doing business in the state are violating unfair-practice laws. These investigations are called *market conduct studies*. If a study is conducted and if a company is found to be engaging in illegal practices, then in theory the company can be fined, but this rarely happens. And when it does, the fine is usually a complete joke. But beyond the amount of the fine, the point is that these "investigations" do absolutely nothing to put even a dime into the pockets of a defrauded policyholder who was cheated out of a few hundred thousand dollars by his or her friendly multinational insurance company.

It gets worse. State insurance commissioners are the ones who run the nation's state insurance departments. These commissioners basically make all the decisions in terms of what a given state does to enforce its regulations. Critics characterize these commissioners as revolving-door, proindustry hacks, appointed (or elected, thanks to "campaign contributions" from insurance companies) based largely on their demonstrated ability to do exactly the opposite of what a watchdog regulator is supposed to do.

To demonstrate, let's take a side trip into the wonderful world of Chuck Quackenbush.

During the 1990s, Quackenbush was the up-and-coming star of California Republican politics. Youthful, trim, and articulate, he was being groomed for big things.

When California's Proposition 103, an insurance reform initiative put before the voters, was enacted in 1988, the office of California insurance commissioner was turned from an obscure position appointed by the governor into a high-visibility statewide elective office. That made it a prime launching pad for politicians hoping to make a run for governor, US Senator, or some other high office.

Quackenbush, who knew nothing about insurance companies except that they had a lot of money, made the rounds, and promised to be a good lapdog if elected. He collected a war chest from the industry, used the cash to buy television ads, and won the job of commissioner in a landslide.

As commissioner, Quackenbush cranked up the department of insurance (DOI) publicity department. He was often photographed having important meetings, thinking deep thoughts, pondering important decisions, and making pithy observations. All of this worked very well—so well, in fact, that Quackenbush might well be the governor today if he hadn't been caught, red-handed, prying millions of dollars for his favorite causes from the coffers of the biggest homeowners' insurance companies in the state. He collected these millions in exchange for his agreement not to prosecute the insurers for having cheated thousands of Californians out of the payments due to them following the horrific Northridge earthquake of 1994.

The whistle on Quackenbush was blown by a highly ethical and gutsy DOI lawyer by the name of Cindy Ossias. She made statewide headlines by exposing the commissioner and what he was doing to the state legislature. The legislature then got into the act, launched an investigation, subpoenaed Quackenbush and his top advisers to testify, and started asking the kinds of questions for which there are no satisfactory answers. When it became apparent that impeachment proceedings were about to be initiated, Quackenbush decided it was time to strike with a bold move.

Instead of finishing up his term as commissioner in the glory of grinning photo opportunities and then moving on to a bid for higher office, he developed a sudden passion for seashells and snorkeling. He quit, leaving not only the DOI but the state. He exiled himself to Hawaii, took up the fine art of blending perfect mai tais, and hasn't been heard from since, at least in the public arena.

Fortunately, California now has a very good insurance commissioner. But despite this, the DOI still can't recover money for cheated policyholders. DOIs simply don't have that authority. For that, we must turn to option three—private enforcement. Now the subject really gets interesting.

Private enforcement occurs when a cheated insured is able to file a civil damages lawsuit under his or her state's insurance regulations. Such a lawsuit is aimed at recovering damages caused by the fraudulent or bad-faith actions of the insurer. For a lawsuit like this to be effective, the remedies provided to policyholders under state law must be effective. The problem is that in most states, such remedies are totally inadequate. Moreover, they differ from state to state.

An individual from New York or Massachusetts who loses hundreds of thousands of dollars as a result of a wrongful claim denial has fewer rights and *far* less leverage than someone who suffered the same fate for the same reason in California. One of the reasons for this difference is (once again) the effective lobbying activities of the insurers. Notwithstanding the inadequacy of the laws and remedies of some states, the fact is that a handful of places, such as California, do have some good protections for policyholders. Unfortunately, insureds even in such states are having those rights stripped from them as we sit pondering all of this. Why? How? ERISA preemption.

ERISA preemption is intended to sound as boring as it does. If something is boring sounding, people probably won't pay attention to it. The less they pay attention, the easier it is to rob them blind.

ERISA, an acronym for the Employee Retirement Income Security Act of 1974, is a federal law that was originally intended to protect the retirement benefits of employees against mergers, acquisitions, and other corporate activities that might otherwise have endangered such funds. ERISA originally had nothing to do with overruling state insurance regulations. To the contrary, it specifically approved of the use of state laws to regulate insurance practices.

That was until the US Supreme Court, in a ruling written in 1987 by Justice Sandra Day O'Connor, changed all of that. In an opinion written in the case of *Pilot Life Insurance Company v. Dedeaux*, the nation's high court eliminated all the legal rights–established over decades under state laws–to protect policyholders from fraudulent and bad-faith insurance practices. The O'Connor ruling simply took a broom and swept these rights under the rug, out the door, down the hall, and into oblivion.

Here's how it happened.

Insurance companies couldn't stand the idea that their cheated customers could actually sue them. The companies wanted to make a big dent in the rights of policyholders to do that.

And so, back in 1987, they took their cause to the US Supreme Court. Help us, they said to the court. If you take away the rights of policyholders to sue us under state laws–at least under policies of insurance purchased at the workplace–if you say that all of the state law protections of these insureds are to be preempted (displaced) by federal law, then because there are no federal protections, we will be *immunized* from fraud. If you do this, said the carriers, at least as to these workplace-purchased policies, we will be able to lower premiums.

This will, reasoned the Supreme Court, encourage the formation of employee benefit plans. Insurance will be more affordable and therefore more people will have it.

Just a second, said the opposition. You can't allow insurance companies to get away with cheating their own policyholders–stealing the very benefits they paid for. That would be ridiculous. And even though an insurance company could increase profits by refusing to pay 5 or 10 percent of its valid claims, there would be no guarantee that they would pass on these illegal savings anyway.

Besides, what about the people who would be losing their homes, their life savings, and everything else? The Supreme Court shouldn't be taking away their right to recover for such losses. You can't substitute federal insurance regulations for state insurance regulations. There *are* no federal regulations. There are no federal deterrents.

Too bad, ruled the high court. We're throwing in with the multinationals. Get out of the way and take your insurance regulations with you. Henceforth, ERISA shall trump, knock out, eliminate, eviscerate, *all* state insurance protections on all policies purchased at work. From this day forth, all consumer rights under state laws on employment-purchased insurance policies are "preempted" by ERISA.

And because ERISA provides no remedies for misrepresentation, with a stroke of a pen, the Supreme Court left insurance consumers who had obtained their policies at work with no antifraud or bad-faith protections under either federal *or* state laws. To this day, such policyholders have no rights to recover for losses caused by such practices. More importantly, a targeted policyholder has no *leverage* whatsoever to get his or her insurer to simply pay what it owes under its policy.

With nothing to motivate them to pay ERISA claims fairly, many insurers simply don't. In fact, UnumProvident, in a highly confidential internal company memo that we got our hands on, actually bragged that it could save more than 95 percent of what it would otherwise have to pay if a claim was preempted by ERISA. (See Exhibit 7.)

"Just a second," you may be saying, "it seems to me that ERISA preemption is inconsistent with McCarran-Ferguson. I thought the federal government was barred from regulating insurance? How is ERISA preemption consistent with that?"

That is a very interesting question. Unfortunately, there is no logical answer.

If you are ever given a choice between buying ERISA preempted insurance coverage through work versus non-ERISA preempted coverage through a group or individual policy purchased other than at work, the choice is easy.

Don't *ever* buy a policy for which the insurance company, in cahoots with the US Supreme Court, is immune from stealing from insureds.

Chapter Three

SO SUE ME

D EPOSITIONS ARE SOMETIMES HELD IN EXPENSIVE HOTEL CONFER-
ence rooms, with sumptuous buffets featuring freshly squeezed
orange juice and croissants, linen napkins, and fragrant floral
arrangements.

Someone in my office, perhaps in a misplaced effort to save the
firm from the appearance of extravagance, had instead scheduled
this deposition in a court reporter's office located twenty-minutes
and two-light-years west of the Four Seasons on Boston Common.
It was obvious that no one from that hotel's housekeeping staff
was moonlighting cleaning this unpleasant little conference room.
It was dirty and damp and exuded the distinct odor of wet, day-old
cigarette butts and leftover pizza.

I was there to question several UnumProvident witnesses in the
Hangarter case. The company was engaged in the seven-veils dance
of termination: if this reason doesn't work, peel off that veil and move
to the next one. The company was now claiming that Joan could still
perform the bookkeeping part of her job and therefore was not disabled. Why the company thought there would be any bookkeeping if
there were no patients shall forever remain a mystery.

∧ ∨ ∧ ∨ ∧

OUR OFFICE ALWAYS TRIES TO SETTLE CASES, AND THE EARLIER THE
better. Claimants–especially disabled, destitute claimants–don't
enjoy litigation. With the attendant lengthy discovery, procedural
delays, motions, trials, and appeals, most clients would rather eat
red ants than litigate.

In this case, given all of Joan's circumstances, I tried especially hard. I pestered UnumProvident's outside attorneys, Horace Green and Lori Bernard of Barger & Wolen LLP, about this constantly. I struggled to get information about the company's internal lines of authority in discovery. I asked everyone I could buttonhole why UnumProvident was refusing to make any kind of reasonable offer. But I got absolutely nowhere. I didn't know why. Sometimes defense firms, which are paid on an hourly basis, advise their insurance company clients to defer settlement discussions until after they've had a chance to take some depositions and file a few briefcases' worth of motions. Who knows? Perhaps they'll uncover information that reduces the value of the claim. Or maybe merely by delaying, the plaintiff will lose patience, have a midlife crisis, and move to Nepal or get run over by a truck on the way to the doctor's office. If any of these happen, poof. No more lawsuit.

I wouldn't give up on trying to settle, but as of the time these depositions commenced, it had been made very clear to me that resolving the case was not in the cards. My settlement attempts fell as flat as a squirrel squished into hot blacktop by a steamroller.

When there's no interest in early settlement, we have no choice but to sit back and try to enjoy discovery, cross-examining insurance executives, claims managers, IME doctors, investigators, and other witnesses, one after the other, until the process has run its course.

∧ ∨ ∧ ∨ ∧

APRIL 25, 2001, WAS A WARM NEW ENGLAND DAY, AND JOSEPH SULLIVAN was clearly unhappy to find himself seated in this conference room. The coffee-stained, brown, loosely adjusted swivel chair to which he had been assigned made him uncomfortable enough as it was, but being surrounded by three somber UnumProvident lawyers, including not only Mr. Green but two senior members of the company's house counsel's inner circle, was compounding his discomfort.

Sullivan was a young, clean-cut, sincere-looking witness. He was also living proof of my theory that UnumProvident didn't hold claims department seminars at the Hyatt to instruct adjusters on how to cheat policyholders, that it didn't have training sessions on "Ignoring Relevant Information and Misconstruing Policy Coverage." I believed that for the company to do something like that would have been as foolhardy as it was unnecessary. It was easier to simply keep employees in the dark as to what they were supposed to do and why. It was just that simple. Ask me no questions, and I'll tell you no lies.

∧ ∨ ∧ ∨ ∧

DEPOSITIONS ARE FACT-GATHERING TOOLS USED TO OBTAIN A TRANscribed record of the sworn testimony of witnesses to events. All or portions of such testimony can later be used to support or oppose various motions, such as motions to obtain certain types of additional discovery or motions to dismiss or affirm specific allegations being made in the case. Portions of deposition transcripts can also be introduced as evidence if the case ultimately winds up in trial. The usefulness of deposition transcripts obviously depends on what a witness says on the record.

Prior to a deposition, deponents are prepared by the lawyers representing their side of the case. Witnesses are usually told what specific kinds of questions they should expect. They may also be instructed as to how they might structure responses to anticipated lines of inquiry. And although witnesses cannot be advised to lie or shade the truth, they can be told that they don't have to provide direct yes or no answers to difficult questions—that it's okay if they equivocate and okay for them to say they don't recall something if there's any doubt about whether they remember it or not. To lie about something is perjury. But if a witness says he or she doesn't remember, how can you prove otherwise?

Lawyers attending a deposition can object, on the record, to questions being posed. Objections such as "The question assumes facts not in evidence" are supposedly made to preserve a party's right to later attempt to exclude or strike certain testimony. If the case winds up in court and no valid objection was made to an improper deposition question, then arguably the right to object may be deemed to have been waived, resulting in otherwise excludable testimony being read into the record at trial.

But beyond preserving legal issues, objections at depositions are often used for other strategic purposes, such as to telegraph a heads-up to the witness. A deponent may have been told to pay close attention to any question that draws an objection, listen to the grounds for the objection, and be especially careful with the answer.

Sometimes lawyers go even further. Even though it's not technically proper, some attorneys will make what are called *speaking objections*. These can be used to actually feed answers to a witness by suggesting a desired response: "Objection. The question misstates the witness's prior testimony. Besides, as you are well aware, counsel, the evidence is that (fill in the answer you want the witness to give)."

Given all of this, it might seem surprising that depositions would ever produce any real surprises at all. But they do.

∧ ∨ ∧ ∨ ∧

SULLIVAN TESTIFIED THAT WHEN HE WAS HIRED BY PAUL REVERE, HE HAD no knowledge of claims handling whatsoever. His training was conducted "in-house" by people "who were employees of Paul Revere."

Following completion of that training, even though he was responsible for gathering and assimilating the information needed to determine what, if any, benefits were payable on a claim, Sullivan did not know whether claims investigations had to be thorough. He didn't recall whether anyone from Paul Revere had ever even instructed him that investigations had to be objective.

Sullivan was responsible for handling a caseload of over eighty claims at any given time. Approximately forty-five other adjusters were in Sullivan's orthopedic claims unit in Worcester, Massachusetts, alone. In addition, orthopedic claims were also handled in claims offices located in places such as Chattanooga, Tennessee; Portland, Maine; and Glendale, California. Sullivan had no idea of the approximate number of orthopedic claims that were open at any given point nationwide. He knew even less about the total number of all claims, beyond just the orthopedic ones.

I asked Sullivan if he could estimate the number of new orthopedic claims–the ones that had just been opened by UnumProvident during the previous year. He couldn't guess.

I asked if he kept track of the number of cases in which he himself had terminated benefits. He did not.

It seemed highly improbable that someone expressly authorized by the company to terminate disability claims would have absolutely no idea how many he was terminating. Perhaps numbers such as these were something the company wanted to keep secret.

Sullivan denied that anyone had ever told him not to keep such records. I asked whether anyone in the company kept track of such information. "Not that I am aware of," he replied.

We turned to the wording of a standard UnumProvident insurance policy. I handed him a copy of the policy's definition of "total disability" and asked him to read the section into the record.

"Total disability," he read, "means that because of injury or sickness, you are unable to perform the important duties of your occupation."

I asked him if, in order to know whether a person qualifies for total disability benefits, he had to know what was meant by the phrase "the important duties."

He agreed that that was true.

I asked whether this meant *all* the important duties, *most* of the important duties, or *any* of the important duties.

Sullivan wrinkled his forehead and squinted as he looked at the policy. He stared at it for several minutes in silence, seemingly puzzled.

I waited for an answer. This was an issue of major importance for reasons that would soon become very clear.

Why was he just sitting there? Was this the first time he had ever thought about it? I waited him out. Finally, he looked up and said, "The important duties. I suppose if it was meant to mean *all*, it would say *all*."

I asked him if this was the first time he'd looked at this policy definition of "total disability."

"No," he said.

It certainly wasn't. He had looked at this language thousands of times. It was the basis for disability coverage in every benefits analysis he had ever performed.

Apparently, in all the time he'd worked for Paul Revere/ UnumProvident, no one had ever taught him how to correctly apply the very definition of disability he was supposed to be using.

DURING THE LUNCH BREAK, SULLIVAN AND GREEN WENT OUT TOGETHER. When they returned and we went back on the record, Sullivan announced that he wanted to make a statement. He had made a mistake before the break, he proclaimed. The "important duties" wording in the policy *did* mean "all of the duties" after all. That, said Sullivan, was what it meant.

I asked him if he wished to change his prior testimony.

He said he did. "I was tired and confused at the time," he asserted.

"We took a break. You spoke to your attorney. You came back and you changed your testimony. Is that correct?"

"That is correct." They had had lunch, he added.

Probably baloney flambé, I thought to myself.

"So are you telling us that someone would not be qualified for total disability if they could perform *any one* of their important duties?"

"Yes," he said.

This was bizarre. It would mean that before any of Unum-Provident's policyholders would be entitled to receive their own-occupation disability benefits under the company's definition of "total disability," they would have to be incapable of doing anything. They would basically have to be comatose.

I decided to shift gears. I asked him about something the company referred to as "roundtable" meetings.

Sullivan was ready for this. He responded that roundtables were meetings held with a number of individuals–claims representatives, medical doctors, supervisors, and others–who had expertise in different areas and could therefore take a kind of group approach.

"Like brainstorming meetings?" I asked.

He said that was correct.

I asked him if the purpose of these meetings was to find pretexts or excuses to terminate benefits.

Sullivan denied this, but he didn't sound very convincing.

I pressed on. "Were agendas prepared prior to these meetings?" I asked.

If his answer was yes, a request for production of the records would be in his hands by the end of the day. I had never seen any written files concerning these meetings.

"Not that I'm aware of," he answered.

How could a company the size of UnumProvident have any kind of important meeting without a written agenda? I'd never heard of such a practice.

Sullivan had no explanation. Out of the thousands of roundtable meetings that had been conducted since they were first launched by the claims department in 1995, the company couldn't produce a single agenda for a single such meeting. And the meetings were continuing to be held to that very day.

Why no agenda? Why did UnumProvident seem to purposely avoid leaving a trail detailing what was going on at these meetings? I wondered.

I wanted to know how the people attending roundtables could possibly prepare to discuss files they'd never heard of, claimants whose conditions they knew nothing about, medical records they hadn't reviewed, and job duties that would remain a secret until the moment the meetings commenced. Sullivan's answer was "You'd have to ask them." An agenda, he said, was not necessary.

What about notes or minutes taken at the meetings themselves? Were any such records kept?

No. No documentation was kept of anything discussed by anyone at any of these meetings. The only place one might find out whether an individual's case was even brought to the roundtable was in that individual's claims file, but all it would confirm was that the file was discussed. No record was kept about what was said or done by whom. And to develop a list of the claims that were subjected to this process, you'd have to go through each and every file in the entire claims department, by hand, page by page–hundreds of thousands of them.

I knew that after these roundtables, UnumProvident would typically have the claimants whose files were discussed followed. Investigators would peer into their houses, film them with hidden cameras, plow through tax and banking records, go through divorce files, and search for information any way they could.

Another common occurrence following a claim being "round-tabled" was that a memo would suddenly appear in the claimant's file from a company medical consultant. UnumProvident apparently had several doctors on call. They would come into the company's offices on a regular basis, go through a stack of files, scan individual medical records, and write skeptical memos about claimants' conditions. "See there," the company could later say about a particular file, "that's why we had doubts about this claim. Look. Our medical consultant himself raised these important issues."

I asked Sullivan whether–again following a roundtable discussion–he had referred the Hangarter case to an "in-house medical consultant" by the name of Dr. John Bianchi.

Yes, he had.

"And what did Dr. Bianchi say to you?" I asked.

Sullivan stated that Bianchi told him Joan's condition should have "resolved." In other words, the company was saying that Hangarter's injuries should have healed. This was totally contrary to the medical evidence from Joan's own treating physicians.

"But why?" I pressed.

He stammered, "Because that was his opinion."

But *why* should her condition have just "resolved"? I continued.

Sullivan didn't have any idea. He apparently had never inquired about this. "You'd have to ask Dr. Bianchi," he said.

Sullivan further acknowledged that, although he had taken Dr. Bianchi's opinion into account in terminating the claim, he knew very little, if anything, about what Dr. Bianchi had done or not done or with whom he had spoken or not spoken before coming to his conclusions.

I asked Sullivan about the company's procedures concerning "independent" medical examinations. These exams were often performed by doctors selected through Genex Incorporated.

Genex, he acknowledged, "is a company that's owned by UnumProvident."

Yet it was brought in to conduct allegedly "independent" medical exams.

In many cases involving orthopedic injuries in Northern California, the IME doctor that Genex chose was Dr. Aubrey Swartz. He was the doctor that Joan was sent to.

Showing Sullivan the termination letter he had written, I pointed out that he had stated that

- Dr. Bianchi said he could see no reason why the insured could not return to work

- Dr. Swartz had stated that she could work part-time

- because she was no longer working she did not qualify for what were called "residual benefits" under her policy

- the insurance policy in question was governed (preempted) by ERISA

It was important that I get these points into the record. What would a jury think when it learned that Bianchi had never set eyes on Joan, much less examined her, and that Sullivan knew this at the time he wrote the termination letter?

What would it think upon learning that even if the claimant could work part-time (which Joan could not), nothing about that fact would disqualify her for benefits under her policy as it was written?

What would it think upon learning that if a claimant was engaging in "any gainful employment," the company was supposed to pay benefits under a formula based on a comparison between present and prior income–a formula that UnumProvident knew was contained right in the policy itself?

What would it think of UnumProvident's concealing the fact that Joan was entitled to three years' worth of *full benefits* under the policy's "rehabilitation coverage"? Or of the fact that when Joan asked about receiving benefits long enough to "get on her feet," she was not told about the rehabilitation coverage in the policy?

Sullivan's letter (Exhibit 6) was filled with misrepresentations.

Three other witnesses were scheduled to testify in this round of depositions. Sandra Fryc (pronounced "Fritz") would close out the afternoon session, and Dr. John Bianchi and Christopher Ryan would give their statements the following day.

∧ ∨ ∧ ∨ ∧

SANDRA FRYC WAS A PLEASANT, THOUGH SOMEWHAT SERIOUS, WOMAN, who came across as all business–tidy, serious, and professional. Over the years, Fryc had served in a variety of capacities with Paul

Revere. She had been an adjuster, claims manager, and claims supervisor. When Provident took over Paul Revere in 1997, Fryc became a regional claims manager for the new company.

I wanted to question Fryc about changes that had taken place during the transition period around 1996 and 1997. Plans had to be made and details worked out for the molding of two claims departments into one. Ralph Mohney, the head of Provident's claims department, would be in charge of the new operation. The entire system had to conform to the Mohney philosophy—as he put it—of claims handling.

Meetings were held in Worcester, Massachusetts, home base for Paul Revere, and in Chattanooga, Tennessee, the headquarters for Provident. Teams of management-level employees from Provident were moved to Massachusetts for months at a time to teach Paul Revere's people the Provident "system." Fryc was an integral part of this transition process.

As I should have guessed, Fryc hadn't taken (or kept) many notes. She said she had no records of what had been said by whom, to whom, or about what in connection with any of the transition activities. Moreover, Fryc's memory about the transition meetings was, she confessed, just terrible. After all, these conferences had taken place several years ago. How could a person be expected to remember the details?

It was such a busy, busy time.

∧ ∨ ∧ ∨ ∧

DR. JOHN BIANCHI, THE "INDEPENDENT CONTRACTOR" WHO PERFORMED what were called "claims reviews" for UnumProvident, was the next witness. Bianchi would come into the UnumProvident offices a couple of times a week. He would be handed a stack of claims files containing the medical reports and records of treating physicians. He would also be given written questions posed by a claims adjuster for each file. He would examine each file and provide the requested response. Bianchi, who was paid well for his opinions, made a good witness for the company. With his white hair and folksy style, he lent an honest, down-home image to UnumProvident's terminations.

In response to my questioning, Bianchi acknowledged that he never actually *examined* claimants. He just reviewed the records. And no, he didn't usually bother talking with the treating doctors. Apparently, he didn't think that was necessary.

He also testified that the company normally didn't provide him with much information on the "usual and customary duties" of particular claimants. It was unclear how he could conclude that a claimant could perform some of her duties if he had no idea what those duties were.

In this case, which involved a claimant with epicondylitis (a condition in which the outer part of the elbow becomes painful and tender), Bianchi testified that in his medical opinion, rendered from some three thousand miles away, the claimant was likely suffering from "radial humeral bursitis."

"Radial humeral bursitis (arthritis of the elbow)?" I said. "Is that a temporary or a permanent condition?"

"It comes and it goes," Bianchi stated.

"Comes and goes?"

"Yes."

"When does it come and when does it go?"

"Who knows?" he shrugged.

"Does it come and go when [Hangarter] is in the middle of a manipulation with a patient?"

"It can happen at rest," said Bianchi.

"How severe is the pain to someone who's a chiropractor?"

"It hurts for a while."

"Would it be debilitating to a chiropractor?"

"You can function with it."

"Do you just kind of grin and bear it?" I asked.

"Yeah," he shrugged.

"Put up with the pain?"

"Right."

Bianchi, in other cases, had rendered his opinions that claimants were not disabled without knowing the applicable definition of "disability." No one had told him what it was—either as spelled out in the policy or under California law.

It was good, I thought, that he hadn't asked Sullivan for the definition.

"Well, you don't have to be dead," I said. "You don't have to be a vegetable. You don't have to be unable to do *everything*. Hasn't anyone from Paul Revere/UnumProvident ever told you that?"

"No," he said.

∧ ∨ ∧ ∨ ∧

CHRISTOPHER RYAN WAS THE FOURTH DEPOSITION WITNESS. AS A UnumProvident claims adjuster, he had paid Joan her initial disability benefits. Ryan was replaced on the file by Sullivan. But that wasn't why I wanted to question him.

I don't know where insurance companies find these people, but Ryan seemed like yet another excessively clean-cut-looking guy–the kind of fellow you might expect to see wearing a white uniform and selling ice cream cones at Disneyland. As a claims consultant and a former senior claims representative, Ryan had been authorized by UnumProvident not only to terminate benefits but to train claims handlers–to tell them what to do in evaluating and deciding on a claim and how to do it.

I asked Ryan the most basic claims question I could think of. "Do you agree," I said, "that insurance companies are required to handle claims fairly?"

Ryan didn't know. Nor did he know whether insurance companies are required to investigate claims thoroughly.

I glanced over at Green to see if this testimony surprised him. It didn't appear to.

Ryan went on to say that he didn't know if insurance companies were required to investigate claims objectively. He didn't know whether claims had to be handled according to the rulings of a state's highest court. He didn't know if insurance companies had the right to have brainstorming meetings for the purpose of finding pretexts or loopholes to terminate legitimate claims. And he didn't know whether the standard for total disability in California was the inability of the policyholder to perform the substantial and material duties of his or her occupation in the usual and customary manner and with reasonable continuity.

As a claims consultant, Ryan was responsible for training and consulting on four to five hundred disability claims at any given time. For someone in that position, not to know these details was like a major league baseball player not knowing how many times he could swing at a pitch and miss before he had to go back to the dugout.

We're not talking about theoretical physics here. Claims-handling requirements imposed on insurance companies come basically from two sources: (1) state insurance codes and regulations and (2) the rulings of state appellate courts. This is not a big secret, so it's hard to imagine any insurance company that is doing business–and making money–in a state not knowing this. It is even harder to imagine an insurance company concealing this rather fundamental information from its own claims department employees, leading them to make decisions on claims without knowing the most basic rules they are required to apply.

It was almost surreal to think that upper management within a huge insurance company like UnumProvident would actually keep its own claims decision-makers in the dark like this. Was this one of the ways the company had come up with to cut off benefits and increase profits? The level of ignorance, the dearth of information, and the paucity of training were almost stupefying.

I asked Ryan, since he had management-level authority, *approximately*, how many individual disability policies the company had in force.

How many claims were pending with the company?

How fast did *his* claims caseload turn over?

How many files did he work on per year?

How many claims, on average, had he terminated per month or per year?

He didn't know and couldn't estimate any of that.

"Do you have a specialty in working on any particular types of disability claims?" I asked.

"Yes," he said. "Orthopedic."

"Do you have *any* kind of background on orthopedic issues?" I asked.

"No," he said. He did not.

∧ ∨ ∧ ∨ ∧

CASES CAN BRING FRUSTRATION IN MANY DIFFERENT FORMS. THE VAST wasteland of apparent ignorance on the part of UnumProvident employees and consultants was enough to drive a sane person into intense therapy. But there were also the personalities of some of the players with which to contend.

Every industry has its share of "unusual" individuals. Two prime examples in the insurance defense field were Chris Collins and Francis Torrence.

Collins was an in-house attorney for UnumProvident Insurance Company. That means he was part of the team of lawyers working inside the company, in the general counsel's office, as opposed to being in one of the outside law firms hired to defend the company when a lawsuit is filed against it. Collins is one of the people who chooses the outside lawyers and firms to be hired. Torrence was a favorite outside lawyer of his.

In my opinion the two were truly a match made in hell. It was hard for me to tell which was worse.

To me, Collins was the kind of guy who could go on a tirade if you dared suggest that he settle a case involving an impoverished single mother with two small children before Christmas.

"What does Christmas have to do with it?" he would probably bellow.

"Well, you know, being disabled, destitute, and in a fight for survival with a multibillion-dollar insurance company would tend to dampen the spirit of the holiday somewhat."

Collins would undoubtedly rant at such an irrelevant and mindless suggestion. He was a *true* company man.

Rumor had it that Collins once wore army battle fatigues to an insurance defense seminar to demonstrate his view that "this is war." His disdain for claimants' lawyers and their clients is legendary.

Torrence has a similar persona and style. He is an issue spotter and disagreement creator without equal. Don't get me wrong about him. It's not that he's not a good lawyer. Torrence is certainly a good lawyer–very skilled, very able. But to me, he did some things that were kind of hard to understand. Really rather strange.

∧ ∨ ∧ ∨ ∧

TO ME, LORI BERNARD WAS VERY DIFFERENT FROM COLLINS AND Torrence. Although she was on the opposite side of the table, I thought of her as a straight shooter whom I felt we could basically trust.

So one day in June 2001 during the discovery phase of the case, just after Bernard had taken Joan's deposition, I tried to reopen settlement discussions. I told her that I was worried, worried that something serious might happen.

"You know, Lori," I said, "she's on heavy antidepressant medication. The doctors are concerned that she's suicidal. This is really one you guys should settle. What do you think?"

"It doesn't make any difference what I think," she said. "It's the client's decision."

"But you can't just say 'it's the client's decision.' You and Horace are their lawyers. They will certainly listen to you. We're talking about life and death here."

"It's the client's decision," she reiterated.

I had seen this attitude before. What was it, I wondered, that allowed some lawyers to back away like this? Had they traded in their compassion for their bar cards? But perhaps I wasn't being fair to Lori. She knew her client, and her client had an agenda. It seemed that UnumProvident's game plan had little room for reasonableness. The company seemed to thrive on going to the mat whenever it thought it had the slightest chance of gaining an advantage by doing so, often using what seemed to be almost any ploy or argument, no matter how ridiculous or specious.

One case our firm had previously handled was that of Susan McGregor. To me, the circumstances of her situation were not only compelling but truly indicative of the difference between a merely outrageous refusal to pay benefits owed and a morally bankrupt one. Like Joan, Susan originally bought her policy from Paul Revere Life Insurance Company. As mentioned, Paul Revere was later taken over by Provident. Provident then merged with Unum.

For years, Susan had been the court reporter for the presiding judge of the San Francisco Superior Court, Alfred Chiantelli. The job entailed accurately transcribing court proceedings at the rate of at least two hundred words per minute while listening to multiple speakers, sometimes including a testifying witness, four or five or more attorneys, plus the judge. Transcripts have to be certified as accurate before they can be filed with the court clerk. They are often used not only by the parties to the proceedings but by the trial court, the court of appeal, and the state supreme court.

The years of constant stress on Susan's wrists took their toll. Her repetitive stress and cubital tunnel (behind the funny bone on the inside of the elbow) injuries were so severe that she was forced to wear braces on both wrists. Chiantelli said that she was the best court reporter he'd ever had and one of the most honest people he'd ever met. She tried, he said, as hard as a person could, to keep working, but she simply reached the point that she couldn't keep up anymore.

Susan had slowed so much that she had to regularly interrupt court proceedings, asking witnesses to repeat themselves or to speak more slowly. At times, Judge Chiantelli found her quietly crying in pain, rubbing her wrists, totally frustrated with her inability to keep up.

Susan was taking high doses of medication every night to avoid being awakened by the pain. Her treating physician said her injuries were severe and permanent. He further stated that continuing as a court reporter would worsen her injuries.

Could there be any doubt that Susan McGregor should receive disability payments because she could no longer perform as a court reporter?

Apparently, the evidence was not sufficient for UnumProvident, which terminated her benefits. According to the company, she simply wasn't injured. And even if she was, said the company, her injuries weren't disabling.

Just in case this theory wouldn't sway a jury, the company's lawyers came up with another defense: that Susan was still able to perform "the substantial and material duties" of her own occupation. Why? Because one of Susan's duties as a court reporter was to scope, or proofread, her work. Since she could still scope, said UnumProvident, Susan was not totally disabled as a court reporter.

It was only after Susan's lawsuit was filed that the company hired a court reporter as an expert witness to testify about the duties of a reporter. Clearly, UnumProvident expected him to support its scoping theory. Under the leading questioning of company lawyers, perhaps he did. However, on cross-examination in his deposition, UnumProvident's expert folded like cheap stationery. He admitted that although scoping *was* one of the duties of a court reporter, that didn't mean that a reporter who couldn't transcribe proceedings but could proofread wasn't disabled. No, it didn't mean that at all.

In terms of damages, under California law, an insurance company that denies a claim unfairly is responsible for paying the present value of future policy benefits in a lump sum, plus damages for its insured's emotional distress, consequential damages (losses that occur as a direct result of the insurance company's actions), costs and fees, and possibly punitive damages. The "present value" part of this simply refers to discounting a lump-sum payment for future benefits to account for the fact that inflation won't take its toll if the money is paid today rather than years from now. If the particular policy includes a cost of living adjustment (COLA), then the benefits don't have to be discounted because the COLA offsets inflation.

In terms of her losses, the value of Susan's policy benefits was less than $300,000. However, her other damages were considerable. The company was forcing Susan to litigate—with all of the attendant commitment of time, energy, and money—when it was aware she needed to be devoting her energy to other concerns: her husband was dying of leukemia. In addition, with her income cut off, UnumProvident's refusal to pay added substantially to Susan's difficulties.

We saw Susan's case as having a settlement value of over $700,000. The company's offer was $200,000—less than the policy benefits alone.

A short time before the McGregor trial began, we were scheduled to attend a settlement mediation. This is a type of private dispute resolution meeting that has become popular as a way of resolving cases short of trial. Each side submits to the other a list of two or three distinguished, retired trial or appellate judges. When a mutually acceptable judge is chosen, a nonbinding settlement conference is held. The judge meets with both sides and tries to bring about a resolution of the case.

These efforts are often quite successful, in large part due to the experience and credibility of the retired judges. It's hard to ignore the opinion of someone who has presided over a few thousand civil trials or appeals. The judges who do this kind of work have seen just about everything. In addition, and almost without exception, they are all very, very smart.

For a mediation to be successful, both sides have to be thoroughly prepared, they must have full settlement authority, and they have to be willing to listen.

UnumProvident started out by simply rejecting all three of the retired judge mediators whose names we had submitted. We then submitted another four names, but they were also rejected. Instead, the company insisted on using Steve Stein, a lawyer. Although we'd had no experiences with Stein, in an effort to move matters along, we agreed to accept him.

Next, the company insisted that Susan and her husband, Bill, both attend the settlement mediation. It seemed to me that the reason for this was to attempt to wear them down and pressure them to undersettle. The company insisted on this despite knowing of Bill's condition. Again, in an effort to resolve the case, Susan and Bill agreed.

Several all-day conferences were then held with Stein. More than ten hours were devoted to settlement discussions. Yet at no time did UnumProvident ever raise its original $200,000 offer. Not by a dime. All the company accomplished was to frustrate its own hand-picked mediator, exhaust Susan and Bill McGregor, and distract us from our trial preparation.

Instead of bringing the two sides closer, the mediation actually escalated the conflict. As soon as the conferences ended, Paul Revere noticed additional depositions and released a torrent of pretrial motions seemingly aimed at sowing chaos and escalating the conflict.

The company and its attorney of choice, the previously mentioned Francis Torrence, were apparently betting that Susan would cave in, as did so many others. That she and her dying husband would give up and take whatever settlement they could get. But they didn't know Susan. And they certainly didn't know her husband.

We went to trial.

During the course of the three-week case, a number of interesting events occurred that I felt could happen only with Torrence and Collins calling the shots. In addition to their "definition of disability" and "definition of court reporting" defenses, the Torrence-Collins team's medical expert, Dr. Richard Rubenstein, testified about his conclusions from what he called a qualified medical examination.

A qualified medical examination, he explained, simply involves the analysis of an individual's medical condition from studying his or her medical records. Citing page and line from Susan's chart, Rubenstein detailed his analysis and conclusions in what seemed to me like hours of some of the most confident and convincing material testimony I'd ever heard. His bottom line was that the records made clear that Susan was not disabled. She simply wasn't.

When Torrence finished his questioning, I stood up with my disorganized-looking notes. Rubenstein had the look of a man who was very pleased with himself. He was poised to smother whatever feeble cross-examination I might come up with. The guy had impeccable credentials. He was a pillar of the community. His confidence was almost palpable.

I asked Rubenstein to again confirm that a qualified medical examination was a process in which the physicians, after thoroughly studying an individual's medical records, drew conclusions about the person's condition.

He looked at me as if he wanted to ask if I'd been paying any attention at all. "Yes," he said impolitely.

"But," I said, "that's not what you did, is it?"

Rubenstein seemed to pretend not to know what I meant.

"You didn't go through the medical records carefully and thoroughly, did you?"

The guy suddenly looked like he had just inhaled a mosquito.

"Uh, no, not all of them," he said.

I asked if he knew that the records he hadn't looked at included those of a doctor who, in fact, had found Susan to be disabled.

He wasn't sure.

This was a major blow to Rubenstein's testimony. For him to have formed his opinions based on incomplete records made his testimony shaky at best.

When I asked him to explain to the jury how much value it should give to a chart review by an insurance company's paid expert witness who hadn't read the entire chart, the good doctor's confident demeanor quickly faded.

The balance of his testimony fell flat. He stumbled a bit as he stepped down from the witness stand and, struggling to recover his composure, cast a weak smile at the jurors. No one smiled back. As the court took a recess, Rubenstein wandered out into the hallway, where I saw him fifteen or twenty minutes later, sitting on a bench in the corridor with Torrence, rifling through some papers. "Just watch," I thought, "I'll bet this guy is going to come back and testify some more."

Sure enough, when court resumed, Torrence put him back on the stand in an attempt to rehabilitate him. Rubenstein's confidence seemed restored. He testified that now he *had* seen all the records. He had studied them carefully, and they made absolutely no difference to his opinion–no difference, whatsoever. I was surprised that he didn't add, "So there."

On recross, I asked him how he had gotten his hands on the additional records so quickly. From whom did he get them?

From Francis Torrence, he said.

"Mr. Torrence called his office and had someone hand-carry a copy of the report over here, correct?"

"Correct."

"Would it be a logical conclusion to draw from that, that he had the report in his office?"

"Yes."

"And he never gave it to you before?"

I guess not, he responded, casting a furtive glance at Torrence. Torrence seemed to be struggling to appear bored.

We then proceeded to go through the previously withheld medical report, page by page, line by line. It was filled with detailed information, tests, procedures, opinions, diagnosis, conclusions–virtually all of it confirming the plaintiff's disability. None of this, according to Rubenstein, had made the slightest difference to his opinion. It was unbelievable.

∧ ∨ ∧ ∨ ∧

THREE WEEKS AFTER THE MCGREGOR TRIAL HAD COMMENCED, THE jury unanimously found Paul Revere guilty of bad faith and awarded damages to Susan in the amount of $1.3 million.

But Paul Revere/UnumProvident and its crew weren't done. Following the verdict, they offered to settle. *But* the offer had a condition. We had to accept a "confidentiality" agreement. Such agreements conceal the terms and amounts of settlements from the public. Although we hate these agreements, we usually swallow hard and sign in order to get the victim his or her money quickly.

But in this case, UnumProvident wanted more than mere secrecy. Not only did it want the terms and amount of the settlement kept confidential but it wanted all the evidence back: all the depositions, all the documents, all the admissions. It wanted every copy of the trial transcript. It wanted the verdict to be sealed and the judgment to be vacated. There was to be no disclosure of anything to anyone. This included departments of insurance, insurance committees of the state legislature, judges in other cases, other lawyers, other clients, the print and broadcast media, the internet world, *everyone*. The case was to be wiped out of existence. Furthermore, any breach of this so-called of this settlement was to be punishable by a $10,000-per-violation "liquidated damages" penalty backed up by an agreement to pay any and all attorneys' fees incurred by Unum-Provident in pursuing this remedy.

I was incredulous–and furious. Years ago, the trend began that was aimed at keeping the *amount* of lawsuit settlements confidential. To do that was one thing, but to use litigation settlement agreements to bury facts and evidence revealing fraudulent or dangerous practices was something else.

To use a settlement agreement to cover up wrongdoing amounted to paying people off to keep their mouths shut so that the defendant can avoid public scrutiny and continue to victimize others.

For UnumProvident's lawyers to think they could buy ours and the McGregors' silence was astonishing.

Instead, we did just the opposite, emailing a memo spelling out UnumProvident's demands to everyone we could think of. Lawyers, clients, the media–everyone. Responses asking for the details poured in from all over the country. Not long afterward, a panel of federal judges from North Carolina issued an order banning these types of agreements in their district. They should be banned everywhere.

Having failed in its cover-up efforts, the defendants next tied up the case in a string of posttrial motions. Motions for a new trial. Motions to reduce the verdict. Motions for a judgment by the court contrary to the verdict and others. The trial judge, Phyllis Hamilton, wrote a twenty-three-page opinion denying all of them.

About seven months after the verdict, Bill McGregor, a courageous and wonderful man, succumbed to his illness. Susan had not yet received a dime. Not on the verdict and not on her policy benefits. Paul Revere/UnumProvident appealed. Going to the mat. Hunkering down. Letting the blood spill where it may.

∧ ∨ ∧ ∨ ∧

I WASN'T SURPRISED THAT MY SETTLEMENT EFFORTS WITH LORI Bernard in the Hangarter case had gone nowhere. She and Horace Green were not the problem. Somebody in Chattanooga or Worcester was. And whoever that was, Chris Collins undoubtedly had something to do with it.

One day about two months before the Hangarter trial, I talked directly with Collins by phone. He delivered a stinging lecture to me about how ethical and fair his company was and on how unethical and unfair plaintiffs' lawyers were. At a subsequent settlement conference, his company wound up offering $500,000 to settle the case. That was it. Take it or we go to trial. Half a million dollars sounded like a lot of money, but it wasn't even half the value of Joan's policy benefits. By the time she paid the out-of-pocket costs in the case, she would wind up with only a fraction of what UnumProvident owed her. We simply weren't going to agree to that.

∧ ∨ ∧ ∨ ∧

ONE OF THE PURPOSES OF FORMAL DISCOVERY IS TO OBTAIN DOCUMENTS and records from the other side. This is often done by subpoena or through what is called a Request for Production of Documents. In our cases against UnumProvident, we've pressed numerous such discovery efforts, searching for records concerning the various initiatives launched by Mohney starting with when he took over Provident's claims department in the early 1990s.

UnumProvident, like many defendants, fought having to release such records. It used arguments of privilege and relevance; it said that gathering the records would be burdensome and oppressive. It fought like hell on every ground imaginable. But we hung on, kicking up so much of a fuss that eventually we were rewarded with more boxes of paper than we had space for in our conference room. If it couldn't get away with refusing to produce documents, UnumProvident's fall-back position was to suffocate the opposition.

Through all of this, I came to wonder if at some point I would discover a checklist for spinning a treating doctor's written records into a justification for terminating or denying benefits. I could envision how it would read.

> Patient history? Was there anything indicating an undisclosed, possibly uninsured, preexisting condition? If not, then did the claimant at one time work with the condition? If so, was it possible the claimant might be able to continue to do so?
>
> Objective/subjective? Most medical diagnoses are based on patient reporting. "Does this hurt? Can you do that?" Can a treating doctor's diagnosis be attacked on the basis that most or all of the medical conclusions were based on subjective information or "self-reporting"?
>
> Different interpretations? If there *was* objective evidence of illness or injury, was that evidence subject to more than one interpretation? "Would this condition *always* cause disability? Would it *always* cause incapacitating pain?"
>
> Inconsistencies? Were there any signs, symptoms, tests, examinations, or evaluations that were inconsistent with the opinions and conclusions of the treating doctor(s)?
>
> How long? Could one say with medical certainty that a particular illness or injury would *never* resolve or improve? (Most doctors used "short window" periods, such as the next six months, to describe disability durations. And rarely would a physician say that a condition could never improve.)

Glass half full? Well, what *could* she/he do? What *was* normal? Was there any atrophy? Were reflexes "normal"? Were motor and sensory test results within acceptable ranges? Did the person stand normally? Hold the head normally? Were the claimant's eyebrows "normal"?

We never found such a checklist, but we found something far more damaging: confidential internal memos—dozens of them found buried among some four thousand documents turned over to us by UnumProvident.

Memos that weren't just smoking guns but smoking missile launchers.

Chapter Four

GO FIGURE

I NSURANCE COMPANIES CERTAINLY DO NOT OWE BENEFITS TO EVERY-
one who files a claim. Many claims are properly denied. In addition,
some insurers simply pay the benefits they owe. But if an insurance
company—any type of insurance company—wants to dramatically
increase revenues by denying or terminating valid claims, it can do
so. Although the numbers used here are based on estimates, in the
case of disability insurance claims the denial analysis might look
something like this.

There are three underlying realities to bear in mind.

First, there's an important difference between short-term and
long-term disability claims. The former include conditions such as
broken arms or wrists. They involve payouts over a limited period
of time and, from an insurers' point of view, are not usually worth
fighting about. The latter claims are for more permanent conditions
and usually involve substantial sums of money.

Second, group policyholders—most of whom have ERISA-
preempted policies—tend to have lower monthly benefits than individual policyholders.

Third, a company seeking to increase revenues by terminating
valid claims has to reject only a small percentage of carefully targeted claimants in order to increase profits by hundreds of millions
and billions of dollars.

For purposes of our example, let's say a disability insurer receives
400,000 claims per year of which 100,000 involve the larger, long-
term disability claims. Let's also say that the *individual* long-term
benefit amounts average $3,500 per month and that the *ERISA*
long-term benefits average $850 per month. Both the non-ERISA

and ERISA claims in our example have an average payout period of twelve years.

The term "reserves" refers to the amount of money an insurer has to set aside to pay for its anticipated claims over the life of the claims. Reserves are counted against company profits. Therefore, a company willing to engage in wrongful benefit terminations can reduce its reserves and thus illegally boost profits. Let's look at the math.

Out of the total of 100,000 long-term claimants, let's say the company decides to target just 5,000. By cheating only 5 percent of its claimants, an insurance company can fly under the public-outrage radar by arguing that those complaining about unfair practices are ignoring all the claims the company does pay.

Assume that 3,000 of the 5,000 targeted claimants are ERISA preempted. Because, as previously discussed, these people have no right to sue for fraud or bad faith and have no right to a jury trial or compensatory or punitive damages, they have no leverage to even get the insurer to simply pay what it owes. They can scream "breach of contract" and they can demand fairness until they gag, but all the company has to say is "we disagree." These claimants are at the mercy of cheating insurers.

In plain English, they're screwed.

To see the extent of this problem, one need only look to a highly confidential internal memo that we pried from UnumProvident's grasp in discovery (see Exhibit 7). In it, the company bragged that it could save over 90 percent on claims preempted by ERISA.

Once ERISA claimants realize they have no leverage, they are only too happy to accept a cash settlement of a fraction of the amount actually owed to them. Even a tiny settlement is better than a worthless lawsuit—especially to a struggling, disabled person.

Back to the math. We don't know what the average monthly benefit would be on carefully targeted ERISA claims, but even using the conservative estimate of $850 per month referenced above, with an average payout period of twelve years, the total value of each of these 3,000 claims would be about $122,000 ($10,200 per year times twelve years). Given that some policies contain cost of living adjustments (COLAs) that keep benefits current with inflation and that others do not, the present value of the amount owed over the lifetime of each claim would probably average about $100,000. Even if a company would agree to pay these ERISA claimants an average of $30,000 (which is a *very* high estimate), the company would still pocket $70,000 per claim. And $70,000 times 3,000 claims comes to $210 million in "savings" on the ERISA claims over the lifetimes of these 3,000 policies.

Moving on to the big money, the individual (non-ERISA) claims, our conservative estimate here is that they are worth an average of $3,500 per month each. That comes to $42,000 per year each. If 200 of the 2,000 non-ERISA claimants are too weak, too trusting, too powerless, or too disabled to do anything effective about being cut off, the company saves more than $500,000 ($42,000 per year times twelve years) on each claim. Again, taking both COLA and non-COLA policies into account and reducing these claims to their present values, the lifetime benefits total comes to about $390,000 each. Multiplied by 200 claims, this adds up to about $78 million in savings to the company.

Assume that the 1,750 claimants remaining all put up a fight. Perhaps 1,000 of them will complain and negotiate with the insurer either on their own or through a lawyer. But these 1,000 insureds all live in the great majority of states–such as New York, Massachusetts, Connecticut, Ohio, Illinois, Kansas, Virginia, the Carolinas, the Dakotas, Texas, and dozens of other places–that have no effective insurance bad-faith laws: no accelerated benefits, no consequential damages, no right to recover out-of-pocket costs expended in seeking benefits due, and limited or no punitive damages allowed for fraudulent claims practices. So guess what? These individuals wind up in the same sinking life raft with the ERISA folks. The company settles these cases in about the same way it handles ERISA settlements: Whap. Then it puts another couple of hundred million dollars over the lives of these policies in the *P* column on its profit and loss statement.

The final roughly 750 insureds are not ERISA preempted, are not too weak to fight, and are residents of states that *do* have bad-faith laws with the threat of punitive damages. Within this group, most will still settle their cases for 60 to 90 percent of what they are owed or less. They will do this either because they buy into their insurer's argument that if they don't, the company will drag the matter out for years and they may not live to see a dime or because they have lawyers who are no match for those of their insurance company. And so, even as to these individuals, the company is able to hang on to another few million dollars per year–$10 to $15 million over the twelve years remaining on the benefit periods.

The last 50 or 75 claimants are the holdouts. About 95 percent of them will eventually settle–but for more money than the rest. Many will obtain the full value of their policies. Some will also be compensated for economic hardship, emotional distress, and the cost and fees incurred in having to sue for their insurance benefits. The company will take a loss on these insureds, perhaps totaling as much as $5 to $10 million dollars in all.

Last, four to ten of the original 5,000 claimants will actually go to trial. Of these, the insurer may defend one or two based on luck-of-the-draw issues such as the unanimous verdict requirements in federal court, antilitigation attitudes among jurors, or other factors such as dislike of the particular plaintiff or the plaintiff's lawyer. There may be a few modest verdicts. Finally, large punitive damages awards may be rendered in two or three cases. The insurer will negotiate to settle the large verdicts, or it will appeal and drag the matter out for another couple of years with the chance of reversal and retrial hovering over the waiting claimant who still has not received a dime of disability benefits.

The questions that have to be answered are these: Out of the original 5,000 wrongfully terminated claims, will the total amount of the settlements, costs, expenses, and paid verdicts exceed the amounts of the benefits owed? Or will the total come to only a fraction of that sum? If it exceeds the amount of the benefits, then the illegal conduct is deterred. If it totals only a fraction of that amount, then the conduct is encouraged. In our example, the company's net profits from its bad-faith conduct would probably be in the hundreds of millions of dollars. But that's for only one year's worth of claims. Next year there's a new batch–a new pool of 400,000 total claims, a new pool of 100,000 long-term disabilities, and a new pool of 5,000 targets.

The math, though based on estimates for illustrative purposes only, explains why and how an insurer can stack the deck so blatantly and why some companies have little concern over whether they might lose a big case now and then. Even tens of millions of dollars in punitive damages are petty cash in the context of the broad picture.

Moreover, as will be discussed in later chapters, when one factors in the personal financial incentives and the possibility of indemnification agreements and other protections afforded to the high-ranking executives calling some of these shots, the bottom line is that it pays to cheat. Big time.

∧ ∨ ∧ ∨ ∧

CHATTANOOGA IS ONE OF THOSE PLACES PEOPLE ARE APT TO CALL "pleasant." Chamber of commerce brochures proudly proclaim it to be "conveniently located near the Georgia border and at the junction of four interstate highways."

In addition to a very nice aquarium and more than five miles of riverbank walking paths, the city boasts the Appalachian Trail, Lookout Mountain, and several Civil War battlefield sites, not to mention the ever-popular Chattanooga Choo Choo. In addition to all of this, Chattanooga is also home base for two thousand five hundred UnumProvident employees. On August 22, 2001, I was in town to depose one of them, Ralph Mohney.

We had obtained thousands of pages of discovery from Unum-Provident, including many confidential internal memos authored by high-ranking company officers and senior management. I was interested in asking Mohney about these documents and about his role in formulating the policies they reflected. I also wanted to get a feel for him as a witness, to see how he answered questions and held up under pressure. Beyond this, however, I was hoping that by appealing to him directly, I might be able to put together a reasonable settlement for Joan that would avoid the necessity of trial.

Following a room service breakfast of canned fruit topped off by a Sara Lee croissant and washed down with a nice warm cup of instant coffee, I was ready for action.

"Look," I said to Mohney before we went on the record, "it makes no sense to drag this out. Can't we just settle it?"

He looked at me with an expression that managed to combine impatience with boredom. He shot a look at two of his lawyers, Sean Nalty and Horace Green, as if to say, "Do I really have to sit here and listen to this?" They got the message.

"We're here for Mr. Mohney's deposition," Green said. "Let's get on with it, shall we?"

Green was a relatively patient man. He had to be. During the past several months, he had listened to my settlement efforts more than once. He knew the pitch by heart. Although boring him wasn't on my to-do list, I was going to make him hear it still another time. This was, after all, my chance to talk directly to a senior vice president and head of the entire claims department. UnumProvident had over twelve thousand employees worldwide, and Mohney had authority over a big chunk of them, including thousands of claims employees working in Chattanooga, Tennessee; Portland, Maine; Worcester, Massachusetts; Glendale, California; and Toronto, Canada.

Who knows, I thought, with all those responsibilities, maybe Mohney hadn't been apprised of the human side of the lawsuit, of Joan Hangarter's suffering. Maybe I could make him see beyond a file's case number to the vulnerable woman. I wasn't about to ignore the opportunity.

"Do you realize," I asked, "that Joan is a single mother? That she has two young children? That she has been forced to declare bankruptcy? That she is destitute? On food stamps? That she was evicted from her home? That she has been placed on antidepressant medication?"

Mohney's response was a glare. He looked as if he wanted to tell me just where to shove it. I wasn't deterred. I guess it's just not in my nature to back off. Some modicum of humanity had to be buried under the armor of mister company man.

"You know you owe the money. Why aren't you just paying the claim?"

Mohney continued to glare. I shrugged, waiting for an answer.

"If we don't get started with this deposition now," said Green, emphasizing the *now*, "I'm going to be forced to terminate these proceedings."

"All right," I relented. "Let's go on the record."

This was not going to be a typical deposition. The court reporter had heard my plea. As she administered the oath, she looked curiously into Mohney's eyes. What was this all about? Who was this person being deposed? And who was the woman whose life had supposedly been destroyed by his company?

I ran Mohney through name, rank, and serial number. The more I knew about his employment experience, history, education, and other background information, the better the feel I would have for him as a person. This would help in structuring my approach to the examination.

We went through Provident's history, starting with the Paul Revere acquisition in 1997 and the Unum merger several years later. In addition, UnumProvident had either acquired or bought the books of business for Colonial Life, John Hancock, Great West, New England Financial, and numerous other companies. In addition to UnumProvident's US operations, Mohney said that the company was active in England, Japan, Argentina, and Canada.

Mohney professed little specific knowledge of the total number of own-occupation policies that had been sold or of other such data. He did say that the company received roughly 400,000 claims per year, of which 120,000 were for long-term disabilities. I was aware that UnumProvident had over 25 million policyholders nationwide.

Mohney saw his duties as the head of UnumProvident's Customer Care Center as including the responsibility to establish the company's claims-handling philosophy. He repeatedly stated that it was his practice to employ the "highest ethical standards" in all aspects of his work.

I knew from the confidential internal company memos we'd obtained that practices established by UnumProvident–and signed off on by Mohney himself–could hardly be characterized as reflecting such standards. But pinning Mohney down on the meaning of those documents or practices, particularly in the context of a deposition where no judge was at the table to overrule defense objections, proved to be impossible. Every effort I made to nail him about specific activities fell flat. Mohney was more than up to the task of dodging my questions. He either wasn't quite sure what a particular phrase meant, or he refused to respond to a question based on attorney-client privilege, or he asserted that words in a memo were being taken out of context and didn't mean what they seemed to say.

After trying for hours to get him to provide answers I'd traveled all the way to Chattanooga to get, I finally realized that all I was doing was spinning my wheels and helping prepare him for what he'd be facing at trial. It made more sense to bring this evidence in through witnesses friendly to our side and through our own experts than to continue to listen to Mohney provide his well-prepared and well-rehearsed recitations.

I'd consumed the canned fruit, Sara Lee croissant, and instant coffee for nothing. Mohney, with his team of skillful lawyers, had proved too slippery for me. At least in the context of a deposition.

One additional line of questioning I decided to defer was the subject of UnumProvident's Hungry Vulture Award. Until word of it leaked out, this award was regularly given to employees who best embodied the values and represented the interests of the company. The award was sometimes presented by President Harold Chandler himself. The award bore the inscription "Patience, my foot . . . I'm gonna kill something" (see Exhibit 1).

∧ ∨ ∧ ∨ ∧

A WEEK BEFORE COMMENCEMENT OF THE HANGARTER TRIAL, WE attended one final settlement conference with UnumProvident's defense team. The present value of Joan's past and future policy benefits alone came to just less than $1.2 million. This did not include Joan's fees, costs, an assessment of her general damages, or anything else. But she wanted to settle and directed us to base our demand on that amount.

The mediator, a distinguished federal judge named Maria Elena James, had the two sides seated in separate conference rooms. This was typical of the usual settlement conference format in which the mediator talks with the members of one side first, peppering them with dozens of questions about the facts and legal issues. She or he then moves on to the second party and repeats the process.

Judge James started with our side. She spoke directly to Joan, watching her closely and sizing her up as a witness, asking her detailed questions about her injuries, current condition, medical prognosis, and former duties. Judge James then turned to us. Who would be the plaintiff's witnesses? Had they all been deposed? What were they going to say? What about the medical testimony? What was the defense contending? Who were the defense witnesses? What was the present value of the past and future policy benefits owed to Joan?

What were our thoughts about why UnumProvident wasn't putting up more money to settle?

She turned back to Joan. Did she realize the value of putting all of this behind her? What was her financial situation? How were the children holding up? Did Joan realize how unpredictable a jury could be?

Then Judge James went over to the other conference room. Undoubtedly, she had a similar conversation with the other side. She was gone for more than an hour. When she came back, she looked drawn. The other side had a different take on the evidence. We assumed that although UnumProvident's lawyers were putting some of their best arguments forward, they were also holding back some surprises that they had in store for the trial.

Although both sides had been required to bring someone to the mediation with full settlement authority, we knew from past experience that UnumProvident's senior management placed severe caps on that authority to make sure the attorneys and company representatives didn't get carried away at settlement conferences based on a judge's comments.

After Judge James had spent seven or eight unsuccessful hours trying to resolve the case, I suggested, as a last-ditch effort, that we get Chris Collins on the speakerphone and talk with him directly. I knew from Sandra Fryc's deposition that Ralph Mohney had to personally approve any settlement above a million dollars. Collins had the ear of Mohney. And Mohney had the money.

We all sat down in one room, and Judge James got Collins on the phone. She introduced herself and explained that the parties seemed to be at an impasse. Not long into the conversation, in response to a comment relating to the plaintiff's allegations, Collins launched into one of his diatribes on how moral and ethical UnumProvident was and how it was being unfairly painted by plaintiffs' lawyers. UnumProvident would never dream of violating the law. The company, he said, was concerned about avoiding payment only on claims it didn't owe. It had millions of policyholders and corporate sponsors from coast to coast. It had the best customer care department in the business. On and on he droned. I listened for as long as I could. And then I listened some more.

Finally, I reached my limit. I calmly asked Collins how moral a company was that manipulated policy language, concealed benefits, twisted medical testimony, put out memos about shredding documents, and came up with schemes to increase profits by millions of dollars a year by cutting off people's benefits? I asked him how an ethical company could intimidate insureds into taking twenty or thirty cents on the dollar, could force people to sue in order to get the benefits they were owed, and could drive single mothers to the edge of their sanity. I asked if he had heard that Bill McGregor had died and wondered when he was going to pay Susan her benefits.

I had more that I wanted to ask, but I never got the chance.

The case was not going to settle. We were going to trial.

∧ ∨ ∧ ∨ ∧

WHEN IT CAME TO LITIGATION, UNUMPROVIDENT HAD A REPUTATION for fighting about everything. Typically, its lawyers would file production request after production request, demand after demand, and motion after motion. They wanted a protective order for this or a limitation on the use of that. This memo was privileged. That one was confidential. They would conduct marathon depositions of the plaintiff. They would seek to discover tax records. They would unearth information from divorce proceedings, take statements from former business partners, and send out surveillance teams and private investigators. When it was time for trial, they would list dozens of prospective witnesses, file countless pretrial motions, and send out late-night faxes announcing their latest demands.

In almost all our cases, often just days before trial, they would file an objection to the introduction, use of, or reference to any of the so-called documents that were generated when Unum-Provident was called Provident Life and Accident or Paul Revere or Unum or the Provident Companies. These documents, the company would claim, were irrelevant, prejudicial, not the "best evidence," and hard to read. They were hearsay. They related to a different company. A different corporation. A different entity. A different "legal person." UnumProvident was not the same company as these others.

It was immaterial, they claimed, that UnumProvident was the successor in interest to all these other companies. It was immaterial that the fingerprints of Chandler and Mohney were on virtually every document.

∧ ∨ ∧ ∨ ∧

DEALING WITH UNUMPROVIDENT MADE ME THINK OF WILLIAM PIERCE, a tough bully that had terrorized so many of us for so long back at St. Joan of Arc Grammar School. He'd gotten away with it for years.

Finally, one of his victims, Tommy, decided that he'd had enough. He hauled off and slammed Pierce in the mouth, knocking him on his backside right in front of everybody. We figured that was the end of Tommy. Pierce was going to kill him.

But Pierce didn't do a thing. He just sat there looking at the blood on his hands and staring at all of us glaring down on him. He didn't bully anybody for the rest of the year. The next fall, he didn't show up for school. We later found out that he had transferred to PS 12.

Chapter Five

THE SEVENTH AMENDMENT

O N JANUARY 14, 2002, SIXTY-SEVEN PROSPECTIVE JURORS WERE herded into the fourteen-row gallery section of Department F on the fifteenth floor of the US District Court Building in San Francisco. The two teams of attorneys, consisting of three lawyers each, were seated with their clients at two large rectangular counsel tables aligned parallel to the empty jury box and perpendicular to the judge's bench. Dozens of cardboard file boxes filled with records, documents, reports, pleadings, interrogatory answers, responses to admissions requests, and other filings lay neatly stacked and labeled on a long bench that ran the width of the room between the attorneys and the gallery.

Weeks before, final discovery had been completed and several hundred pages of pretrial motions filed with the judge. Both sides, as required, submitted to the court their witness lists and indexed exhibit binders, with copies sent to opposing counsel. Three four-inch volumes were filed by the plaintiff, four by the defendants.

As the prospective jurors were selecting seats, the court deputy, Wings Hom, handed each attorney a printout listing the names and assigned numbers of the panelists. A young law clerk for the defense immediately scurried out to the hallway with a printout, returning a few moments later empty handed.

Once everyone was settled in, Hom called the roll. He then picked up his telephone, cupped his hand around the receiver, and whispered softly into the mouthpiece. A few minutes later, he stood and asked everyone to rise.

"Department F of the United States District Court for the Northern District of California is now in session, the Honorable James Larson, presiding."

Judge Larson entered and stepped up to the bench. He was a serious, athletic-looking man with penetrating eyes and a no-nonsense demeanor. He had a reputation for being an extremely smart, savvy judge. If a lawyer neglected to ask an important question of a witness, Larson wouldn't hesitate to step in and do so. He didn't believe in legal chess. He believed in fairness. I felt he was a good judge to have in this case. He was not the type of person to put up with any nonsense from the lawyers or from their clients. Like all exceptional judges, Larson had an exceptional law clerk, Kathleen Campbell.

After smiling a warm good morning and welcoming everyone to his court, Judge Larson briefly touched on the importance of jury service. He then introduced the attorneys: Ray Bourhis, Alice Wolfson, and David Lilienstein representing the plaintiff, Joan Hangarter; Horace Green, Lori Bernard, and Edward Corrigan for the defendants, Paul Revere, UnumProvident Insurance Group.

"The case that you have been called upon to serve in today is a civil matter," he said. "We will be calling approximately fourteen jurors to wind up with a final jury of six plus two alternates.

"I will be asking each of you who's called upon to sit in the box a number of questions about your backgrounds in general, where you live, what your family consists of, what your occupational history has been, some of your interests . . . and so on. Those who turn out not to be particularly well suited to sit on this case may be challenged for cause. If that happens, you'll be excused and sent back to the jury room to find a case that might be better suited to you.

"In addition to these challenges for cause," said Judge Larson, "there are what we call peremptory challenges. These are the challenges that the attorneys are entitled to exercise based on various intangible, subjective factors. The goal in all of this is to do the best we can to obtain a fair and open-minded panel of jurors that will consider the evidence and law presented."

Judge Larson proceeded to read a brief, neutral statement, previously agreed to by both sides, describing the case.

He explained that the plaintiff contended that she had purchased an individual disability insurance policy from the defendants; that at some point she had filed a claim that she was disabled; that the company had begun making payments to her; and that despite evidence from the treating doctors that she continued to be totally disabled, it had subsequently terminated the benefits.

The defendants, he said, asserted that its decision was reasonable and proper. The company further alleged that Joan was not disabled from performing her duties as a chiropractor and that she was not entitled to any of the damages she was seeking.

∧ ∨ ∧ ∨ ∧

LITIGANTS WITH DEEP POCKETS ARE ALWAYS LOOKING FOR NEW AND improved ways to buy a strategic advantage. Jury-consulting firms, focus groups, and mock juries are three examples.

Jury-consulting firms can quickly provide detailed information about individuals listed on prospective juror lists. This information can include political party affiliations, voting histories, subscriptions, home ownership data, credit reports, motor vehicle registration records, organization memberships, and histories of internet and credit card purchases.

Focus groups consist of carefully selected teams of individuals who are given a general outline of the case. The teams are then fed additional pieces of information that might surface during trial. This information is given (or in the vernacular, "spun") to each team differently. Individual and group reactions are then measured and evaluated.

Mock juries involve the staging of an entire case before a paid jury in a simulated trial. In a defense mock trial, the roles of the plaintiff and the plaintiff's counsel are played by others. The defense attorneys play themselves. The results, along with comments and observations from the mock jurors, are carefully assessed.

All of this is supposed to help in making numerous strategic decisions: what kind of jury to select, which facts to emphasize, how to approach particular allegations, how to deal with difficult evidence, and so on.

After swearing in the entire panel, Hom began randomly picking fourteen numbers from a tumbler. These numbers corresponded to the numbers on the printout of prospective jurors. One by one, those called stood and were directed to their place in the jury box. Those not called remained in the gallery. As prospective jurors were excused, additional names were called to fill their places.

How people react to voir dire questioning varies greatly. Some are guarded and noncommittal, obviously not wanting to share personal information with a bunch of strangers. They give short answers: "Yes," "No," "Sometimes," "I'm not sure." It's hard to know what they might be thinking, even with pressing follow-up questions. Then there are the "yackers." They'll enthusiastically provide details about subjects they haven't even been asked, often about matters not even their closest relatives might want to know.

Hom began to call the names.

Juror number one was Mariaelena Arriaga. As she moved up to take her position in the box, Hom called number two, Elizabeth Halliburton. Next was David Romero. Then came Jeffrey Goldfine, Phillip Cecchettini, Robert Johns, Shirley Paganini, Oscar Ayala, Adriana Smith, Cheryl Burr, Donald McCause, Dan Malstrom, Carlos Giron, and William McKinley.

First, Judge Larson read a list of all the witnesses who might possibly be called to testify. He asked if any of the prospective jurors were acquainted with any of them. None were.

"Okay, Ms. Arriaga," he said, "I'm going to start with you."

Larson asked Arriaga if she had seen or read anything about the case, where she resided, and how long she had lived there. She replied that she had heard nothing about the case; lived in Richmond, California; and had moved to Richmond from Mexico several years before. In response to additional questions, she stated that she was married, had three children—aged six, five, and eleven months—and was working as a case manager at the Marin Community Clinic. She was a registered nurse with a specialty in pediatrics.

Judge Larson asked Arriaga questions about her hobbies, whether she regularly went to the movies or had a favorite television show. After asking a few more questions, Larson moved on to prospective juror number two, Elizabeth Halliburton.

Residence, educational background, training, experience, employment history, questions about relatives, personal experience with litigation, recent movies, books, subscriptions, etc. Halliburton said she was a graduate of Lewis and Clark College with a major in Spanish literature. She had a farm, raised horses, and was learning to play the piano. Her husband was a freelance photographer. She had never served on a jury before.

"What's the last book you've read?"

"*Dancing Naked in the Mind Field*," replied Halliburton. It was a book about the DNA chain written by Berkeley scientist Kary Mullis.

While Larson questioned, the lawyers listened, watching reactions and jotting notes.

David Romero worked in customer service for a prism manufacturing company. He subscribed to *Newsweek*, *Sports Illustrated*, and the local newspaper. His wife was a legal secretary for a large insurance defense firm.

Jeffrey Goldfine was an attorney who specialized in municipal law and land use. His undergraduate degree was in psychology. His most recent read was *The Art of War* by Sunzi (Sun Tzu).

Phillip Cecchettini was married. His wife was an art historian, and he had a twenty-nine-year-old son. Cecchettini, who had a master's degree in sociology, ran a small company and produced websites in the United States, Italy, and France. He loved to cook. He also had what he described as an extensive collection of "things dealing with the *Mona Lisa*."

When asked if he could be fair and impartial as a juror, Cecchettini volunteered that he had built a website for Dr. Richard Rubenstein, a forensic neurologist. "I don't know how relevant that is," he said, seeming to be holding something back, "but it could possibly be relevant." Judge Larson decided that rather than proceeding on this subject before the entire panel, he would hold off until Cecchettini could be questioned individually, out of the presence of the others.

Robert Johns, who was born in Martinez, California, lived in Napa. A retired construction worker and former marine, Johns at one time worked as a casino security guard. He now volunteered as a trailer attendant collecting contributions for the Salvation Army.

The more Johns talked, the more his personality charged forth. Pretty soon he had everyone smiling and nodding.

"What's the last movie you saw?" asked Judge Larson.

"*Dead Man Walking* with Sean Penn."

"And your favorite TV show?"

"I like *L.A. Law*. I like them late shows," said Johns.

"What about *Judge Judy*?" kidded Larson.

Johns shook his head firmly. "I'm not crazy for her."

"Good," replied Larson, "then you and I see eye to eye. Can you think of any reason, sir, that you can't be fair or open minded to the parties in this case?"

"No," said Johns. "I'm pretty levelheaded as far as judgment on people."

By the time the judge finished asking questions, Johns had many people in the courtroom agreeing with his self-assessment.

Shirley Paganini was from San Ramon. Now retired, she had worked as an accountant for a steel construction company for more than forty years. Her husband, who had served in the airborne in World War II, was retired from PG&E (Pacific Gas and Electric Company). Shirley had three grown children, subscribed to *Sunset*, *Kiplinger's*, and *Reader's Digest*, and was the former president of the local chapter of the Native Daughters of the Golden West.

On it went. Judge Larson questioned the rest of the potential jurors one by one.

Adriana Smith said she had been involved as both a plaintiff and defendant in a lawsuit and that she wasn't sure how that experience would affect her ability to be fair in this case. She also mentioned that she had experienced personal problems with an insurance company pertaining to a serious medical condition involving her daughter.

Dan Malstrom somewhat pointedly stated that he had a relative whom he would characterize as "chronically disabled." He had some doubts as to the authenticity of this condition.

William McKinley stated that he didn't know if he could be fair to both sides because of experiences he'd had in the merchant marine involving injuries to crew members that he thought were being exaggerated.

As Judge Larson reviewed his notes and prepared to proceed with the individual follow-up questions to be asked out of the earshot of the other panelists, I reflected on how much effort our legal system places on attempting to secure fair and impartial citizen juries. How different our system was from justice systems in which government employees or professional appointees make all the decisions.

Yet rather than recognizing and protecting this system, so many in our country are trying to dismantle and destroy it, weakening the power of juries, giving trial and appellate judges the power to second-guess their decisions, and proposing legislation to reduce the role of jurors in our civil justice system.

Halliburton was the first to be questioned privately. Judge Larson asked her to elaborate on her comment that she had recently heard a report on National Public Radio about a disability case against an insurance company. She said she really didn't remember the details. Judge Larson also asked her about a condition she had mentioned concerning an injury to her wrists. What, if any, effect might this have on her ability to be fair and impartial in a case involving a somewhat similar problem? Halliburton answered the questions matter-of-factly, without any sign of emotion. She thought she could serve in an objective and impartial manner.

Paganini was questioned about her high blood pressure and stress level and the effect jury service might have on her condition. This was a matter of obvious concern to Judge Larson, and although I wouldn't have minded having a juror empaneled who had experienced, firsthand, the effects of impairments on functional capacity, it was obvious that Paganini was going to be excused.

Cecchettini was asked to explain his comment about whether his website design experience with his medical expert witness client would tend to bias him against the insurance company in this case. He understood that some experts tried hard to see situations from the "glass-half-empty" perspective of those who had hired them to testify. He seemed to imply that this might be a particular problem in situations involving the kind of lucrative repeat business a large insurance company could provide.

Smith was asked about her experience involving her daughter. The little girl had Down's syndrome and congenital heart disease. Smith was forced into a fight with her insurer, which had refused to pay for covered surgeries based on the argument that they were "experimental."

Malstrom was quizzed about his mechanic cousin who he seemed to feel was exaggerating a disability claim. What did he know about the condition in question? Why did he feel it was being exaggerated? Whom had he spoken with about this?

McKinley was examined about his experiences in the merchant marine.

In the end, Paganini and Smith were excused. The others were not—at least not at this point.

I hoped we wouldn't ultimately have to waste peremptories with some of the folks remaining but thought Larson was probably right in not knocking them off for cause at this point—at least not based on the answers given to his questions. It was frustrating to me that the anti-insurance people always seemed to express self-doubt about their ability to be objective in reviewing evidence, while the pro-insurer types usually insisted that they could be fair and impartial despite their views. This was not the first time I'd witnessed this phenomenon. It wouldn't be the last.

∧ ∨ ∧ ∨ ∧

FOLLOWING THE LUNCH RECESS, WE WERE BACK IN COURT TO PICK UP where we'd left off. The first order of business was to explain to the panel that two jurors had been excused and would be replaced. Hom called Moralyn Giles and Sasha Saibi.

In answer to Judge Larson's questions, Giles stated that she was married, lived in San Ramon, had three children, and worked as a ticket agent for Northwest Airlines. Her husband was a youth administrator for a local church. The family liked to travel. She could think of no reason why she couldn't be a fair and impartial juror.

Saibi was employed by Hyatt Hotels. He was originally from Framingham, Massachusetts, and now lived in San Francisco. He was single, played the harmonica, and had never served on a jury before. He said he could be fair and impartial.

Judge Larson explained that he would turn the questioning over to the attorneys. The plaintiff would question the entire panel first, followed by the defense. After both sides were done, Judge Larson would take a brief recess to hear additional challenges for cause outside the presence of the panel. If any replacements were necessary, the new jurors would be questioned. Then a sheet of paper would be passed back and forth between the two sides. The attorneys would alternate writing down their peremptory challenges. Those panelists remaining would constitute the jury.

∧ ∨ ∧ ∨ ∧

I STARTED WITH MARIAELENA ARRIAGA, ASKING HER TO FILL IN SOME blanks about her work with the Marin Community Clinic. Did she have any experience with MRIs? With patients who had cervical disc disease? With epicondylitis? Was there anything in her work that required her to make repetitive, stressful movements of her arms, neck, hands, or wrists?

Had she ever had an occupation that required her to make repetitive strenuous use of any of those parts of her body? Did she have any personal experience with own-occupation disability insurance? Any close friends or relatives in the insurance or legal business?

The purpose of these questions was to determine whether anything in Arriaga's background might give her preconceived notions about issues that would be surfacing in the case. A prospective juror's answers and nonverbal reactions to such questions could sometimes give clues concerning the person's attitudes about these matters. In this instance, I got no clues.

Because jury selection is the first opportunity the attorneys have to address the people who will be deciding the case, it's a very important process. It sets impressions—one way or the other—that may be hard to unset. I find it a somewhat uncomfortable process. For one thing, I have trouble remembering names. I've tried everything from facial associations to repetition to memory books, but nothing works. It's really upsetting to me that some lawyers can just stand up after listening to the judge's questions and remember everyone's occupation, marital status, medical history, and favorite restaurants while I'm still struggling to figure out who's McDermott and who's Olsen.

In addition, there's a thin line between probing and prying, and I have to be careful. I'm not talking to just the person I'm questioning. The whole panel is listening. And if I'm not on my toes, I can turn off half of the people in the room before I sit back down in my chair.

On the other hand, I've learned from bitter experience that I'd better root out the potential problems whether it's uncomfortable to do so or not. One of these problems has to do with attitudes about punitive damages.

"Do you have any feelings," I asked Arriaga, "about the notion of creating a financial deterrent to discourage a corporation from doing something illegal but profitable?"

Arriaga had no feelings against punitive damages if the evidence supported such a step. Likewise, she had no maximum limit in mind, beyond which she wouldn't go, regardless of the evidence, the conduct, or the need to financially discourage a company's behavior.

Awarding damages for emotional distress was another subject that had to be addressed. Some people have the idea that such damages are really baloney. Life is stressful and you should just be tough and deal with the problems that come your way instead of whining about "mental suffering."

At first, Elizabeth Halliburton seemed as if she might be one of those people. She felt that "if we choose to dwell on loss of money or other loss, that would take you down a trail that could drive a person crazy. I can't really see," she said, "awarding anybody for emotional distress."

"Would it be a fair statement," I asked, "that as you sit there today, you feel you have a strong–I hate to put it this strongly–but do you think you have a feeling of bias against emotional distress damages?"

"Probably, yeah, I would say so," she said.

Having said what she did about emotional distress, I was somewhat surprised when Halliburton indicated that she had no reservations against awarding punitive damages in appropriate situations. Her answers were also somewhat surprising to me on the subject of her own experience with injuries that were preventing her from doing certain activities.

Halliburton had done some professional massage therapy but after injuring her hands had been forced to stop. "I started to feel it in my elbows and arms, and I stopped. I stopped and chose to do something different, to not continuing doing that, and I do it just periodically now. My hands–they're fine. I just . . ."

"Are you saying that they're fine because you stopped doing that?"

"Yes. Yeah, exactly. I'm sure if I went back to what I was doing before, these pains would continue and then it might become something. I just listen to my body."

"And you don't do [this work] at all anymore?" I asked.

"No, I do it periodically, but it's not my income. I do it because I enjoy it," she said. "I would love to be able to do it more, but I don't do it because it hurts me."

David Romero was next. I knew the defense was going to claim that Joan was trying to blame her insurer for problems that were caused by other factors in her life. This was a potentially explosive issue. If the defense could paint Joan as someone trying to make UnumProvident pay for her own mistakes, this could hurt her credibility and her case. I knew this allegation wasn't true and felt that I had to beat the defense to the punch.

"Mr. Romero, the facts in this case, without going into them in any detail now, are going to indicate that there are a number of different factors that played into Ms. Hangarter's financial problems and difficulties. Only one of them has to do with the insurance companies. The others may be only indirectly related to them. Do you think as a juror you would be able to balance in your own mind those aspects of her emotional distress . . . for which the insurance company is responsible versus those things that they have nothing to do with and are not their fault?"

I cast an eye at the defense table. I could tell that UnumProvident's team didn't like my stealing their issue before the opening statements were even given.

"Would you be able to make your decision in this case," I continued, "fairly to the insurance company and fairly to Dr. Hangarter with regard to what was the cause of her problems?"

Romero said he wouldn't have any trouble at all making this distinction. What was Joan's fault was hers, and what was the insurers' fault was theirs. I knew that Joan took full responsibility for her own mistakes and would say so without equivocation. Every prospective juror in the room now knew that.

The questioning continued. Jeffrey Goldfine expressed some moderately conservative attitudes about punitive damages.

Phillip Cecchittini said he was unaware of whether his client, Dr. Rubenstein, had ever charged more than $20,000 to testify in support of an insurance company's position on a case in which he hadn't even examined the claimant. (We knew he had because it happened to be in one of our disability bad-faith cases.)

Dan Malstrom talked a bit about the fact that most of his clients were business owners. He stated that that wouldn't give him a pro-business bias of any kind.

Carlos Giron said his English wasn't very good, and he was concerned that he might have some problems keeping up with the testimony. Judge Larson excused him, and he was replaced by Craig Larson.

The time I was allotted for this phase of the case was winding down, so I ended with a question to the entire panel.

"Do all of you promise, if you're selected as jurors in this case, that you will listen carefully to the evidence, follow the instructions of the court, and do what's right? Will you give us your commitment to do that?"

They all nodded. It was Green's turn.

Green started with Arriaga and went down the line, asking the panel members whether they would give a fair shake to his client even though it was an insurance company and the person suing was an individual.

When he got to Cheryl Burr, she mentioned that she was a student and that she was afraid that she would be dropped from some of her classes if she had to serve. Judge Larson asked both sides to stipulate to releasing her. She was replaced by Gavin Distasi. The good news was that Distasi was a musician. The bad news was that he also worked for a financial planner who had sold half a million dollars' worth of UnumProvident policies in the past year. That was it for Distasi. He was replaced by Deborah Paine, juror 142.

Green continued questioning the panel, but it looked as if we were just about done. Malstrom mentioned that he had a small business and might have some problems if he was tied up in trial for weeks. Judge Larson seemed to be sympathetic but deferred doing anything about it for the moment.

The potential jurors were asked to step out in the hall while the court took up the matter of any additional challenges for cause. I asked the court to excuse Romero, the juror whose wife worked for a huge insurance defense law firm whose clients I had sued on more than one occasion. Judge Larson had a one-word response: "Denied."

Next, I asked that Cecchittini be excused because of his involvement with Dr. Rubinstein and the possibility of their discussing this case in the context of our encounter in the previous trial. Green doubted that Cecchittini knew anything about the previous case and thought it unlikely that the subject would come up.

Judge Larson agreed with Green. Cecchittini would remain on the panel.

Due to her admitted bias against awarding emotional distress damages, I next asked that Halliburton be excused. Again, I lost.

The only challenge I won involved Malstrom, the man with a cousin he considered a malingerer and who admitted to having a pro-defense bias. Judge Larson excused Malstrom.

Green's only challenge was to Deborah Paine, the woman who had experienced some physical problems of her own. This was denied.

When court reconvened, Paulette Hillyer was picked to replace Malstrom. Hillyer told the court that her employer said he would not pay her for the time she spent on jury duty, and so, following the judge's pointed criticism of the company in question, she was excused and replaced by Theresa Alvarado. Alvarado, in turn, was excused based on language difficulties. She was replaced by Maria Cantese.

The next morning, Judge Larson agreed to excuse Romero on hardship grounds. The two sides used their peremptory challenges to excuse Cecchittini, Arriaga, Giles, Paine, McKinley, and Halliburton.

That was it. We had our jury.

Judge Larson excused the jurors for the rest of the day. Evidentiary matters needed to be taken up with counsel. Jurors would return the following morning at 9:30 to hear opening statements.

∧ ∨ ∧ ∨ ∧

DEPUTIES, COURT CLERKS, COURT REPORTERS, AND EVEN JUDGES— people who have spent years watching trials—will all agree that it's close to impossible to read a jury with any accuracy.

Juror A smiled at the defense lawyers. Juror D took copious notes on certain testimony. Juror H was a loner who never associated with the other jurors. Juror B rolled his eyes when a particular witness was being cross-examined.

When a case is finally submitted to them—when they go into that jury room to deliberate—things happen. One may pick up on something that the others missed. A second may interpret certain evidence differently than her fellow jurors. A third may have heard specific testimony but not believed it. Their take on the parties or the lawyers may be entirely different from what you're expecting.

Some observers believe that many jurors make up their minds on key parts of the case early based on opening statements. Others say that jurors typically change their minds back and forth as their impressions change during the course of the trial.

Because the plaintiff has the burden of proof, he or she gives the first opening statement, puts on the first witnesses, offers the first evidence, gives the first summation, and so on. Sometimes this is viewed as an advantage because the plaintiff gets to form the first impressions and set the initial agenda.

However, going second has some big advantages. The defense gets to sit back and see how the plaintiff has chosen to present the case. The defense also gets to lie low with evidence that the plaintiff may not even know about, allowing the plaintiff to make allegations that will be troublesome in light of what the defense may later establish.

In addition, it is generally accepted that the plaintiff can put on an almost-flawless case but then have it blown apart by a single powerful piece of defense testimony. Television and movies have people conditioned to accept, even to look for, the "big *Law and Order* turnaround": "So you were never on Washington Street the day your spouse was killed? How then do you explain this parking ticket issued to you at the corner of Washington and Sansom at the very time of the murder?" People are always waiting for the big payoff. Sometimes witnesses oblige them beyond their expectations.

Insurance companies have all of the financial, technical, and personnel resources that an unlimited budget can provide. They are like herds of giant Energizer bunnies that can just keep going and going and going. Their lawyers have lawyers, and they file motions by the kilo. This makes matters even more uncertain.

During a trial, it's the plaintiff who tends to worry. To a defendant insurance company, it's often just another case, one of thousands. A claimant who has lost savings, a home, dignity, self-respect, or all four has one chance and only one. If he or she loses, the blow can be devastating and permanent.

The consequences can be severe for the plaintiff's lawyers. Taking a large case on a contingency fee and advancing all the out-of-pocket costs is a very expensive proposition. In an insurance bad-faith case, plaintiff's lawyers will pay, upfront, for twenty or thirty depositions, half a dozen expert witnesses, and travel expenses to fly back and forth across the country for days and weeks at a time.

They will have three or more attorneys working for the twenty-plus months it takes to prepare for trial. They will spend more hours than they wish to count developing evidence, preparing to examine witnesses, responding to motions, and attending conferences. By the time they get to trial they may well have $300,000 to $400,000 dollars invested in the case. They become strangers in their own homes.

They worry about doing something wrong or dumb to blow the whole case at the last second. They constantly ask themselves if they're missing something, if they're presenting the case well. They fret about the jury, the judge, or both. They don't know until the last minute what's going to happen on key evidentiary questions or last-minute motions or jury instruction requests.

But the biggest question mark of all is the jury. They know that in the end, they will wind up entrusting the entire case to a group of complete strangers. And they wonder if perhaps they shouldn't have gone into some other line of work.

Because of them, a good and decent woman, someone who is depending on them, someone who is living in poverty, may remain penniless for the rest of her life.

Because of them, a greedy and nefarious company may have the last laugh.

Chapter Six

OPEN FIRE

O PENING STATEMENTS, AS JURORS ARE REPEATEDLY REMINDED, are not evidence. Furthermore, they are not a final argument. They are merely an organized recitation–a road map–describing what the actual evidence in the case will be. That being said, to most people opening statements sound an awful lot like both evidence and argument. They are an important early opportunity for the lawyers to talk directly to the jurors about the facts. More importantly, they are a strategic watershed, a chance to outmaneuver opposing counsel and cut him or her off at the knees early in the process.

Of all the many givens in trial practice, one of the most tried and true is that you never want to appear to have played "hide the ball" with a jury. If there are bad facts in your case you had better get them out there yourself, and early on. If you wait for the other side to do this, you're dead. I can hear the taunt in my sleep: "Well, Mr. Bourhis gave a very nice opening statement to you. Yes, very nice indeed. The only thing is, he didn't tell you everything. He must have forgotten. He didn't mention that his client is (fill in the blank)."

In this case, the blank as far as UnumProvident was concerned was that Joan lost her life savings because of bad investments, bad judgments, and bad business habits. UnumProvident was going to argue that Joan was trying to blame her insurance company for her own mistakes, that she was bankrupted because she poured her savings into her abusive boyfriend's business venture, that she got tired of doing chiropractic work and wanted to be a dot-com millionaire, that her disability claim was bogus, and that when she got called on it, she shifted to plan B, which was to exaggerate her medical and financial condition and sue the company for bad faith and for her emotional distress.

Since we had fought with UnumProvident about this in numerous settlement conferences and mediations aimed at resolving the case, we knew exactly what the company's arguments were. We also knew they were wrong.

So in our opening, I told the jury that Joan had made lots of mistakes in her life, that she blamed herself for all these mistakes, and that she wanted to make sure the jury knew she did not blame the insurance company for them. She had picked her fiancé–not UnumProvident. She had invested her savings in his internet company–not UnumProvident. She had agreed to sell her chiropractic practice to Dr. Sugarman–not UnumProvident. Joan did not want a dime from her insurance company for anything caused by the mistakes she had made. The issues were whether Provident owed her disability benefits under its policy, and whether if it had paid, would Joan have been evicted, have been forced into bankruptcy, had her car repossessed, and have been driven into a deep depression and to the brink of taking her own life. These were questions the jury would have to decide.

Horace Green did an excellent job of responding in his opening statement. He went into all the arguments we knew he'd be making, and he did so very persuasively. He told the jury that the plaintiff got to go first but asked them to keep an open mind until the defense got to present its part of the case and until all the evidence was before them. He explained that the evidence would show that UnumProvident's corporate philosophy was to pay all proper claims fairly, promptly, and fully. It would not, said Green, be the nation's leading disability insurance company if it didn't do just that. In addition to being a good lawyer, Green was a very charming individual. Unassuming, humble, good-humored, nice, quick, ready with an easy grin, he was the perfect choice to set the image UnumProvident wanted to create, and wanted to hide behind.

With the opening statements out of the way, we were ready to call our first witness. Most lawyers will carefully script the order of witnesses and the manner in which the evidence is to be presented. Juries need to be led from A to Z in a logical, understandable fashion. This is not always easy to do. The attorneys have lived with the case for years sometimes. They know every detail, every argument, every nuance, every wart. But in trial they have to start from scratch.

The whole case has to be conceived of, produced, and directed to an audience of strangers in a matter of weeks. Usually, the plaintiff testifies first. He or she tells the story, sets the stage, and establishes the tone and theme of the case. But there's no set formula. Every situation is different.

We were faced with UnumProvident's contention that Joan was not disabled because, according to the medical doctor it had hired, she could still work part-time. In addition, the company had made what I thought to be the bizarre contention that she could still do the bookkeeping aspect of her work and that since bookkeeping was *one* of her duties, Joan was not totally disabled in her own occupation. With regard to residual or partial disability, the company's position was that to qualify for partial disability payments under the wording of the policy, the claimant had to be working at least part-time. Since Joan wasn't doing that, she wasn't entitled to the residual benefits either.

With issues like these floating around, and with the underlying question of what the standards of the industry require of an insurer, we wanted to begin our case with an insurance expert as our first witness—to start out with some explanations that would put some of these points into a framework.

To begin a bad-faith case in this way is—to put it mildly—unusual. Unlike lay witnesses, whose testimony is ordinarily limited to what they have personally observed, expert witnesses are permitted to testify about their opinions and conclusions.

In order to qualify as an expert, a witness has to have sufficient education, training, or experience in a particular field or concerning a particular subject. A properly qualified expert can give opinion testimony concerning just about anything from a scientific subject to the value of a baseball trading card. In an insurance practices case, it is important to have an expert who can testify about applicable industry standards and obligations.

To be credible, an insurance expert witness has to come across as knowledgeable, reasonable, honest, and thoroughly prepared. He or she has to be able to testify convincingly on direct examination and to withstand intensive cross-examination. It's not for the faint-hearted. We had Frank Caliri as an expert witness on the claims-handling standards applicable to the insurance industry.

During the past twenty-five years, Caliri had worked as an insurance consultant and a forensic expert in insurance litigation. He had been retained approximately 150 times as an expert in this field, and he'd testified in more than forty depositions and a dozen or more trials–about 40 percent of the time for the defense and the balance for plaintiffs.

In preparation for his testimony in Hangarter, Caliri thoroughly studied all the depositions. The plaintiff's transcript alone consisted of three volumes and hundreds of pages. In addition, there were depositions of company officials, claims handlers and supervisors, treating doctors, the insurance company physicians, and more. Caliri had also carefully read the voluminous claims file plus the hundreds of pages of internal company memos turned over in discovery.

It's no easy task to absorb all this material well enough to formulate opinions capable of withstanding rigorous challenge by an aggressive and highly trained cross-examiner. We worked hard with Caliri to prepare him for his direct and anticipated cross-examination. But no matter how much you work at it, surprises are inevitable. We knew that, and we were worried about it.

∧ ∨ ∧ ∨ ∧

ALICE WOLFSON, MY PARTNER, NEVER WENT TO MEDICAL SCHOOL, BUT she was probably born with a stethoscope around her neck. She knew the impairment issues relating to disability insurance as well as anyone in the country. A graduate of Barnard College with a master's from Stanford University and a degree from University of California's Hastings College of Law, she was a Fulbright scholar with a deceivingly soft-spoken manner for a relentless cross-examiner. She was a walking land mine for any defense expert foolish enough to try to step on her. Fortunately for Caliri, he was being called by Alice on direct.

Alice started out by asking him to describe claims-handling standards to which insurance companies must adhere.

"Claims evaluations," he explained, "must be fair and thorough. A company cannot avoid obtaining, or ignore, information that supports payment of the claim. It cannot misinterpret or misrepresent or misstate the policy benefits. It cannot put its own financial interests above those of the insured. It cannot force a policyholder to sue in order to collect benefits owed."

Alice asked Caliri if he had reviewed Joan's insurance policy in preparation for testifying.

"Yes," he said. "I did."

"How is total disability defined in this policy?"

Caliri, who looked a bit like Dustin Hoffman and had similar mannerisms, was a very good witness. "There are three parts to the definition of total disability," he said. "One is the inability to perform the important duties of the occupation you were engaged in at the time you became disabled. Two is that you are not engaged in any other gainful occupation. Three is that you are under the regular care of a doctor."

"Were there other benefits, besides total disability benefits, provided under this policy?"

"Yes. There's what's called a residual disability benefit. There is a rehabilitation benefit, and there is a recovery benefit. Residual is applicable if the insured is disabled but is working at something else. There's a formula for determining the amount of the benefit under residual. The rehabilitation provision is supposed to allow an insured to receive full disability payments while they are in an approved rehab program. Last, there is something called a recovery benefit. This has to do with loss of earnings protection."

Alice handed Caliri a thick binder filled with exhibits and asked him to turn to the tab for plaintiff's exhibit 34, the UnumProvident internal document entitled "Individual Disability Claims Performance Objectives." "Is it acceptable," Alice asked, "in the processing of individual disability claims to have 'objectives' for how many claims should be terminated?"

"No," said Caliri. "And this document describes just that. It says that for every new dollar in claims, the claims department should terminate eighty-four cents' worth of existing claims. The company actually developed a formula called a 'net terminations ratio' to track this and set goals for the termination of ongoing claims."

This was a crucial point. The jury had to understand that a policyholder, who in good faith paid premiums for years, was going to be wiped off UnumProvident's books for the company's bottom line.

"Have you reviewed any documents concerning Mr. Mohney's 'claims initiatives'?"

"Yes, I have."

"Do you know what the purposes of these claims initiatives were as stated in the documents?"

"Yes. To use what they called roundtable meetings, surveillance, new claims approaches, so called independent medical examinations, and other techniques to improve the net terminations ratio [see Exhibits 8 and 9]. If you look at exhibit 37, it shows right on the second line an improvement of the ratio to 90 percent. That meant they were now terminating 90 cents' worth of existing claims for every dollar in new claims."

Caliri then referred to exhibit 47, which described a "Top Ten List" (see Exhibit 10): "Each adjuster will maintain a list of ten claimants where intensive effort will lead to successful resolution of the claim. As one name drops off, another name will be added." *Resolution* was the key word. Caliri noted that Ralph Mohney and Sandra Fryc had admitted in their depositions that the term *resolution* was merely a polite way of saying *termination*. In the terminology, or code, of UnumProvident, they meant exactly the same thing.

"So what you see here," explained Caliri, "is that each claims adjuster was directed to provide a 'top ten' list of claims that 'with intensive effort' could be terminated."

Alice had another key question. "Mr. Caliri, do you know whether it falls below the standards of the industry to instruct claims personnel to shred sensitive documents related to a claims file?"

"That would certainly be improper," he said.

She asked him to turn to exhibit 44 (see Exhibit 11). "Do any portions of exhibit 45 describe activities that would fall below the standards of care in the insurance industry?"

"Yes," said Caliri. "An insurance company cannot destroy or shred documents that relate to claim handling or investigations. This Provident internal memo tells people to do exactly that—to 'shred' documents or records pertaining to investigations.

"Then, section B.4 of this document states, 'For matters that are especially sensitive or confidential, consider conducting most of your communication in person, not on paper. If you do write something that's sensitive, be cautious. Say only what's necessary, and copy only those who need to know.'"

I thought back to Mohney's Chattanooga deposition. The strategy of introducing these documents through Caliri rather than Mohney was appearing to be a good one.

Caliri next turned to exhibit 43, an internal company memorandum to field managers dated February 21, 1996. Field managers were responsible for conducting on-site investigations. Their job included obtaining information, taking statements from the insured or from witnesses, and so on. The memo stated: "Effective immediately, recommendations and/or conclusions should not be included in the written report. They should be communicated verbally to the home office or submitted in a separate memo."

Other memos discussed avoiding putting information in writing "that could hurt the company in court" or making sure files backed up what "the company was trying to prove." Some memos talked about "profiling" high-value claims and claims from Florida and California. And the jury heard about the memos referring to termination-of-claims goals.

Caliri testified that all these memos revealed business attitudes and practices that violated even the most minimum insurance industry requirements and standards.

Alice asked whether Caliri had drawn any other conclusions about Provident's claims-handling practices from the material he had reviewed.

"Yes," he said.

"What opinions did you form and what were they based on in this case?"

"For one thing, the company authorizes employees to terminate claims who have not even been trained as to the required standards of disability. Second, it appears from the record that Provident relied on the opinion of an IME doctor who provided them with a biased report. Third, they misrepresented both the terms of their policy and the claimant's occupational duties in order to assert that she was not totally disabled. Fourth, they misstated the requirements of their residual disability coverage, and they specifically told their insured that she wasn't qualified for that coverage either, when she was. Fifth, they concealed from their policyholder her rights under the thirty-six-month rehabilitation coverage. In fact, she specifically asked whether there was any way she could be kept on claim for at least a little while longer while she tried to get on her feet. They simply said no."

At this point, Horace Green asked for a sidebar conference, out of earshot of the jury. He wanted to take up two matters with the court.

Judge Larson excused the jury.

Green proceeded to make UnumProvident's usual argument that the documents Caliri had put before the jury were inadmissible. They were privileged and irrelevant. In addition, Green argued, they were authored by individuals at a time when they had been working for Provident, before the company had grown into UnumProvident (through the acquisition of Paul Revere and the takeover of Unum). Now, went the argument, the company was a different corporate entity. The memos Mohney wrote when the company was Provident Life and Casualty should not be admissible now that the company was UnumProvident.

This argument was a real stretch. It was the corporate lawyers painting an elephant yellow and calling it a chicken. The fact was that Chandler and Mohney had served, respectively, as the CEO and the head of claims ever since the days of their appointments back in 1993 and 1994.

The "separate entities" theory made me cringe and think about all the lawyer jokes at cocktail parties ("it depends on what your definition of *is* is").

Judge Larson didn't buy UnumProvident's contention. He immediately cut to the heart of the matter, overruling Green's objection and noting that UnumProvident was clearly the successor in interest to all these companies.

Green had another issue. "I believe, Your Honor, that Mr. Caliri may be asked to testify about other cases, cases other than this one. I think that would be improper, and I would request that counsel be admonished not to get into that."

Judge Larson turned to Alice and me. "Do you intend to go there?" he asked.

"Yes, we do," replied Alice. "Part of plaintiff's case alleges that the defendants are guilty of unfair business practices in violation of Business and Professions Code Section 17200. We believe we are entitled to show that the defendants are engaged in a pattern of conduct and that what happened in this case was not an isolated incident."

Judge Larson looked back at Green, inviting his response.

"If Mr. Caliri talks about other situations, we will have to cross-examine on the specifics. We will be here forever trying minitrial after minitrial. Who did what? Why did they do it? Was this proper or was that improper?"

Larson stopped him. "I think you're right," he said. "We're not going to have a dozen other cases tried as part of this case. Ms. Wolfson, you're going to have to find some other way to put on the evidence you need to establish. You may not do it by asking about other specific cases. That's my ruling. Understood?"

"Understood," she responded.

This was a blow to us. We had planned on going into a number of these other cases in some detail. We wanted the jury to hear about what the company had done to Dr. Stuart Gluck. We wanted to question Caliri about Dr. John Tedesco, an eye surgeon whose benefits were terminated even though he couldn't control his trembling hands due to Parkinson's disease. We wanted to discuss a CPA whose benefits had been cut off even though she had multiple sclerosis and brain lesions; a human resources worker whose benefits were terminated despite having post-polio syndrome, a progressively debilitating neuromuscular disease.

We wanted Caliri to be able to testify about the contractor with cancer, the dentist with a permanently severed clavicle, and the businessman with spinal disease so severe that he was unable to read a newspaper without tacking it to a wall. We wanted to ask Caliri how many fraud and bad-faith lawsuits had been filed against UnumProvident by claimants in the past three years.

We felt that all of this was pertinent in establishing the business patterns and practices of the defendants. We thought it was all relevant to the jury's consideration of punitive damages.

Judge Larson's concern was that such testimony would open the door to a case-by-case defense, resulting in countless minitrials involving other claims. This, he felt, would unduly prolong the trial.

We were not going to be able to present the evidence we wanted to offer–at least not on a case-by-case basis. We would have to approach this point differently.

UPON THE JURY'S RETURN, ALICE CONTINUED.

"Mr. Caliri," she said, "in forming your opinions in this matter, did you review anything other than the depositions, the claims file, and the memos that you have described so far?"

"Yes," he replied, "I looked at the records and depositions in numerous other matters."

"Without discussing the particular facts or details of any of those matters specifically," said Alice, "did you observe any patterns in the defendants' conduct?"

"Yes, I did," said Caliri.

Without going into the facts of other cases, Alice was driving the point home.

"What did you conclude from what you observed?"

"That there were clear patterns of wrongful claims practices that ran from case to case in all of the cases I looked at. That this case is not an isolated situation at all."

That was about as far as Alice dared go. Jury members would simply have to figure out for themselves why she didn't ask any detailed follow-up questions. She hoped that they wouldn't conclude that we could not come up with any other examples or that there were no other cases.

"Thank you, Mr. Caliri," she said. "That's all I have for this witness, Your Honor."

Cross-examination began with an attempt to undermine Caliri's qualifications as an expert on industry standards. The defense argued that despite his extensive education and experience, Caliri had never actually worked as a claims adjuster. This was tantamount to saying a surgeon could not testify about hospital cleanliness standards if he had never worked as a janitor. This effort went nowhere.

Next, Caliri was asked if he had any evidence that regulatory authorities, such as the California Department of Insurance (DOI), had specifically found Paul Revere or UnumProvident guilty of wrongdoing. We would take care of the innuendo that the companies had clean hands because the DOI hadn't come after them on redirect examination. A handful of questions about the DOI would be enough to quash that notion.

Green then asked Caliri about his allegations that Sullivan and Ryan had been inadequately trained. "Isn't it true that you were not even present during their training?" Green asked. Caliri acknowledged he hadn't been present.

"And have you ever seen the materials that were used in their training?"

"No."

"So how can you say the training was insufficient?"

This exchange reminded me of the old story about cross-examination in a maiming case. The defendant was accused of biting off the victim's thumb. The defense lawyer, questioning an eyewitness, said, "Isn't it true, sir, that you did not *see* my client bite off Mr. Allessio's thumb?" "That is true," the witness answered. "Then how can you testify that he did it?" snarled the attorney. "Because," replied the witness, "I saw him spit it out."

"Because," Caliri said, "they didn't even know the definition of *disability*. He didn't know it when the claim was terminated. He didn't know it when his deposition was taken over a year later. He still doesn't know it—even to this day. The adjusters have never been trained as to what it is.

"Besides," he continued, "Mr. Ryan testified in his deposition, on page sixty-one, that he didn't know whether insurance companies were required to handle claims fairly, didn't know whether they were required to investigate them thoroughly, and didn't know whether their assessment of a claim even had to be objective.

"This is an individual who has been promoted numerous times, who has been authorized to cut off claims, and who has been put in charge of training other claims handlers. It's difficult for me to recognize that a person in his position would not understand the simple concept that you have to treat claimants fairly and that investigations have to be objective and thorough."

It was time for the defense to move on.

Green turned to State Insurance Regulation 2695.3. This section requires insurers to "retain all documents, notes, work papers, correspondence and other papers pertaining to a claim in sufficient detail that the pertinent facts and dates can be reconstructed."

"It doesn't say that you can't shred documents, does it?"

"No," said Caliri, "but you shouldn't need a formal regulation to realize that you can't be shredding documents."

"That's *your* interpretation," UnumProvident's lawyer argued.

"That's a *reasonable* interpretation," Caliri retorted. "Maybe *you* believe that it is reasonable to shred documents like this. I don't."

Moving on, Green attacked Caliri's testimony concerning the claims termination letter, residual disability standards, and recovery benefit.

Caliri held on pretty well. He was able to back up his testimony with specific references to the depositions of witnesses, to internal company memos, and to exhibits.

With regard to further cross-examination on the rehabilitation benefits, Caliri volunteered that he had reviewed numerous other cases involving Provident and had not found a single one where the rehabilitation benefits had been offered. "In fact," he said, "in a case that I was recently working on, the insured specifically asked for rehabilitation benefits—by name—and the company refused them."

"Was that this case?" UnumProvident's lawyer asked weakly.

"No," Caliri said. He may as well have added, "But so what?"

Green asked if Joan understood her policy, and again Caliri had the perfect answer, one that would resonate with the jury.

"The average layperson doesn't understand these policies. The company knows that."

UnumProvident then mounted an offensive on the internal documents. Selectively going through them and picking out ones that were missing dates, recipients' names, or authors' identities, Green asked a series of questions.

"You were not there when this document was written, correct?"

"You don't know who wrote it, correct?"

"You don't know who actually read it, correct?"

"And you don't know whether anyone who worked on the Hangarter case ever saw this document, correct?"

Pick, pick, pick. It was hard to tell if Green was making any headway with the jury. It's not a bad ploy to obfuscate with a deluge of not terribly relevant questions. Someone on the panel might glean great importance from Caliri's not knowing who did the writing, reading, and possibly arithmetic.

Following a lunch break, the cross-examination continued.

"Mr. Caliri, not all claims terminations are bad, are they?"

"No. They're not all bad."

"If the company helps a claimant get back to work, that claim terminates, doesn't it?"

"Yes."

"That's not a bad thing, is it?"

"No."

Nor is it a bad thing, Caliri agreed, that if a policy says that benefits end at age sixty-five and the person reaches that age, the benefits terminate.

Nor is it a bad thing that benefits are stopped if the person gets better. Green wanted to implant in the minds of the jury that termination didn't necessarily equal misconduct.

Green had further questions, which included trying to taint the witness as a hired gun willing to skew his testimony for the side paying the bill.

"What is your hourly billing rate, Mr. Caliri?"

"Two hundred and fifty dollars per hour," he said.

"And how many hours did you spend on this case?"

"About seventy-five hours."

"That would come to about $18,750. Correct?"

"That sounds about right."

As usual, the lawyer had saved his best questions for last.

"Sir," he said, looking up at Caliri with barely concealed glee, "do you have a disability policy for yourself?"

Uh-oh, I thought, here was one of those surprises that comes up out of nowhere.

Caliri looked slightly embarrassed while Alice tried to pretend she'd known this was coming all along. Feigning nonchalance, she was pretending to write notes on a pad.

"Yes, I do," Caliri responded.

"And with whom do you have these policies?"

"With Unum and with Provident," he said.

"Redirect?" asked Judge Larson.

"Yes," Alice replied. She had to defuse Green's last bombshell.

"Mr. Caliri," said Alice, "knowing what you know about Paul Revere, UnumProvident, why do you still carry a disability policy with them?"

"First of all, insurance companies don't sell these own-occupation policies anymore. They haven't since interest rates plummeted in the early nineties. If I dropped my policy, I would get nothing despite all the premiums I have paid them thus far. Plus, I frankly doubt that they would try to take advantage of me. I don't really fit the profile for the type of person they tend to take advantage of."

Alice then responded to Green's documents tactic by going through all the documents that *were* dated and identified: exhibits 31, 43, 60, 123, 125, 127, 128, 138, 139, 142, 143, 144, 145, 146, 147, 148, 149, 151, 152, 153, and 155.

As she went through each document, she asked the same questions over and over: "What is the date on this memo?" "Who wrote it?" "To whom was it written?" "Do you have any reason to believe that it was never sent to the recipient[s] listed?" "Or was never received?" "Or was never read by those it was sent to?"

She hoped the jurors got the point.

∧ ∨ ∧ ∨ ∧

THE WORLD IS FULL OF EXPERT WITNESSES, BUT WHAT IMPRESSED ME most about Caliri were his preparation and his ability to cite minute details from a voluminous record. He had done a very good job, but I worried that perhaps he had come across as too confident, too smooth, too opinionated about UnumProvident. Toward the end of his testimony, I thought I'd caught a couple of jurors casting their eyes downward somewhat skeptically. I hoped I was wrong. Maybe they were just tired.

Following his testimony, I pulled Caliri aside in the hallway before he left for the airport to thank him for all the hard work he had put into Joan's case.

"Wish Joan good luck," he said.

Luck? I thought. After all we're going through? But the truth was that UnumProvident *had* been lucky in the past dodging the bullet.

People were hardly enamored with lawyers, lawsuits, or litigation. And when all was said and done, jurors were people.

Chapter Seven

SO HELP ME GOD

T HE MOST IMPORTANT WITNESS IN ANY CASE IS THE PLAINTIFF. If the jury can identify with her and agree that she is doing what's right by bringing a lawsuit to recover damages for events that happened to her, then the battle is half won. On the other hand, if the plaintiff comes off as a whiner, an angry person, or someone who's exaggerating or looking for a windfall, then problems are created that may be insurmountable. This is not shocking. People have empathy for someone who was cheated, but they don't like woe-is-me crybabies.

Someone who appears angry, upset, tearful, or vindictive can really turn a jury off. A good cross-examiner can exploit this very effectively, making the plaintiff her own worst enemy. In preparing Joan for her testimony, Alice and I tried to anticipate as much of this defense tactic as much as possible. We wanted to give her a bigger dose of sour medicine than she would ever get from the defendants at trial. The problem was that in many ways Joan *was* angry, upset, tearful, and vindictive. She felt, and with good reason, that she had been knocked down, stepped on, crushed, and ruined by Ralph Mohney and Joseph Sullivan and Sandra Fryc and Chris Collins of Provident. And a part of her wanted to get them all back. The truth of the matter was that if she could have sent them all somewhere for a week of thumb bending, she would probably have done it in a flash. That is not the Joan we wanted to present.

So just before trial, one day after a failed settlement conference, Alice and I got Joan in my car and went to work. Playing the role of a defense lawyer from hell, I explained to Joan the importance of how she appeared to the jury. "Be ready," I said, "for anything."

"Like what? What can they say?" Joan asked.

"They may try to get you upset. To imply that you're a phony. That you're just trying to set up UnumProvident. Why did you supposedly squander your savings over a flaky dot-com business? Why did you expose your family to living in the same house with this allegedly violent, unpredictable man? It doesn't make any sense that these things all happened the way you're saying they did. The only explanation is that you're exaggerating all of this as part of an effort to get rich quick in this lawsuit at the expense of a big faceless target defendant. A big unsympathetic corporation. An insurance company."

"B-But . . ." Joan stuttered.

I pressed on. "Most parents would be willing to take a bullet to save their children. Why couldn't you have endured some pain in order to feed your own kids? You could have protected them from poverty. From welfare. From food stamps. From humiliation. You still have your arms and legs. You still can see and hear. You're smart. You're well educated. You could have found work. Isn't it true you were tired of having to deal with employees, billing, bookkeeping, and all of that? That you were tired of the long hours and the hard work? That you just didn't want to practice chiropractic anymore? You wanted to set this company up; that's what you wanted. That's what this is all about. Isn't that so? That you let it all go in an effort to nail this company? So that you could cry and carry on and exaggerate and blame and be a victim? Poor Joan. Poor Joan."

Naturally, she became upset. Could this really happen? Is this what she was going to face in front of everybody? Was she going to have to endure this?

Probably not–at least not to this extreme. But this little session gave Joan a bucket of ice water in the face, a reality check to force her to rethink who she was and what this was all about. No matter what the defense threw at her on the witness stand, she would be ready. There would be few, if any, tears. There would be no frustration or recrimination or whining. The theme would not be "woe is me." It would simply be "I don't think that what this company did was right." If anyone was going to get angry at UnumProvident, it would be the jury, not Joan.

∧ ∨ ∧ ∨ ∧

ON DIRECT EXAMINATION WE WENT THROUGH THE NORMAL, GET-TO-know-the-plaintiff background information: length of time in the area, family, the reason for her interest in chiropractic, her education, the launching and building of her practice, the referrals she received from physicians and other medical professionals, her relationship with and interest in her patients, what her plans had been for the future. Next, I asked Joan about her purchase of the policy and the representations that had been made to her about what would be covered if she ever became unable to practice chiropractic.

Joan remembered Patricia Meyers specifically telling her that the policy she was purchasing was the best policy because it would specifically cover her as a chiropractor (see Exhibit 12). "So if I was injured and I couldn't be a chiropractor anymore, then it would protect me. She told me that."

When asked if there was any discussion of what the "important duties of her occupation" were, Joan responded, "Well, no, because Pat was very–Pat Meyers was very adamant in the beginning that even if I did paperwork, it wasn't my–she was the one who kept saying: 'Look, Joan, you are a chiropractor, your important duties are chiropractic; it doesn't matter if you do paperwork, it doesn't matter–you are a chiropractor; that is why [you are getting this] policy."

I asked Joan about her injury and how it occurred, about her medical treatment, about her efforts to save her practice, about her hiring additional help to assist her in the office, and about her failed attempts to continue performing patient treatments after her injury.

I asked about Joan's IME.

"You were signed up for an insurance medical examination, or an IME, . . . with a Dr. Swartz, right?"

"Yes." In March of 1999.

"And what happened during the exam?"

"He did some–he didn't touch me. He didn't do any palpation rather, where you touch. He just looked at me. I think he had me do a few range of motion (tests) and squeeze the dynamometer. That may have been it. . . ."

"Dr. Swartz ultimately rendered an opinion that he thought you could see, I believe he said two or so patients per hour."

"Yes . . . which is totally contradictory to the way I practice."

"Do you agree that you could see two patients per hour?" I asked.

"Not without a great deal of pain and discomfort, and probably unsuccessfully treating them," she said. There was no way Joan could even pay the overhead by treating such a small number of patients.

I moved on to Joan's benefits termination. "What was your reaction when you found out for the first time your UnumProvident claim was being denied or terminated?"

"I was really shocked. I felt sick. I realized, all of a sudden, that they were saying that because I owned the business, I [wasn't qualified to receive benefits as a chiropractor]."

I asked her about her conversation with UnumProvident claims representative Ken Seaman.

"Were you told by the insurance company that they were going to be terminating your benefits?"

"No. I called Paul Revere to ask where my check was, and the guy said—I think it was Joe Sullivan—said that their representative Ken Seaman was going to be coming to visit me soon."

"Did he come?"

"He did."

"And what did he discuss with you?"

"He told me that I wasn't considered disabled by the company anymore and that the [Dr. Swartz] IME showed that I wasn't disabled, and it was time for me—I wasn't going to be getting any more benefits."

I asked Joan about the circumstances surrounding her eviction and about her relationship with Bruce Wexler just before she moved to Southern California to be with her sister.

"Bruce was getting very agitating to be around. He threatened me, so I just—in any case, we were evicted. And when I showed up in court to try and fight the eviction notice, who was there but an attorney who had been one of my patients. So I felt totally humiliated."

I asked Joan what effect the eviction had on her.

"All of a sudden my world was upside down . . . and I ran away to my sister's [in Encinitas]."

Joan explained that while she was there, she tried to obtain work. "I tried to do a few different things. I tried to find a chiropractic office to practice in. But you've got to understand that I was crying all the time . . . I don't know what was wrong with me . . . So it was extremely hard. But I went and interviewed a whole lot of different doctors down in Southern California, to look for a place that I would practice in if I was going to practice. That's the first thing I did." Joan explained that when she tried to do chiropractic work, it was extremely painful.

Shortly after her failed attempt to return to chiropractic she made an appointment with an employment agency. During her interview she began to cry and wound up running out to the parking lot, where she sat in her car and sobbed.

I asked Joan why she came back to the Bay Area.

"Well, truthfully, Bruce convinced me that he respected who I was and knew who I was, and he wouldn't make me, you know, like, just go [work in] McDonald's, that he would help me recover my self-esteem and help me build a new kind of business in the chiropractic field and he would help me. He promised that he would help take care of me and the kids."

Bruce and Joan then came up with the idea of starting a chiropractic website business. Bruce had the computer knowledge and would do the website design and Joan had the marketing ability within the chiropractic community, so it seemed to make sense.

"Did you make any money doing this?" I asked.

"Yes," said Joan, "I actually sold seven or eight websites. I was really proud of myself, I really was." But it didn't last. Starting a business takes money, money that Joan didn't have. Without the funding to keep the business going, Joan couldn't hold on. Ironically, in addition to the total and residual disability coverages that were supposed to be provided by UnumProvident, the policy also contained a "rehabilitation" provision that was supposed to pay a disabled claimant thousands of dollars per month if she wanted to try to transition into another occupation. This money might well have provided Joan with the resources necessary to allow her consulting firm to survive long enough for her efforts to have been successful.

However, in UnumProvident's termination letter, and in Sullivan's conversations with Joan, this rehabilitation benefit was never mentioned. Joan had specifically asked UnumProvident if it couldn't provide some kind of financial assistance to just help her get on her feet. "No," the company said, it could not.

"And did you stop trying to start your business at some point?"

"Yes. And Bruce and I had a huge fight. . . . And he hit me. He punched me; he threw me on the bed. He raised up his guitar. He had this huge, black, electric guitar that he held over my head, and he threatened to kill me with it. And he threatened to–"

"Did your children see this?"

"They heard it. They heard it. They heard the whole thing. And I started screaming, 'He is hitting me, he is hurting me, help, call 911.' So my daughter and my son . . . ran to the phone and called 911."

"If we can take a snapshot of this point in time that you are describing, what was your financial status?"

"Well, I had zero. My financial situation at that point was I had no money. All I had was a Shell credit card and a Chevron credit card. That was it. So, I could eat at the Shell station. That was it. . . ."

Joan explained her bankruptcy, applying for welfare and food stamps, having to put her furniture and personal property in storage, and then defaulting on her payments to the storage facility and thereby losing all of her possessions. Joan described putting her children on a free lunch program at school.

I asked her how it felt to have to do these things–how it felt to be suddenly poor.

"You know," she said, "I wrote an article about what it feels like to be poor. I don't know if you got that. But . . . it's the most humiliating thing that has ever happened to me. It's extremely embarrassing. I tried to avoid the market where all my kids' friends were, and I felt totally embarrassed by this."

I made the point that not long ago, Joan had been earning a very good living.

"You had furniture?"

"Yes."

"Clothes?"

"Yes."

"Nice car?"

"Yes, I had a nice car."

"The insurance company," I asked, "how do you feel about their role in connection with these events?"

"You know," she said, "I don't blame the insurance company for the loss of my savings or the money that I put out. That was my risk; it was a calculated risk. But if I had the insurance–every day that I have to get a welfare check or get help or I don't have money for food or I don't even . . . I would not have this problem if I was getting my benefits. I am concerned about my whole life. I chew my inside of my mouth. I have had to go on anxiety medication just to deal with my anxiety about my day-to-day life."

I pressed on a bit. "I think you said something earlier to the effect that you could use the money, the disability payments. What did you mean, you could use it?"

"I don't want to be flippant, but I'm out–I have no money. Even just to come here today is–do you know what? Just to come here is an enormous expense. It may seem like a little, but it's a big expense to me. So when I said I could use the money, it's true." I started to worry a bit. I could see it in her eyes. I could see her anger coming.

"I deserve the money, you know," she said, glaring at the Unum-Provident side of the courtroom.

"Did you think," I quickly interrupted, "when you bought this policy, that if you ever became unable to perform the important duties of your occupation as a chiropractor, you would have to go through all of this in order to get your benefits?"

"I never expected to have to go through any of this. To think that I injured myself and went from having a career and income to being almost homeless and on welfare, I don't think . . . I wasn't prepared for this."

On cross-examination, Horace Green had fairly limited options. Although he asked a lot of questions, it didn't seem to me that he was making much headway. He parried around the policy terms and played about the edges of Joan's testimony.

He asked Joan whether it wasn't true that she had liked Dr. Swartz until she saw his report.

"You know what?" she said. "I actually expected, naively enough, that Dr. Swartz would be fair and impartial. Okay? I literally thought this man would be fair and impartial."

"Okay," pounced Green. "So you thought that he had been fair and impartial until you got the report?"

"No. No . . . I said I expected him to be fair and impartial . . . I expected him to be professional, and I expected him to do a thorough evaluation and examination for me, and I don't know that I could tell you ahead of time what his findings would have been."

Green also asked numerous questions about corporate entity, overhead, and tax-related issues. I didn't understand the point of any of that and hoped the jury didn't either.

Green finished with one last attempt to make it seem as though Joan had wanted to get out of chiropractic for years and that she had simply decided to sell her practice and use her disability insurance as a quick road to a premature retirement. The idea that UnumProvident seemed to be pushing was that all of this disability business had somehow arisen out of Joan's desire to do something else. I didn't understand the reasoning behind this, but maybe the company had an investigator who was going to pop out from behind a tree holding a tape recorder in one hand and a video camera in the other—poised to testify that Joan had told him she hated her profession and had finally found a way to get out of it. I really didn't know what Provident was up to with this, but one way or the other, Joan was ready for it.

"After having been in your practice for twenty years," Green smiled, "isn't it true that you just didn't want to do it anymore?"

Green seemed to be hoping for a slight grin or a flash of some kind of acknowledgment from Joan. He didn't get it.

"Mr. Green," Joan said, looking him square in the eye, "I loved my patients. I loved my patients so much that I had trouble letting them go. I had trouble in turning them over to someone else. It was extremely hard for me. I really cared about my patients. I would go back today and take them back under my wing and adjust them, whether they paid me or not, if I could. . . .

"I was really enthusiastic. If you had any of my patients in here to testify, they would tell you how enthusiastic I was. I loved it. I had a lot of benefits and perks from being a chiropractor. I had a good living. I had my home. I paid for my own life. I paid for my own way.

"I loved the perks of being a chiropractor. I got to travel. I got to speak and lecture and be respected. I was never on Medi-Cal, you know. I could pay for dinner. There were too many—there were a lot of benefits of owning my own practice and being a doctor."

Undaunted, Green forged ahead. "During the time of your claim, isn't it true you told your employees that you didn't want to be a chiropractor anymore?"

Finally, Joan smiled. "I also told my employees I wanted to be a famous actress; I wanted to marry Robert Redford. I had fantasies of all sorts of things, but I never wanted to leave my practice."

∧ ∨ ∧ ∨ ∧

MY REDIRECT WAS SHORT. THE MAIN POINT I'D BEEN SAVING WAS ABOUT ERISA.

"I'd like you to assume, Joan, that there's been testimony in this case from an expert witness as to the significance of an ERISA preempted claim and that the testimony is that if your claim is preempted by ERISA, you lose the right to sue for fraud and you lose the right to a jury trial."

Several jurors seemed to suddenly lean forward.

"Right," said Joan, "I understand that."

"Joan," I asked, handing her Provident's termination letter, "did UnumProvident ever tell you that your claim was preempted by ERISA?"

Green sprang from his chair as though he'd accidentally irritated a swarm of hornets.

"Objection. Lacks foundation. Calls for speculation," he said, trying to look nonchalant while his eyes bulged out of control.

"Overruled," responded Judge Larson.

"When I read this," said Joan, referring to the termination letter that was now displayed on an overhead projector, "they told me that it was ERISA. And also, I think Ken Seaman said something about that, which came as a total shock to me."

If Joan had accepted that lie, and God only knows how many UnumProvident claimants have, she wouldn't have been sitting in court at that moment. She and her two young children would have been back in her little apartment eating their food-stamp dinner and wondering how their insurance company had been able to rob them of what they'd thought was their constitutional right to a trial by jury–this jury or any jury.

For much of the remainder of her case, we intended to keep Joan out of court. After all she had been through, she was fairly fragile, and the last thing we wanted was for her to break down crying or to display anger in front of the jury.

It was hard to know exactly how the jury had reacted to Joan's testimony, but I felt that one way or the other, the real Joan had come out and that she had stood up well on her own behalf. She had done a good job in my eyes. Time would tell whether others would agree or not.

Chapter Eight

PINPRICKS
AND PRETEXTS

P LAINTIFF MAY CALL HER NEXT WITNESS," JUDGE LARSON SAID. "Thank you, Your Honor," Alice said. "The plaintiff calls Dr. Edward Katz."

Katz, a highly respected orthopedic surgeon, graduated from medical school at Northwestern University. He spent his early years treating disabled children at the Chicago Shriners Hospital. During the Vietnam conflict, he served two years as assistant chief at the Great Lakes Medical Center, performing orthopedic surgery on complex war-related injuries. For the past twenty-five years, Katz had a private practice in Northern California, treating hundreds of patients and performing ten to fifteen surgeries per week.

Katz was a pleasant, unassuming, and casual man, with whom most people felt instantly comfortable. He testified that when he examined Joan, it was his understanding that prior to her injuries, Joan's usual occupation had been that of a chiropractor in active practice. That is, he explained, she was a hands-on chiropractor that did myofascial manipulations (stretches and movements done on soft tissue), manual traction, and spinal adjustments.

As part of his examination, Katz took a "patient history." In addition, he obtained and reviewed Joan's medical records. From this, he learned that her arm problems had started years before with pain in the right shoulder, right elbow, right forearm, and upper shoulder region of the trapezius muscle. The pain was aggravated when she moved her head and neck. She described its severity at the time as about an 8.5 out of a pain range from one to ten.

Katz described the examination he conducted, which included range-of-motion and lateral bending tests and the palpation, or feeling, for muscle spasms.

"Can you actually feel a muscle spasm?"

"Yes, you can, and you can compare one side [of the body] to the other when you palpate."

"Do you consider this type of palpation to constitute an objective test?"

This was an important issue because an insurance company searching for a basis to deny or terminate a claim will often argue that the medical tests that were administered could have been faked. If they were all subjective tests, they were susceptible to this kind of attack. Claimants, on the other hand, look for objective evidence of injury or disease in order to counter this.

Katz explained that as a doctor performing palpation for thirty-six years, he could feel a muscle spasm if it is present. "In Joan's case, it was clearly present," he said.

Katz next described a Spurling test. "It's a test for cervical disc disease where we compress the head in extension and we put pressure downward. On a symptomatic patient–a patient *with* a disc problem–they will get pain to the posterior cervical spine radiating down the arm. And that indicates disc compression and a bad disc."

The Spurling test he performed on Joan was positive.

"Is a Spurling test subjective?" Alice asked.

"No. Performed by a specialist who knows what he is doing, it's objective."

"Did you make any other physical findings on your examination?"

"Yes, there was a depressed biceps reflex on the right side and a positive pinprick test verifying decreased sensation or numbness on the long finger of the right hand."

"What is the significance of the pinprick test?"

"First of all, you take a pinwheel, which has sharp metal protrusions on it, and you actually run it over the skin. We performed this test, and the results were positive. It showed nerve-root compression affecting the sensory portion of the nerve in question, going down the right arm."

Katz went on to explain that the muscle spasm he had observed meant that the muscle was irritated by either local irritation or through the nerve going to muscle, causing it to compress. This spasm was caused by degenerative disc disease that Joan had in the cervical spine at the C5–C6 disc.

Katz had also examined three MRI reports, plus the actual pictures. He put the pictures on the overhead projector and explained them to the jury.

The first two were taken five years before. The third about three years later. All three MRIs were positive. The most recent showed that Joan's condition was worsening.

Katz also testified that the MRI reports confirmed the physical findings and were consistent with Joan's physical complaints.

"What is your diagnosis of Joan Hangarter's condition, Dr. Katz?"

"She has cervical disc disease and lateral epicondylitis," he said.

"Is there any doubt in your mind about that?"

"No."

"Would her condition prevent Dr. Hangarter from performing manual traction, spinal adjustments, myofascial manipulations, and the other procedures performed in chiropractic?"

"Yes."

"What, in your medical opinion, would happen if she went back to her work?"

"She wouldn't be able to do it. If she forced herself, she would exacerbate her injuries significantly."

"Is her condition permanent?"

"Yes. The arm is chronic. The disc disease cannot resolve spontaneously. Her condition is permanent."

We had nothing further.

᭞ ᭝ ᭞ ᭝ ᭞

"MS. BERNARD," SAID THE JUDGE, "IS THIS YOUR WITNESS?"

"Yes, Your Honor."

"Very well, you may cross-examine."

Lori Bernard, like her partner, Horace Green, was a skilled lawyer. She was pleasant, composed, and smart. Right at the moment, she was also conspicuously pregnant.

Recently she had been the subject of some very personal and nasty commentary on an internet message board. The commentary was written by someone with no lost love for her or for her current client. Horace believed that we had something to do with all of this. We didn't. In fact, I believed that we were being set up by somebody–perhaps somebody working on behalf of UnumProvident, somebody who might be trying to destroy our credibility in the eyes of Judge Larson.

If our fears were correct, the ploy may have come dangerously close to accomplishing its purpose. On the first day of trial, Larson, justifiably furious at the internet messages that were being published and that had been brought to his attention by the defendants, came close to accusing the plaintiff or her counsel of having a hand in the matter. "Only someone intimately involved with this case would have had the information that appeared on the website," he said.

Because we didn't know where any of this was actually coming from, we had earlier opposed issuance of a subpoena for the website's records. But now, we offered to join the defense in requesting a subpoena for the production of all records and information on the website in question.

Suspiciously, our offer, and the resultant silence from the defense, was the last we heard of the situation.

∧ ∨ ∧ ∨ ∧

AFTER ASKING DR. KATZ SOME GENERAL QUESTIONS ABOUT THE PROCE-
dures he had used for dictating his notes from the physical examination and about his normal customs and practices in reviewing MRIs, Bernard turned to the topic of cervical disc disease.

Referring to a medical journal article that Dr. Katz had attached to his report, Bernard asked if the article referenced certain specific symptoms as being consistent with Joan's condition. The symptoms included pain in the thumb and index finger, of which Joan had not complained. Katz agreed but pointed out that not all patients have all the symptoms. In Joan's case, she had pain in the middle finger, which was consistent with the diagnosis.

The article also said that patients who are suffering from lateral epicondylitis will often show wasting and weakness of the biceps muscle, which Joan did not. Katz explained that such wasting depends on the degree of nerve-root compression. The fact that Joan didn't exhibit such wasting did not change the diagnosis.

Bernard moved to the subjective/objective arena. Could this symptom be faked? Could that one?

Katz maintained that it would be difficult to fake the absence of reflexes, hard not to react when stuck with a pin, and virtually impossible to fake a muscle spasm, much less an MRI result.

Bernard suddenly shifted gears.

"Is there a procedure," she asked, "whereby a patient can get cortisone into the affected area without actually having injections?" I didn't know much about cortisone treatments, but it seemed as though Bernard was laying a framework for later testimony by UnumProvident's IME doctor.

"Yes," replied Katz. "It's called iontophoresis. It's done in physical therapy with a machine. They put cortisone on the skin and then work a machine over you. The cortisone is passed through the skin cells to the tissue. It doesn't go very deep. That's the problem. It will go a layer or two to the subcutaneous tissue, but I don't think it gets deep enough into the area where the tendons take off. So you really have to stick a needle in there and inject them."

"When patients come in to you with 'tennis elbow,'" asked Bernard, using the term in as pejorative a way as possible, "do you usually expect the condition to resolve with conservative care? In other words, without surgery?"

"Most do get well," he said, "but Dr. Hangarter's condition is chronic. And chronic conditions like this do not simply 'resolve.'"

That brought up the subject of cures. "Could treatment for what you believe to be Dr. Hangarter's conditions include immobilization?"

Katz agreed that treatment for the condition could include immobilization, as well as cortisone shots, elbow surgery, and cervical surgery.

"Doctor, would you agree that the success rate would be as high as 90 percent for the elbow and 80 percent for the spine?"

"It could."

Finally, Bernard was ready for her best-shot question. "You testified that even if Dr. Hangarter received successful surgery for both the elbow problem and the disc, she could not return to chiropractic without putting herself at risk. Correct?"

"Yes."

"Handing you your deposition in this case, page 52, line 14, I asked you, 'Is it also your opinion that should she take any actions to seek additional treatment, that she at a later date may be able to return to her occupation?' Can you read what your answer was to that question?"

Squinting, Katz read, "Yes. She needs good treatment."

"Thank you," smiled Lori. "That's all I have."

∧ ∨ ∧ ∨ ∧

"Briefly, Your Honor.

"First, Dr. Katz, putting aside the inherent risks involved, you mentioned a possible surgery success rate of 90 percent for the elbow and 80 percent for the neck. Does that mean that the balance fails?"

"Yes, the balance fails. In the case of the neck, if the bone graft fails, the person has to do another operation. They actually get worse."

"Dr. Katz, let's assume for the moment, as Ms. Bernard has been suggesting, that Dr. Hangarter has immobilization. How long would that immobilization last?"

"We would immobilize the arm for a year."

"If Dr. Hangarter went through that and had cortisone shots, elbow surgery, and cervical surgery, would you after that ever recommend that she return to chiropractic?"

"No."

"Why not?"

"Because that would put her at serious risk for further complications. It would make her worse."

"Thank you. That's all I have, Your Honor."

"Thank you, Dr. Katz," nodded Judge Larson. "You are excused."

Lori Bernard was still smiling. I suspect she knew what Unum's IME doctor, Dr. Swartz, was going to say when it was his turn to take the stand.

OUR NEXT WITNESS WAS DR. LINDA BERRY. BERRY WAS A CHIROPRACTOR who had treated Joan for the first time in April 1997. On direct, Berry produced an MRI taken on August 30, 1997, and testified that based on her review of the MRI and the medical records and her physical examination of Joan, her initial diagnosis as entered in her chart was "lateral epicondylitis, cervical intervertebral disc syndrome, and tendonitis." Using a plastic model, Berry demonstrated for Judge Larson and the jury the area of the cervical spine involved in Joan's injuries.

"If there's a bulging disc," she said, demonstrating, "it displaces the nerve. It pushes it up out of the way, and that puts pressure on the nerve [causing] pain, numbness, and tingling.

"These nerves come out of our spinal cord to make our muscles move. So if there's pressure on a nerve root, it doesn't get to send all its information to the muscles, and so the muscles can start to wither and get weak and die."

Berry next produced a second MRI taken on May 12, 2000. This MRI showed that Joan's condition had worsened. Berry described how growths, or spurs, had developed, causing bony projections to penetrate into the area where nerve roots were based. This, she said, would interfere with the transmission of nerve impulses, causing pain, numbness, paresthesia (a tingling sensation), and weakness in the muscles.

Berry treated Joan with ice to control the inflammation, braces for compression, and a variety of chiropractic modalities. She saw Joan from 1997 to 2000 and treated her on more than thirty occasions without seeing any lasting improvement. She ultimately referred Joan to Allen Ling, a physical therapist, but his treatment was not successful. By May 1998, Berry had determined that Joan was not going to be able to return to the practice of chiropractic.

Berry testified that Joan really loved being a chiropractor and that it was very difficult for her to give up her practice. During the course of Joan's treatment, Berry encouraged her, on a number of occasions, to attempt to perform adjustments. But these attempts all resulted in terrible pain.

"Is there any doubt in your mind about the diagnosis of Joan's cervical intervertebral disc syndrome?"

"No."

"What about your diagnosis of her lateral epicondylitis?"

"No doubt."

"Do you have any opinion of what would happen to Joan if she could somehow force herself to continue treating patients as a chiropractor?"

"I don't believe she could even get through a week of doing it without getting severe pain." Berry was asked if anyone from the insurance company had ever contacted her to ask for the basis of her opinion that Joan was totally and permanently disabled.

"No," she replied, "they did not."

Berry was cross-examined by Lori Bernard. She was asked about her training with interpreting MRI reports, the accuracy of closed versus open MRIs, and whether the degree of narrowing of disc spaces noted in 1997 wasn't "minimal."

When asked whether she had ever recommended cortisone injections to relieve Joan's pain, Berry responded that she was not licensed to recommend medical prescriptions. When questioned about Joan's various attempts to perform chiropractic manipulations, she responded that this had occurred three or four times and that she had ultimately instructed Joan to stop these efforts.

Bernard then asked a question that caught me completely by surprise. She asked if Berry's opinion concerning the permanence and severity of Joan's condition would change if she were to learn that Joan had continued to perform chiropractic after she said she had stopped.

Everything froze. The courtroom fell so silent you could hear your own breathing. The suggestion that Joan had done this clearly implied that she was lying to her insurance company. And perhaps to everyone else, about her condition. Our objection to this question as assuming facts not in evidence was sustained.

Bernard said she would return to the subject later on.

What did Bernard know that we didn't? What was the basis for this question? Did UnumProvident have some kind of surveillance film or investigators' report that we hadn't seen? Whatever this was about, it certainly had planted a seed that perhaps Joan was not telling the truth.

∧ ∨ ∧ ∨ ∧

AS THE NEXT ORDER OF BUSINESS, WE WANTED TO OFFER IN EVIDENCE brief excerpts from the April 2001 depositions of Joseph Sullivan, Chris Ryan, Sandra Fryc, and Dr. John Bianchi. These witnesses were all out-of-state residents, so they were beyond the subpoena range of the California federal court. Therefore, even though we believed that some or all of them would probably be called to testify by UnumProvident's lawyers as part of their defense, we had no choice but to read from their depositions during the presentation of our case.

In doing so I established from Sandra Fryc's deposition that the correct definition of *total disability* was the inability to perform one's duties in the usual and customary manner and with reasonable continuity. I also read her admissions that claims had to be investigated fairly and objectively and that it was not permissible for the company to conduct a biased investigation aimed at finding a way to cut someone off.

From Chris Ryan's deposition, I read the sections of his testimony revealing that he didn't know what Fryc was talking about. He neither knew the correct definition of disability nor did he know that insurance companies were required to handle claims fairly, objectively, or thoroughly. He had never been taught any of this, even though he worked under none other than Sandra Fryc.

The portion of Joseph Sullivan's testimony I read to the jury included his statements that he too was unaware of the definition of disability applicable to Joan. I also read his contradictory and retracted testimony about whether the inability to perform "the important duties" of one's occupation meant *all*, *most*, or *some* of those duties.

Portions of Bianchi's deposition were also read, including his statement that some disability claimants should just work in pain. I also read the part of his testimony in which he admitted that he had never spoken to any of Joan's treating doctors before coming to his diagnostic conclusions about her condition.

∧ ∨ ∧ ∨ ∧

DR. WILLIAM FEIST WAS THE FORMER MEDICAL DIRECTOR OF UNUM-Provident. He resigned several years after Chandler had come on board and after Mohney had taken over the claims department.

I had taken Feist's deposition in another case against Unum-Provident—not in Joan's. But we were seeking to introduce it in the current case.

Green objected. He sought to exclude it on two grounds: one, that the deposition wasn't formally "noticed" (taken) in the Hangarter case, and two, that because Green had not been present at the Feist deposition he had not had the opportunity to cross-examine Feist himself.

This was the type of legal challenge that could suddenly pop up in the middle of a trial, sending everybody's assistants scurrying about to resupply the Tums. But we had done our homework. We'd carefully researched this issue and felt confident that we were right on the law. As long as the issues were substantially similar in both cases and the lawyer representing the defendant had done a thorough job, the deposition could be introduced.

After studying the Feist transcript, Judge Larson came to the same conclusion. First, he noted that the issues in the two cases were virtually identical. Second, he observed that Sean Nalty had done a comprehensive job in his cross-examination.

Comprehensive wasn't the word for it. I remembered that Nalty had gone on in such detail and for so long in his cross that I could have qualified for state residency and gone home with an Alabama driver's license by the time he was finished.

∧ ∨ ∧ ∨ ∧

AFTER READING SOME OF THE BACKGROUND QUESTIONS AND ANSWERS to the jury—to give them a feel for Feist—I dove into his testimony.

Before Chandler and Mohney had assumed their positions, testified Dr. Feist, nothing was ever said about shredding documents or omitting and deleting information from claims files. But everything changed with their arrival. "For one thing," Feist testified, "Mr. Mohney issued an edict prohibiting doctors from writing on a file that an insured was disabled.

"I recall specifically," he said, "a case, probably in November of '95, in which there was a very unfortunate man in his midforties who had had several myocardial infarctions [heart attacks] and had severe incapacitating angina. This man literally could not walk across the length of the room without getting severe chest pain.

"I wrote on the file–just as clear as I could write it–that this man was permanently and totally disabled. I was called on the carpet by Mr. Mohney. 'Dr. Feist,' he said, 'you are *not* to write on any file–this file or any file–that someone is disabled. That is for the *claims* department to decide.'

"That may sound like a simple procedural thing, but it was really a profound philosophical change." That change meant, Feist explained, that Mohney and his associates would always be able to make the call as to whether or not someone was to be considered disabled. If for some reason the claims department didn't want to permit disability benefits, it could deny them.

"That is a small but good example of the philosophical change that came in when Mr. Mohney and Mr. Chandler took over."

With regard to the roundtables, Feist testified that they were held for the specific purpose of finding "any way or modality to try to terminate claims. Questioning the integrity of the treating physician, using surveillance inappropriately, getting an IME to prove their case, saying that the individual was fraudulently trying to get money out of Provident–all of those modalities were used."

Feist had actually attended roundtables that had profiled more than 250 claims. The company targeted high-value claimants and "brainstormed," as he put it, for "any excuse or pretext" to cut off their benefits. "The whole tenor of these meetings was 'We have got to find some way to terminate [this] claim whatever it takes or however we can do it.'"

The terminations themselves did not occur at the meetings, he said. Instead, the adjusters who were in charge of the files "were given their marching orders and off they went."

Feist also confirmed that no agenda was prepared for the cases and subjects that were to be discussed at roundtables. Any notes that were taken at the meetings were subsequently destroyed.

It was clear that Feist had seen what the company had done to reduce claim payments, increase profits, and make up for losses resulting from its inaccurate interest rate projections. He had seen what Mohney and Chandler had done–and he didn't like it.

In response to a question from Nalty, Feist testified that he was being paid nothing for his deposition or for anything in connection with his testimony against UnumProvident.

On redirect, I asked him why he had agreed to give this testimony when he was still in the insurance industry. "Why are you willing to do it?" I asked.

"Well, the bottom line," he said, "is I want to help individuals who I feel have been, over the years, wronged by Provident. I have no ax to grind against Mr. Chandler or Mr. Mohney, but when individuals are harmed by a process like this, if I have a chance to speak out against it, that is what I would like to do."

∧ ∨ ∧ ∨ ∧

NEXT, WE READ FROM THAT PORTION OF RALPH MOHNEY'S DEPOSITION in which he named the numerous distinct subsidiary companies owned by UnumProvident whose claims he was responsible for overseeing. We also read the testimony in which Mohney stated that UnumProvident received about 400,000 new disability claims per year, of which about 120,000 were long-term claims.

With this, plus the presentation of Christine Davis, a CPA specializing in insurance accounting who was examined by Alice concerning "discount rates," the calculation of the present value of Joan's future policy benefits, and other esoteric matters beyond my comprehension, we were done.

When the plaintiff rests, before the defense calls its first witness, it usually makes a number of motions. These motions are based on the idea that the plaintiff has what is called the burden of proof in a civil case. If he or she has failed to establish at least a prima facie case (one that creates at least the inference of liability) sufficient to allow the trial to proceed to the next phase, a motion for a directed verdict in favor of the defense is granted by the court and the case is dismissed right then and there. The defendants congratulate each other while the plaintiff's lawyers take ballpoint pens from their briefcases and commit hari-kiri at counsel table. (If they neglect to do this, their partners will certainly assist them when they return to the office.)

Chapter Nine

CUSTOMER CARE

W E HAD RESTED OUR CASE. THE DEFENSE WAS UP. FOR UNUM-
Provident's first witness, Horace Green called Sandra Fryc.
Fryc was finally going to get to answer questions from a friendly
examiner. She testified that she began working with Paul Revere in
1987 as a claims examiner. She worked in that position for two years.
Through various promotions she moved to the positions of development manager, claims manager, and claims quality performance
consultant. Fryc said that as a claims manager, she was involved in
the training of claims personnel and in mentoring them–helping
adjusters with specific problems or questions involving claims.

She stated that Paul Revere's philosophy concerning claims
handling was to perform a "thorough, objective, and fair handling
of every claim."

After the merger between Paul Revere and Provident, Fryc noted
no change in the company claims philosophy. She said that the merger
was good because it increased the resources necessary to handle
claims properly.

Fryc was asked about her company's process for handling claims.
She said that resources such as medical, financial, legal, vocational
rehabilitation, and underwriting services were all available to the
claims department. In addition to evaluating claims thoroughly
before they were denied, Fryc insisted that the company would also
consider any new information made available by a claimant after
the denial. If appropriate, the claim denial would be reconsidered.
She said that the reason for sometimes ordering surveillance was
to ascertain whether a claimant was being accurate with what he
or she told the company, "to substantiate what the claimant was
telling us."

Fryc acknowledged the existence of roundtables but asserted that they were not set up for the purpose of finding excuses to order terminations but only to provide a "group think" to help assess certain claims.

Green asked Fryc in the context of the company's terminology whether the phrase "resolve" a claim meant the same as "terminate" a claim. She denied that this was the case.

"Do you have friends in the claims department?" asked Green.

"Yes."

"Do they deny legitimate claims in order to save money for the company?"

"No."

"Has that ever been the company's philosophy?"

"Absolutely not," said Fryc.

"Has there ever been any corporate scheme to deny legitimate claims in order to save money?"

"No," she said firmly.

On cross-examination, Fryc acknowledged that she had been deposed about fifty times in other cases.

I questioned her about the definition of disability in the UnumProvident policy, which stated that claimants were to be considered disabled if they couldn't perform the "substantial and material duties of their occupation. Does this mean *any* of your duties, *most* of your duties, *all* of your duties, or what?"

Fryc said claimants were asked to fill out a form listing their duties.

"Do you tell them when you ask that question how you [Unum-Provident] are going to interpret the phrase 'the important duties'?"

"No."

"Do you reveal to them that if they are able to perform *any* of the duties on the list they are providing, the company will say they are not totally disabled?"

"No."

Fryc said the company looked at all of a person's duties in evaluating a claim.

I asked her, if a concert violinist filled out the form saying that her duties included reading music and playing the violin, whether this person would fail to qualify for total disability payments just because she could still read music even if she couldn't play. After trying to dodge the issue, Fryc finally replied that she could not provide a yes or no answer because it was a hypothetical question.

The rest of my cross-examination involved various company memos and a number of issues relating to her interpretation of the provisions in the policy. Green did a pretty good job of rehabilitating Fryc on redirect. I had nothing further on recross.

On the way home that night I worried that my examination of Fryc had been rambling and poorly focused. Fryc had done a pretty good job as a witness–better than the job I had done as Joan's lawyer.

∧ ∨ ∧ ∨ ∧

FROM OUR EXPERIENCE, IT SEEMED TO BE A COMMON TACTIC FOR UnumProvident to defend itself from charges of engaging in fraudulent claims practices not by justifying its conduct but by searching for ways to attack or undermine the claimant. Perhaps it had some kind of a study showing that the best way to prevail before a jury was to smear the policyholder. In the Hangarter case, the defense put on the stand two former employees of Joan's: Rhonda Corey, who had worked as an office administrator, and Parissa Peymani, the chiropractor Joan had hired to pitch in and take over her practice while she tried to recuperate.

Corey, a strong, no-nonsense-looking woman, walked to the witness stand with an air of purpose about her. She began her testimony by explaining that she was once forced to leave the office because she was being sexually harassed by a male employee. Joan, she sniffed, had refused to do anything about it.

I could have objected to this entire line of questioning–which was clearly irrelevant–but I didn't. I was hoping, instead, that the jury would see through UnumProvident's tactics.

In my view, it was difficult to imagine Corey being harassed. She gave the impression that any man foolish enough to try anything with her would be singing soprano in short order.

Next came the issue Bernard had referred to in her cross-examination of Dr. Berry. Corey was asked whether she had made an anonymous call to the company informing it that Joan was continuing to treat patients *after* she had gone on disability. If the information were true, the clear implication would be that Joan was exaggerating her injuries in order to collect disability benefits to which she was not entitled.

Yes, said Corey, she had made the call. And it was true: Joan was continuing to treat patients regularly. She was doing it, she said as she held her head back and looked down her nose, "behind closed doors and with the shades drawn."

I wondered how Corey could tell what was going on behind closed doors–given that the doors were, well, closed.

Bernard asked why Corey had called UnumProvident to report that Joan was still treating patients while she was telling the company she couldn't do so. Corey responded, with a confident nod to the defense table, that she had done this because it was the right thing to do. She had no motive other than to tell the truth.

On cross-examination I handed Corey a UnumProvident form she had signed just weeks before she'd anonymously called the company with her "closed door" story. On the form, Corey had unequivocally stated that Dr. Hangarter was *not* adjusting patients at all. Corey had no explanation for this.

Under questioning, Corey was also forced to concede that her denial of "any ulterior motives whatever" in making her call wasn't exactly correct. That in fact, the very day before the call, Corey had become furious with Joan for laying her off in a cost-cutting effort.

I had a hard time believing that UnumProvident's claims people, with the extensive surveillance they had conducted in this case, could ever have really believed Corey's story. What was going on here? Was there more to this than they were admitting?

∧ ∨ ∧ ∨ ∧

UNUMPROVIDENT'S NEXT WITNESS WAS A THIN, FRAGILE-LOOK-ING woman with dark hair and a calm, resolute demeanor. Parissa Peymani had been employed by Joan on two occasions, from July 31 until the end of October 1996 and from June 30, 1997, to April 3, 1999. She had voluntarily left the practice the first time to take care of what she obliquely referred to as "personal business." When she returned in 1997, there was a two- or three-day transition during which Joan explained the status of her patients and prepared Peymani to take over for her. Peymani's second departure was not voluntary.

Lori Bernard questioned Peymani on direct. "After this two- or three-day transition (after Peymani had been hired the second time), did Joan Hangarter stop seeing patients altogether?"

Here it was again.

"No," she said, tossing her head as she avoided looking at Joan.

"Do you have an idea of the number of patients that she continued to see?"

"Between five to seven."

"And how long did she continue to see these patients?"

"Pretty much the whole time."

Bernard asked Peymani to describe the circumstances surrounding her leaving Solano Chiropractic the second time.

"On April the third, which was a Saturday," Peymani said. "I came home, and Ms. Hangarter fired me on the answering machine."

Bernard paused to let the point sink in.

"And I have the tape too," Peymani added.

I didn't doubt it.

Bernard changed the subject. There was something else despicable to be presented.

"Were you contacted by Ms. Hangarter's lawyers to testify in this case?"

"Yes," Peymani said.

"Did you leave Solono on good terms?"

"No."

"When you left Solano Chiropractic, were you paid in full for the services you had provided to Solono?"

"No," said Peymani. "And I actually bounced checks as a result. Checks and bonuses."

Bernard thanked Peymani and withdrew to the defense table. She had nothing further.

On cross-examination, Peymani admitted that she filed an action with the state labor commission to try to obtain the money Joan owed her. The reason, she confirmed, that she had recovered nothing in that case was because Joan was found to have no assets.

The part about being fired on her answering machine wasn't "exactly" correct either. In fact, it was downright incorrect. Under questioning, Peymani acknowledged that what had really happened was that Joan had taken Peymani aside at the office and told her about her financial problems. Joan said she was sorry, but she was afraid she was going to have to let Peymani go. When Peymani asked Joan to reconsider, Joan reluctantly agreed to think about it. She did so but couldn't find a way to keep Peymani on. She simply couldn't afford it.

To talk to Joan further about this, Joan called Peymani at home repeated times to let her know of her decision. Unable to reach her, Joan finally left a message on her answering machine, explaining the situation.

With regard to the number of patients Joan had attempted to treat after going on disability, I asked Peymani if she had previously testified that Dr. Hangarter had seen only four patients plus one friend in the entire twenty-one months after she came on board.

Peymani saw me reaching for the certified copy of her deposition transcript.

"Yes," she said. She admitted that she herself had seen thousands of patients in that same period.

Did Peymani know that the reason Joan had seen some patients after becoming disabled was that she had been encouraged by her doctors to try and do so?

"No."

"Or that her doctors had finally given up and told her to stop?"

"No."

"Or that even after her doctors had told her to stop, until the time she finally gave up and sold her practice, she continued to try?"

"No."

It seemed to me that for Bernard to twist Joan's efforts to see how much she could do into an attempt by her to lie about her condition was really a stretch.

"Did you ever hear Joan complaining of pain in her arm, her shoulder, her hand?" I asked.

"Very, very few times."

"Did you ever see her wearing ice?"

"On the elbow," Peymani admitted.

"Did you write a letter," I asked, "to Ken Seaman on May 29, 1998?"

Bernard objected but was overruled.

"Yes," she answered.

From this letter, I read, "I am performing all of the patient treatment and patient care at Solano Chiropractic because Dr. Hangarter has been unable to perform her regular work activities. I have been the treating doctor for Solano Chiropractic since July 1997. Should you have any further questions, I will be more than happy to answer them for you. Sincerely, Parissa Peymani.'"

"Did you write that letter?" I asked her.

"Yes."

"Did you ever receive a response from Mr. Seaman?"

"No."

"Did *anyone* from Provident ever call and say, 'Would you please explain this to us? We would like you to elaborate on what you've said in some way' or 'We have some additional questions'?"

"No."

I wanted to clear up the matter of Peymani's call to our office.

"Were you aware that you had been served with a subpoena to testify in this case?"

"Yes," Peymani conceded.

And that if we didn't make other arrangements with her that she would have had to come to court and sit in the hall, waiting to be called as a witness. And that instead, we had offered to put her on a twenty-four hour standby. That this was not a threat. That it was simply an offer made to her for her own convenience.

"Isn't that right?"

"Yes. I guess so."

"And your response was that you were not going to come in, and that we would have to send a federal marshal to get you, right?"

She didn't deny this.

"And then you demanded to be paid $350 per hour to testify."

"I said that, yes, because that's the money I'm losing being here."

I wondered how much money the jurors were losing "being here." "Nothing further, Your Honor," I said, sitting down.

Bernard mumbled that she had no redirect. I thought that was probably a good decision on her part.

∧ ∨ ∧ ∨ ∧

HORACE GREEN WAS READY WITH HIS NEXT WITNESS. RALPH MOHNEY walked stiffly to the witness stand. Tall and slightly balding, he had a kind of wooden, starched look. But as I knew from past experience, he was an incredibly tough and able witness, confident and poised. He was also very experienced. He would be well prepared and cool under fire, likable to the jury, and tough to cross-examine. I was nervous about him.

Green started out by asking a number of background questions: marriage, family, education, and so on. He segued into Mohney's occupation and job duties, which the UnumProvident executive described as having overall responsibility for the customer care operation. There was that name again: the "Customer Care" Center. I wondered if Mohney was the one who'd renamed it.

I wondered whether UnumProvident's customers "cared" about whether their insurer was defrauding them out of their benefits? Or "cared" about whether the company was forcing them into bankruptcy? Or "cared" about whether they had to sue UnumProvident to get the money it owed them? Mohney wouldn't have liked these questions, and they would have been too sarcastic for me to ask in front of the jury.

Green's questions would be more to his liking.

"When you were in charge of Provident Life and Accident's Claims Department, did you develop and put into place a 'philosophy' regarding claims handling?"

"Yes, I did," Mohney said. "And that consisted of four parts: to ensure thorough, fair, and objective evaluation of all claims; to pay legitimate claims promptly; to assist insureds in getting back to work; and to defend the company against illegitimate claims."

Mohney mentioned that he was going to be in Glendale, California, later in the week to talk with employees about this claims philosophy. He didn't mention that the reason he was going to be in Southern California in the first place was to testify in another bad-faith case against his company.

Next, Mohney talked about the "extensive training programs that we have for customer care specialists. When we hire a new customer care specialist, they go through a program to help them spread the philosophy around."

That's not all they were spreading around.

As I sat there, I found it impossible to look at Mohney without thinking about those people whose lives he and his "initiatives" had destroyed–the lives of people like Stuart Gluck.

∧ ∨ ∧ ∨ ∧

DR. STUART GLUCK, A WONDERFUL, BRILLIANT, AND EXTRAORDINARILY talented man and a board-certified psychiatrist, was sold a disability insurance policy through the American Psychiatric Association in 1984. The policy was originally underwritten through the Centennial Insurance Company. Centennial was later bought out by UnumProvident.

In 1988, Gluck was sold a second disability insurance policy–this one by Paul Revere. In 1992, he bought another policy from Paul Revere. Without it, his existing coverage was insufficient, said the agent. All the policies covered Gluck should injury or illness ever prevent him from performing the duties of his own occupation as a psychiatrist.

In 1996, Gluck was diagnosed with HIV and soon suffering from a constellation of AIDS- and medication-related symptoms, including persistent fatigue, chronic diarrhea and incontinence, impaired concentration and memory, personality changes, and halting speech. In 1999, Gluck was further diagnosed with a nervous system disorder called peripheral sensory neuropathy. As a result, it became impossible for him to hold small objects. This condition also caused a constant burning sensation in his hands.

On February 2, 2000, after he had pushed himself to work in his condition for almost four years, Gluck filed with UnumProvident (which now owned both Paul Revere and Centennial) for disability benefits under his three policies. A month later, Gluck was diagnosed with coronary artery disease.

In May 2000, he had triple coronary bypass surgery. Due to a complication of the heart surgery, Dr. Gluck suffered organic brain damage. In addition, subsequent to the operation, he continued to have significant, ongoing coronary artery disease, resulting in cardiomyopathy, disease of the heart muscle. His cardiologist considered him a class II congestive heart failure patient and found him to be completely disabled from his occupation on the basis of his heart condition alone.

Approximately a month after the bypass surgery, UnumProvident began paying disability benefits. In August 2000, Gluck was awarded Supplemental Security Income (SSI) disability benefits. SSI found that Gluck's total disability began on February 19, 2000, around the time he applied to UnumProvident for benefits. As UnumProvident was well aware, the definition of disability under SSI is much stricter than under its own policies. The SSI standard requires that an individual be disabled from performing *any* occupation.

On January 5, 2001, UnumProvident field representative Chris Moffatt called Gluck. As of that date, UnumProvident was aware that Gluck was taking enough medications for his various medical conditions to stock a good-sized pharmacy. UnumProvident was also aware of Gluck's heart condition.

On March 30, 2001, when he called to inquire about the delay in his March payment of benefits, Gluck was informed for the first time that his claim had been terminated. Although he had not received it and it's unclear when it was mailed, a letter in the UnumProvident file to Gluck indicated that as of March 27, 2001–without a single IME and without a single telephone call to any of his treating physicians–UnumProvident had terminated his benefits. The company did this on the basis of an "opinion" from an in-house "medical consultant." This medical consultant, we learned, was a nurse.

Totally ignoring his treating doctors and basing its decision on its in-house nurse's opinion, UnumProvident told Gluck that the medical documentation did not support any restrictions or limitations that would affect his ability "to perform the duties of your own occupation beyond October 23, 2000." To add insult to this injury, and in order to gain leverage, UnumProvident threatened to collect alleged overpayments. The company then fraudulently alleged that Gluck's long-term disability policy, which he had paid for himself, was governed by ERISA. If he had been duped by this or had asked a lawyer who did not specialize in this field what it meant to be governed by ERISA, he would have believed that he had no right to sue UnumProvident for the damages it had caused.

On June 20, 2001, we met Gluck for the first time. On August 6, we sued UnumProvident on his behalf. As soon as we filed suit,

UnumProvident offered to pay the benefits, claiming that a "clerical mistake" had been made. The offer was made with a "reservation of rights," which meant that the company was leaving open the possibility of attempting to get its money back. We rejected the offer.

On October 16, 2001, UnumProvident wrote Gluck, informing him that it was removing the condition to seek reimbursement of benefits. In addition, for the first time in the more than seven months since the company had terminated his benefits, UnumProvident requested an independent medical examination.

We refused to drop our lawsuit. Not long thereafter, the case settled for an undisclosed sum. The amount of the settlement was the only detail Gluck would agree to keep confidential.

∧ ∨ ∧ ∨ ∧

"MR. MOHNEY," INQUIRED GREEN, "DIRECTLY OR INDIRECTLY, HAVE YOU ever instructed anybody in the customer care organization to deny a legitimate claim?"

Mohney pouted and looked taken aback by even the suggestion of such a possibility. "Absolutely not." He repeated it for emphasis. "Absolutely not."

"Why not? Isn't that a good way to save the company money?"

"No, no," he said. "I'd say we wouldn't want to do that for several reasons. Number one, it is the wrong thing to do, and it is—it would be an ethical violation. Secondly, it flies in the face of this philosophy we have been developing over these years. Third, financially it would hurt our company." In addition, he added, "If we were perceived to be a company that did not pay legitimate claims, we would not grow."

Mohney explained that the company, naturally, does not pay *all* claims. Some are fraudulent or exaggerated or involve malingering. To pay claims that are not compensable would drive up the cost of insurance.

He also talked about the money the company had invested in "clinical resources," computer systems, impairment-based management, and other investments. He denied that the purpose of the roundtables was to find excuses for terminating claims. He denied that the company had ever set goals for terminating claims, saying that the number of claims was something the company simply monitored. They weren't goals; they were "expectations." And of course, any shredding was done only to protect the privacy of insureds and their medical records or to get rid of extra copies of documents.

"Did you ever have the expectation that any of the customer care units for which you were responsible would save $60 million per year by denying legitimate claims?"

"Again," Mohney exclaimed, "it would be the wrong thing to do. It's contrary to our philosophy, and it hurts the company financially."

"Thank you very much," said Green. "I have no further questions."

I did.

"Mr. Mohney," I said, "I would like to start by addressing your comment that your company would not be doing well if it had a reputation for wrongfully denying claims. Do you recall testifying about that?"

"Yes."

"How many policies are outstanding right now in what is called the 'bad block' of business [own-occupation policies] sold in the 1980s?"

"I'm not sure I understand your question about the 'bad block' of business of policies sold in the 1980s." However, he added, "I am aware that the business issued in the 1980s was not performing as well as it was expected."

To follow up, I asked, "How many of those policies are still out there?

"I do not know," he asserted. This was hard for me to believe.

"How many people, approximately, do you approach every year to buy individual disability policies? Do you have any idea?"

After his attorney objected and was overruled by the court, Mohney responded, "I don't know how many people we approach each year."

"Well, when your salespeople go out and approach these people to buy policies, those individuals would have to *know* about your claims-handling history in order for them to be negatively affected by your practices. Isn't that correct?"

Mohney knew very well that only a small percentage of policy-holders ever make claims for serious disability problems. He also knew that the rest of them never found out about what happens to such claimants. The company hardly advertises how many claimants have had their benefits cut off for phony reasons.

"Have you ever had anything to do with what's called the 'confidential settlement agreement'?"

"I'm not sure," said Mohney.

How he could be "not sure" about this was hard to fathom. Just a few months ago I had questioned him about his role in the confidentiality proposal in the McGregor case.

"If those agreements are, in fact, used . . ." sidestepped Mohney, "it's done on advice of counsel." In other words, he was saying, what I know about this subject, I know from attorney-client privileged communications with company lawyers. Therefore, I don't have to testify about it.

I asked Mohney if the company had other bad-faith or fraud cases pending against it that were currently in litigation.

Again, Mohney asserted the attorney-client privilege. "The only thing that I know about the litigation of our companies is what has been shared with me by counsel."

Apparently, whenever Mohney attended meetings in which the number of terminated claimants who had the temerity to sue was discussed, the company made sure a lawyer was in the room. That allowed him to claim attorney-client privilege and refuse to ever discuss the subject.

∧ ∨ ∧ ∨ ∧

THIS WHOLE CONCEPT OF "ATTORNEY-CLIENT PRIVILEGE" IS A BIT mind-boggling to me. Lawyers, of course, are very protective in guarding anything that could be perceived as causing the slightest erosion in their father-confessor relationship with clients.

I'm not so sure about the wisdom of this. In fact, I once wrote a letter to the editor of the *New York Times* on the subject. It had been reported in the *Times* that at the annual meeting of the American Bar Association, two important subjects were on the agenda: one, whether there should be modifications to the lawyer-client privilege, and two, whether it was acceptable for attorneys to have sex with people who had come to them for legal services. I wrote that the two issues were really about similar problems. Namely, did the ABA think it should be sanctioning lawyers to get paid for screwing the public?

The *Times* didn't print my letter.

∧ ∨ ∧ ∨ ∧

"LET ME ASK YOU ABOUT THE $60 MILLION MEMO." THIS WAS MARKED AS plaintiff's exhibit 36 (Exhibit 4). I read from the 1995 memo: "'Due to the significant financial leverage associated with individual disability claims, the return on these claims improvement initiatives is expected to be substantial. A 1 percent decrease in benefit costs due to more effective claim management translates to approximately $6 million in annual savings. We believe that aggregate improvements in the 5 to 10 percent, $30 to $60 million annually, range are possible—once the initiatives have been fully implemented.' Do you see those words, sir?"

He did. The $60 million figure seemed very low to me, but this memo was written before the Paul Revere acquisition, Unum merger, or other expansions.

I then asked him a simple math question: "If you take claims that have an average benefit of $2,000 per month . . ."

"I hear you so far," he said.

"So would you just say that an average of $2,000 per month equals $24,000 per year?"

"That math is right."

"Two thousand claims like that per year at $2,000 a month would be worth $50 million a year. Correct?"

"If you're asking whether two thousand times twenty-four thousand equals $50 million, the answer is no," said Mohney. He looked very self-satisfied. I had deliberately made the mistake, counting on him to react as he did.

"Maybe my math is not exactly correct," I apologized. "What would it come to?" I noticed that several jurors were writing, apparently making calculations on their pads.

"Forty-eight million," he declared.

"Forty-eight million," I said. "I stand corrected. I apologize. To get to $50 million a year you'd have to add some more claims."

Mohney acted as though he didn't get it.

I asked him how many total claims, roughly, had been made from the individual disability block of business in 1995, the year he wrote the memo.

He said he didn't know.

"Well, let's just say even if it was only one hundred thousand claims, two thousand claims would only be 2 percent of that. Correct?"

It seemed that Mohney didn't want to be pinned down on a specific number. He started throwing around confusing terms such as the names of different types of claims. I didn't mind changing the subject. The point was made: two thousand claims hardly amounted to a fraction of the company's total claims, yet the amount of money that could be saved terminating those claims was in the tens of millions of dollars *per year.*

"I believe you said that the company never set goals for terminations. Is that correct?"

"I said we never had a—it was never our intent to have a set number of claims to terminate. We did have expectations around if we did things, what would the impact be on the number of claims that close?"

"What I'm trying to find out is whether the company ever set 'goals' for terminations."

Mohney refused to acknowledge the memos that specifically talked about "termination goals." "I think I testified earlier that there was something that was prepared in 1995 that was headed '95 Objectives. Something that was headed '96 Objectives that was prepared in 1996 . . . and it did include on that sheet of paper something about a 'Net Terminations Ratio,' which, again, my belief was that that was our expectation, that if we carried out these improvements all within the context of our philosophy, all within the context of paying every claim that should be paid, that we would see that movement."

I followed up this response with "I think you indicated that most of your terminations were people who simply went back to work."

He answered that that was correct.

But UnumProvident didn't need roundtables just to count the number of people that went back to work. "That wasn't the purpose of the roundtable, was it?"

"I'm not following your question," said Mohney.

Right, I thought. I repeated the question, but Mohney still said he didn't follow it.

Since he wasn't going to answer me, I turned to the "formula" UnumProvident was using to measure claims terminations. I asked Mohney to take a look at plaintiff's exhibit 152, which he admitted he wrote and sent to Executive Vice President Tom Watjen on January 21, 1998.

"Do you see where it says claims resolutions of $165.6 million for the quarter reached a record high and were $10.8 million, 7 percent above the previous quarter four average?"

"Yes."

Moving down the page, I asked Mohney if he saw where, referring to the old Paul Revere operation, it said, "Claims resolutions of $138.2 million were $.2 million higher than the average for the four previous quarters for Worcester."

"Yes."

I then asked him to turn to plaintiff's exhibit 148, from which I read, "Terminations reached a record level of $166.7 million, up $16.5 million, 11 percent, from the previous fourth quarter average.

"Did I read that correctly?" I asked.

"Yes."

We went through other exhibits relating to termination amounts. They talked about $140 million here and $160 million there, up 16 percent here and up 24 percent there. After a while the numbers were all just a blur—a slice of reality from a day in the life of Ralph Mohney, a day in the life of the Customer Care Center, a day in the life of UnumProvident.

"Okay," I said, ready with a question I knew he wasn't expecting, "with reference to your comment about customer satisfaction earlier, isn't it true that you got to the point with the company that your claimants, the ones that were filing disability claims, became so angry, so upset with your company that you had to respond to a rash of threats from claimants?"

"You're mischaracterizing–" Mohney fumed.

Green shot up. "Objection. Lacks any foundation whatsoever. Argumentative."

Judge Larson asked for the answer to the question.

"Well, he's mischaracterizing something that he knows," stumbled Mohney.

"Restate the question," ordered Judge Larson. "And if you're referring to a document, identify it."

Handing Mohney a copy of plaintiff's exhibit 143, I asked him to identify it for the record. He indicated it was an internal memo from himself to Mr. Tom Heys.

I asked him if he saw the section labeled "Issues and Concerns."

"Mm-hmm," he responded.

I read from the memo. "'In response to a rash of recent threats from claimants, a multidisciplinary task force has been assembled to develop training procedures and security recommendations.' Did I read that correctly?"

First, Mohney claimed that he thought the company had received only two threats. Then he said that in any event, the company had to deal with a fair number of people with "psychiatric disabilities." He reiterated that the company pays legitimate claims.

Later, I asked him to tell the court about the recent case where the company cut off a dentist's disability benefits, the one where the claimant's clavicle was broken in half such that it would never grow back together and no surgery could be performed. I hoped we could bring up other cases in cross-examination that we had been barred from asking about in Caliri's direct examination. First, lawyers are permitted more latitude in cross than in direct. Second, should a party "open the door" to a topic on his direct, the opposing side is allowed to ask questions about that topic, in response, on cross.

It wasn't going to happen.

"Objection. Irrelevant. Argumentative," said Green.

"Sustained," said the judge, with a hint of annoyance. "We are not going to be adjudicating other claims here, Mr. Bourhis."

Moving on, I asked if, as part of his claims-handling process, he ever considered the issue of whether people can afford to take on his company or not.

"Objection. Argumentative."

"Overruled."

"Our intent is to pay every legitimate claim. I talked a lot about our process. I talked a lot about our training. I talked a lot about the resources we bring to bear to make sure we make the right decisions." Mohney then indicated that "we don't want lawsuits."

He also didn't want to answer the question. It was inconceivable that the company didn't consider the financial leverage it had over poor or disabled people. UnumProvident could hire four-hundred-to five-hundred-partner law firms—one on top of the other. The company could afford to have lawyers that were in charge of one case spending days in the visitors' gallery observing another trial. Many times, UnumProvident representatives had said that clients who didn't accept what we considered lowball settlement offers wouldn't see any money for years.

Mohney wouldn't cop to it.

"Have you ever considered in terms of your claims practices the issue of how many or how few attorneys there are out there that can take your company on?" I asked.

"Same objections."

"Overruled."

"Again, our commitment is to pay every legitimate claim."

"Sir," Judge Larson said to Mohney, "I think you can answer that question yes or no."

Mohney denied any awareness of this.

"That's all I have for this witness, Your Honor."

Horace Green asked Mohney two final questions on redirect. One had to do with clarifying who had written a particular document. The second question sounded like a broken record—Had Mohney ever directed anyone in customer care to deny legitimate claims?

Of course, he had never done such a thing.

Now might have been an appropriate time to launch my addition to the evidence code, the bullshit objection. Appropriate, perhaps, but most unwise. Judge Larson would be the first to agree that it was good I kept my mouth shut.

Mohney adjusted the sleeves of his shirt, uncrossed his legs, brushed away a slight wrinkle in his slacks, flashed me an odd smile—bordering on a smirk—nodded to the jury, and departed for Los Angeles. It was a pity the jury couldn't be told precisely where he was headed and why. The very well-to-do head of UnumProvident's

Customer Care Center was on the way to his next testifying gig—in another bad-faith case. If they had known this, the jurors might have wondered how he had time to give customers any care at all.

I couldn't put my finger on it, but something about the way Mohney had looked at me as he left made me uneasy. UnumProvident had so much going for it in the way of resources. It could hire all the jury consultants, stage all the focus groups, do all the background checks, and investigate all the witnesses it wanted to. What did he know that I didn't?

∧ ∨ ∧ ∨ ∧

UNUMPROVIDENT'S NEXT WITNESS WAS JOSEPH SULLIVAN. SULLIVAN looked the same as he had during his deposition in Boston: scrubbed clean with toothpaste-commercial teeth.

According to Sullivan, he became a claims adjuster because he liked helping people financially when they needed it, when they were disabled. The worst part of the job? Litigation.

He stated that he had never heard of any "net terminations ratio," was never trained to shred documents, and received regular training on state laws in the states in which he handled claims. Not only that, he knew that UnumProvident had to be fair and objective in its claims handling. In fact, that was part of the company claims philosophy.

As a claims examiner, he had never been paid bonuses for denying more claims nor did he have any goals for the number of claims he was supposed to deny in a year.

When Green asked him if the purpose of the roundtables was to deny claims, Sullivan's left eyebrow quivered when he said no. I wondered if anyone else noticed.

They moved on to specifics concerning Joan's file. Green had a number of questions about what Sullivan thought and did. All and all, Sullivan was doing a nice job for his company on direct.

On a high point, in his examination Green suggested that it might be a good idea to break for lunch. When we returned, Green announced that he had no further questions of Sullivan.

"Your witness, Mr. Bourhis," said Judge Larson.

On cross, Sullivan acknowledged that he had written the termination letter to Joan. It had been approved by a higher-up before being sent to Joan.

I examined him, once again, on whether he knew the correct definition of "disability." I certainly assumed that by this point he would know it. I was just setting him up, preparing to read his deposition testimony into the record to demonstrate that at the time Joan's claim was cut off, he didn't know the standard that had to be applied–on Joan's claim or on anybody else's. I was shocked to learn that even now, after years of depositions on this and countless other cases, Sullivan still didn't know the answer to this question.

We went through Joan's termination letter, paragraph by paragraph. He tried gamely to explain what he had written in the context of the policy coverage. Why wasn't Joan entitled to total, residual, or rehabilitation benefits? What was his analysis of the specific procedures that Joan was required to perform in her work? Wasn't it true that Joan's claim was *not* governed by ERISA? Why had he tried to persuade her it *was*?

I didn't think Sullivan's responses to these questions were very convincing.

Surprisingly to me, UnumProvident, even after the answers he had given in his earlier deposition in this case, had never provided Sullivan with any additional training. Not only had the company not done this, but Sullivan acknowledged that it had never even criticized him for anything he had said or done in his termination letter or with respect to any other aspect of Joan's claim.

To the contrary, he had actually been promoted by the company since his termination of Joan's claim. He had been elevated to the rank of claims consultant and given authority and training responsibilities over other adjusters and over some 450 to 500 disability claimants.

I asked him if, in his new position, UnumProvident had actually given him the power to cut off the benefit of any one, or any number, of these people. Did he actually have that authority?

Yes, he said, he did.

With regard to his testimony that he knew nothing about "net terminations ratios," he admitted that the memo about the net termination formula had been sent only to "senior management." He didn't know about the memo simply because he was not a member of the senior management team.

I asked him if he could provide any estimate of the total number of claims he had terminated or was terminating—per day, per week, or per year. He didn't know and couldn't estimate the number.

I thought Sullivan's testimony had been pretty good for us. His admissions were almost unbelievable. I was therefore shocked to see that at least two of the jurors smiled warmly at him when he stepped down from the witness stand. Shyly he smiled back.

∧ ∨ ∧ ∨ ∧

DR. AUBREY SWARTZ WAS NEXT. HE WAS EXAMINED ON BEHALF OF UNUM-Provident by Bernard. Swartz, a graduate of the University of Southern California and the University of California, Irvine, interned at Los Angeles County Hospital. He performed a year of general surgery at Cedars-Sinai Hospital and three years of orthopedic surgery at the University of Miami in Florida. He testified that he was in private practice—mainly in San Francisco and Oakland—and that most of his work was devoted to treating patients with orthopedic injuries. About 25 percent of his practice involved medical-legal evaluations. He was retained by UnumProvident to perform a medical evaluation of Joan on March 11, 1999.

Swartz stated that in his examination of Joan, he noted that she could stand well on her toes and heels, squat well with both knees, and hold her head erect. Her posture was relatively normal, the curve in her low back was fine, and her hips and pelvis were level. He found no muscle spasm in the neck or upper or low back and no tenderness in the neck. Tenderness in the low back and between the shoulder blades was minimal. Lateral bending and rotation of the spine were mildly limited, but that, he said, could be "patient exaggerated."

Reflex, motor, and sensory testing showed a "normal neurological examination." Grip strength, measured using an instrument called a Jamar dynamometer, was slightly below average, but that, he said, could also be patient controlled. He observed no atrophy, and the muscles of the right upper extremity seemed to have normal girth and to be working well. The range of motion of Joan's right elbow was "normal."

Swartz characterized the MRI studies as showing only "minor, very minor disc changes."

Given his physical examination, his strength and range-of-motion testing, and his review of the imaging studies, Swartz concluded that, even giving Joan the benefit of the doubt concerning her reports of pain, she could certainly continue to treat several patients per hour. "Frequently," he said, "that's what we will do. Sometimes we will see three an hour, sometimes four. . . . You don't need to do . . . twenty, do such an assembly line. . . . Just do what other doctors do and you will get along fine."

In the years following his examination of Joan, Swartz reviewed a number of reports from other doctors, including Katz, Berry, and Donald Bishoff. Nothing in any of those reports changed his opinion in any way. Specifically, Swartz went through several of the findings contained in Katz's medical records and concluded that Katz's diagnosis was inconsistent with those findings.

On cross-examination by Alice, Swartz acknowledged that in addition to San Francisco and Oakland, he had offices in Las Vegas, San Jose, Modesto, Sacramento, and Reno. He admitted that he actually performed "very few surgeries." He mostly performed medical exams for insurance companies.

Swartz was handed copies of the seventeen most recent reports that he had prepared for UnumProvident. In one report after the other, he had used phrases such as "cannot find a sufficient basis for disability," "could see no evidence of impairment," and "insured is capable of performing the usual and customary requirements of his occupation."

Alice gave Swartz a copy of a detailed, computer-generated procedures summary, stamped "Received" on February 20, 1998. This was received by UnumProvident almost a year before Swartz's IME. She pointed out that the summary listed hundreds of "myofascial releases," "cervical, lumbar, and thoracic spinal manipulations," "manual tractions," and other procedures, performed within a period of nine months, all required to be performed as part of Joan's practice.

"Were you given a copy of this document by UnumProvident?"

"No," he said.

"Did the company ever give you *any* description of the activities Dr. Hangarter performed in her practice?"

"No."

Alice asked him if he'd ever asked Joan for such a description himself.

"No."

Just how Swartz could bring himself to testify that Joan could go back to work without knowing what she did in her practice was, to put it mildly, puzzling.

"What percentage of Joan's practice before her disability involved manual traction?" asked Alice.

"I don't know," said Swartz.

"What percentage involved myofascial release?"

"I don't know."

"How about spinal manipulations?"

"I don't know."

Alice then asked him about his allegations on direct concerning "patient exaggeration." "Can a patient voluntarily create a C3-4 right lateral protrusion in the cervical spine?"

"No." Swartz also admitted later that a patient cannot voluntarily create a C4-5 broad-based disc bulge.

Alice showed Swartz copies of medical records that he had not been given by UnumProvident. These included records of several visits by Joan to the emergency room at Kaiser Permanente.

"Do you see that she was prescribed a sling for her elbow?"

He did.

"And do you see the [Kaiser] diagnosis of chronic lateral epicondylitis?"

Again, he did.

Had UnumProvident even given Swartz the definition of disability in Joan's policy? No. He had never even seen the policy and did not know the definition.

With regard to the issue of the number of patients per hour, Alice asked Swartz if he knew how many patients it was necessary for Dr. Hangarter to treat per day or per month just to meet her office overhead expenses.

Swartz didn't know. He appeared not to understand the significance of the question. This seemed odd to me. One would have thought that Swartz, with offices in Las Vegas, Reno, Modesto, Sacramento, San Jose, San Francisco, and Oakland, would well have understood the concept of meeting one's overhead.

Chapter Ten

FACT OR FICTION

F EW PEOPLE REALIZE THAT IN ADDITION TO THE MORE COMMON privileges, such as the attorney-client privilege, which conceals from public exposure verbal or written communications between a lawyer and client, something called the *work-product privilege* also exists. Under this, virtually everything an attorney does in preparation for litigation is out of bounds to discovery.

For example, if a lawyer is fishing around for an expert witness to testify on a client's behalf, the lawyer can talk to any number of experts before choosing one. The identities of all the rejected experts can be hidden from the other side, concealed forever. The "designated" expert's identity is disclosed only after he or she is formally "declared" as an expert. Those not ultimately chosen are considered "consultants." They, along with whatever opinions they may have rendered, are kept secret. So even if an attorney goes through ten or fifteen candidates before finding one willing to say what the lawyer wants to hear, the other side has no way of knowing that.

Plaintiffs can seldom afford to engage in these expensive expert-consultation exercises. But to insurance companies, where money is rarely an object, it's more of a tax deduction than an impediment.

For this reason, an insurance company looking for someone to testify that a claimant is not disabled can shop the records around to any number of doctors. If the first eleven say that the claimant is disabled but number twelve says otherwise, the defense can hire number twelve and forget about one to eleven entirely. It's as though they had never been contacted.

Insurance companies and their in-house or outside lawyers can go even further with consulting reports if they want. Some attorneys will insist on getting a verbal report from a proposed expert before he or she puts anything in writing. This gives the lawyers a chance to influence the substance of the report–what's said or how it is worded–before it's too late, before the final report has been completed.

Sometimes companies request a rough draft. Such a draft can then be reviewed, discussed, and edited before the final version is written. When the final is done, the draft can be used to light a cigar or folded into an origami swan.

If this all sounds to you, to put it nicely, a bit sleazy, you are not alone. This game-playing nonsense is enough to make most normal people cringe.

But not everyone is *normal* in this sense.

An insurance defense lawyer once tried to get a Paul Revere defense expert to change his written opinion before submitting it. But the lawyer picked the wrong guy. Not only did the expert refuse, but he went a step further by testifying, at trial, about what the lawyer had wanted him to do.

Sadly, it is uncommon for such tactics to backfire in this way. Usually insurance companies, or any party providing substantial repeat business, can get one of their well-paid experts to do or say just about anything.

In the Hangarter case, another law firm had been handling the defense before Green and Bernard's firm took it over. The first firm wanted to find a second IME doctor so Swartz wouldn't be its only insurance medical expert. We had no way of knowing how many other experts, if any, it screened before coming up with Dr. Donald Bishoff.

Bishoff was a neurologist. He went to medical school at Cornell University and did his three-year residency at the Neurological Institute of New York. At the time of the trial, he was a clinical professor at the University of California. He performed his IME of Joan for UnumProvident on November 9, 2000. Now he was sitting to the left of the jurors, a thick file resting on the witness stand before him.

Bishoff reviewed the 1997 MRI. He said that the degenerative conditions discussed in the MRI report were very common.

"They occur in everyone," he said. "I say to my patients sometimes, along with the wrinkles and creaky joints and going bald, these are the things that happen to you as you get older. The central canal stenosis means that the discs deteriorate, and you get a little arthritis in the bones. The central canal through which the spinal cord runs becomes a little narrower."

In his opinion, the MRI findings indicated that the degeneration was minimal, no more than would be expected in anybody Joan's age. And it was on the left side of her body. "There was no way damage on the left side would cause any impact on the right," he said.

Regarding the 2000 MRI, "The short version," he said, "is that by 2000, she had a little more of the same. And three years from now, she will have a little more, and six years from now, she'll have a little more than that. And so will we all."

The physical examination that Bishoff conducted involved what he called a "standard neurological examination" focused on her neck, upper torso, and upper extremities. She had a normal neurological examination, he said, almost a full range of motion for the neck both in turning and tilting. She had no symptoms or signs attributable to irritation of the nerve roots.

Bishoff also performed some manual muscle testing. These, too, he said, were normal.

Bishoff's response to Dr. Katz's findings was that he "simply disagreed with them." "Since neurologists know that grip strength is often spurious," he lectured, "we test *all* the muscles that you need for grip: the long finger flexors, the intrinsic hand muscles, and the thumb muscles–all of that. And we test them individually. For some reason, patients often give full effort to that part of the exam. So we test all the muscles you need for good grip strength. . . . And, in this case, they were all normal."

Bishoff disagreed with using the Spurling test. Katz, he sermonized, "must be an orthopedist. *We* don't use that test. I mean it's not *really* a sign. A sign is something where you can see that there's a difference between two sides."

Bishoff disputed Katz's finding that Joan had a depressed biceps reflex on the right side. It was simply not true, he said. She did *not* have a depressed biceps reflex on the right. When he checked, all of Joan's reflexes were normal.

"When I supervise the residents or the medical students at UC, they often tell me about one reflex being different than another reflex. But it's usually a matter of technique. They're usually not doing it right. I'm not casting any aspersions, but *we* neurologists like to think that we are the best in the reflex department."

Of course, Bishoff also disagreed with Katz's conclusions. "Katz says she has a degenerative C5–C6 disc with C6 radiculopathy [disorder of the spinal nerve roots]. I mean that's simply not true."

According to Bishoff, Joan didn't have tennis elbow either.

I remembered the experiment in which a ball is placed in the center of a square table. Four subjects are seated, one at each side, and asked the color of the ball. The first person says green. The second says white. The third says white on the left and green on the right. The fourth says green on the left and white on the right. Of course, the ball is half green and half white; its color depends on the subject's point of view. It was not going to be easy on cross-examination to shake a guy who was saying, "The ball is green; not white, not green and white, not white and green, just green. I saw it with my own two eyes." But we would try.

"Do orthopedists and neurologists ever disagree on diagnosis?"

"Oh, yes," he said.

"What's the difference between the two?"

"In neurology, we deal mostly with the nervous system: brain, nerve roots, nerves and muscles, spinal disorders. Our role is mostly diagnostic. We don't operate. Orthopedists are surgeons. Some of them have a special interest in the spine, but it's mostly surgically oriented."

"You say that in your examination, you noted no limitation of movement in the cervical spine. But you agree, do you not, that Dr. Swartz also found limitation in that area?"

"That's what it says here, in his report. Yes."

"And did Dr. Swartz comment that he found any kind of symptom exaggeration?"

"No, I don't remember seeing that."

"You also, I think, stated that orthopedists use the Jamar dynamometer test for measuring grip strength?"

"Yes."

"Are you aware of whether the patient who is gripping the dynamometer can see the results of it as they're doing it?"

"I would assume they can't."

"Okay. Were Dr. Swartz's results on the dynamometer, the grip strength test, normal?"

"Sorry," he said. "You know, I didn't really scrutinize this. Let's see. Grip strength as measured on the Jamar dynamometer: right was 35, 35, 35; left was 35, 35, 33."

"Is there any standard with regard to the dynamometer concerning the dominant versus the nondominant hand?"

"There probably is, but I don't know it. I don't use it."

"Okay, so you would have no way of knowing whether or not Swartz's findings were normal or abnormal?"

"No. I mean it looks pretty close on the two sides, but I couldn't comment on that."

"And you disagree with Dr. Katz's conclusion that grip strength was abnormal. Is that correct?"

"Yes."

"What is the difference in the time between when you saw Dr. Hangarter and when Dr. Katz saw her?"

"I saw her in November of 2000, and he saw her, I think, in August of last year [2001]. Whatever that is. Nine months."

"I believe you talked about a number of tests that you performed on Dr. Hangarter?"

"Right."

"Palpation, correct? Different kinds of biceps tests, correct? That is another thing you said you disagreed with Dr. Katz about? He found a depressed biceps on the right?"

"Right, right."

"And you said that would not be uncommon if someone were, as you wrote in your report, 'guarding'?"

"Right."

"And one common reason for a patient to be 'guarding' an arm would be if, in fact, the arm hurt. Correct?"

"That's possible." Bishoff said that reflex tests were objective when conducted by a neurologist but "not valid in this case" because they had been conducted by Katz, an orthopedist. He had similar feelings about palpation.

At least he conceded that a disabling condition can worsen by engaging in certain activities and that it can improve if the person stops performing those activities.

One point that should be noted about Bishoff's testimony was that he did not examine Joan until three and a half years after she had stopped practicing and a year and a half after her benefits had been cut off. How could the insurance company have relied on Bishoff's opinions in terminating Dr. Hangarter's claim eighteen months before he had even set eyes on her?

A "no-hindsight test" rule is used when it comes to claims decisions. That means that the evaluation of whether an insurance company acted properly has to be made based on what it knew *at the time it made the decision*, not on what someone says a year and a half *after* the decision. Obviously, an insurance company shouldn't be allowed to claim it used an opinion to cut off benefits that it didn't have at the time of termination.

It was hard to gauge how successful Bishoff was as a witness: credible and professional or arrogant and biased?

∧ ∨ ∧ ∨ ∧

EVERY DAY FOLLOWING COURT, I WOULD MEET WITH ALICE AND DAVID Lilienstein, another lawyer from our office, in the closed cafeteria on the second floor of the Federal Building to relax at one of the empty tables, run through the events of the day, and talk about the next day's session.

The parking lot attendants across the street kept everyone's keys so they could move cars around and shuttle people in and out throughout the day. The guys working there were very nice, but they went home every night at five thirty *sharp*. If you weren't there to pick up your car by then, you had a problem. So no matter what else we were doing, at 5:20, we had to pack up and head for the lot. It was a good thing too; otherwise, we would have sat around that closed cafeteria until nine or ten every night. Instead, we would usually drive to the office and sit around *there* until nine or ten.

The topic of that evening was what to do about Dr. Bishoff. A few of the jurors seemed impressed by him. He acted so damn sure of himself.

It was hard to know what to do. We talked about it for a while—and then a while longer. Finally, we decided: we had to put Dr. Katz back on the stand in rebuttal. This was easier said than done. When I called Katz the next day, he was reluctant. He had a full surgery schedule the following day. That was the problem in dealing with practicing doctors and not professional witnesses. I practically begged him to find some way to do it, telling him how worried I was about the effect Bishoff may have had.

"Call me back in thirty minutes," he finally said. "I'll see what I can do."

I knew it was going to be expensive. Surgeons don't cancel surgery schedules just for the fun of it. In addition to his own scheduling problems, I was sure he was going to have to do some patient handholding as well. His patients were not likely to respond happily to having their operations postponed.

Alice, David, and I worked at the office, hoping for the best—hoping that when we called him back, it wouldn't be to hear him say that he was sorry, truly sorry. He had tried, but it was just impossible. He couldn't do it at the last second like this.

But that didn't happen. He agreed, I think in part because he could see what was really going on here, and he wasn't about to let Joan's life be ruined by a bunch of swindlers and con artists. Not without a fight.

∧ ∨ ∧ ∨ ∧

IT WAS THAT QUIET TIME IN THE MORNING BEFORE COURT BEGINS. THE lawyers were standing at their respective tables, unloading trial binders and stacks of paper, getting depositions and deposition outlines ready for the day, and chatting with Judge Larson's assistant, Kathleen Campbell, and his court reporter, Joan Columbini.

A court like this could never function without someone like Kathleen. She made sure that submissions prepared by the attorneys for the judge were in order before presenting them, often saving attorneys considerable embarrassment in the process. Beyond that, she kept everything together and functioning in an orderly way. The same was true of the judge's court reporter. As I watched her ready her transcription equipment for another day of perfect work, I wondered how she and all other court reporters were really able to do what they do so consistently and with such effortless precision. It was one of the mysteries of the legal system that I would never understand.

The defense had rested. And whatever they knew, however they knew it, they seemed disturbingly confident–animated and smiling, joking around with each other.

People–faces that I hadn't recognized–had sat through various parts of the trial, in the back of the room, taking notes and looking thoughtful. In addition, both sides had obtained "dailies" from the court reporter–transcriptions of each day's testimony completed within twenty-four hours and ready for analysis and reanalysis. Maybe the defendants had a shadow jury working behind the scenes, giving the defense continuing input on what was working and what wasn't, on which witnesses were "selling" and which were not. It didn't make any difference at this point. We didn't have time to worry about it.

We were going to present two brief rebuttal witnesses. Then we would have the final arguments, jury instructions, and the long wait.

And that would be it.

∧ ∨ ∧ ∨ ∧

JUDGE LARSON WAS SEATED AT THE BENCH, SCRIBBLING SOME NOTES and whispering to his court clerk. As the jurors filed in, there was an almost tangible aura in the courtroom that the case was winding down and entering the final phase. Joan, whom we had kept from the courtroom during portions of the trial that we felt might be difficult for her to deal with, was seated at the counsel table, fidgeting lightly with the edge of one of the dozen or more binders that were strewn about the walnut surface. It seemed oddly quiet for the minute or so that Judge Larson took to finish whatever he was writing.

"I understand there will be some brief rebuttal by the plaintiff," he said finally. After explaining to the jurors what rebuttal was, Judge Larson directed us to proceed.

First, we recalled Dr. Katz. He ambled amiably past the jury box and up to the witness stand and sat down with a patient, matter-of-fact look on his face. Alice questioned him.

"Dr. Katz, the other day the defense brought in a Dr. Bishoff who testified, among other things, that the MRIs of Dr. Hangarter were 'normal.' Do you agree with that?"

"No," he replied. "They were not 'normal' in any way."

"Why do you say that?"

"Because the 1997 read [of the MRI] by Dr. Cardozza shows changes at C5-6 with left neuroforaminal narrowing, which is not normal. Then the May 12, 2000, report shows multiple-level disc disease that is worse than the one in 1997."

"Doctor, do you have any experience with nerve surgery?"

"Yes. During my two years in Vietnam and as assistant chief at Great Lakes, we did a lot of wound surgery and nerve surgery involving upper and lower extremity wounds in marines with blown-out nerve segments. We did anastomosis [surgery] to repair those nerves, radial and median ulnar nerves, and the sciatic nerves for injuries to the pelvis. I know a bit," he smiled, "about nerve surgery."

"Dr. Bishoff also said that if Dr. Hangarter had any injuries, they were on the left side, not the right. Is that correct?"

"The major C5-6 problem is on the left side. At C4-5, it's on the right side, accounting for her right arm pain and radiculopathy. The C3-4 level–I have a diagram here. Can I show it to the jury?"

"Let me see it first," said Judge Larson, "and Ms. Wolfson, show it to defense counsel, please."

Bernard studied the diagram for a minute. "No objection," she said.

Katz put his diagram on the overhead projector and continued. "The C5 root that comes out here," he said, pointing at the image on the screen, "affects the volar side of the arm, or inner portion of the arm going down to the hand right here."

"Is it your opinion," asked Alice, "that [the condition you see in] the MRI from 2000 showing the stenosis at C5-6 and the right neuroforaminal narrowing at C3-4 is, in part, responsible for the pain that Joan reports in her arm and neck?"

"Yes," he said. "The C3-4 would give her neck pain. The C4 nerve root covers the back of the neck area on that diagram. It's the rear area in the back of the neck. The C5 root goes down on the right side. It covers her right arm."

As for Bishoff's contention that many people are running around at the age of fifty-two or fifty-three with nonpainful, bulging discs,

Katz agreed that maybe 30 to 40 percent of those with the condition would be asymptomatic (having no pain or other effects). This meant, of course, that 60 to 70 percent *would* be symptomatic.

"But," he continued, "we only do an MRI in the first place because someone is complaining of the pain. What the MRI can do is to confirm or fail to confirm a physical basis for the complaints. In Joan's case, the MRIs confirmed it."

"Dr. Bishoff said his neurological exam was normal. Can you account for why that may have been?"

"The exams were not done within the same time frame. I saw Dr. Hangarter after she had been working part-time collating materials in an office. She had been using her arms and hands, and she suffered even from that amount of usage. That accounts for the muscle spasm that I found. It also demonstrated what would happen anytime Joan were to engage in protracted activity involving the repeated use of her hands, arms, shoulders, or neck."

"Dr. Bishoff also said that tenderness and tightness of the right trapezius muscle is a subjective test. Is that correct?"

"It's *objective* because I put my hands on a patient and palpate the muscle. One cannot *fake* spasm."

"Dr. Bishoff also testified that he couldn't understand how Joan's range of motion in her cervical spine could be limited based on the MRI findings. Is that correct?

"No. It's not correct."

"Why not?"

"Because she's got multiple changes at multiple levels."

"Dr. Bishoff also disagreed with your findings on the Jamar test. In fact, he said that orthopedists use them, but neurologists don't. Do you have an opinion on that?"

"Neurologists," smiled Katz, "are a different group of people. Orthopedists take care of people and operate." He added that a form issued by the state of California and approved by the California Industrial Welfare Commission specifically included Jamar dynamometer studies. "I brought one along with me if you would like to see it."

It wasn't necessary. Lori Bernard could wade into that one if she wanted to.

Bernard limited her cross to a handful of questions about when Katz had read the MRI reports versus when he had read the actual films. Hadn't he testified in his deposition that he had read the MRI reports but not the films themselves at the time of his examination of Joan and that he had read the actual films later?

"That's correct," he said.

"No further questions," said Bernard.

∧ ∨ ∧ ∨ ∧

JOAN HANGARTER WAS OUR LAST REBUTTAL WITNESS. SHE WALKED TO the witness stand with a look of weary determination, like someone who had been paying a very high price for simply living her life. I thought of how she must feel going through all this–to be looking at the faces of the attorneys and company representatives sitting so smugly, so confidently at their table. Preparing to pounce on her every word.

My questioning of Joan would be very brief, but I almost wished I could have introduced into evidence an article Joan had written about poverty for the *San Francisco Examiner* shortly before the trial began.

> We need food as well as light bulbs. Toilet paper, detergent and other such items. One hundred and fifty dollars are required, not the paltry twenty dollar bill that I have in my hands.
>
> Each month on the 9th or 10th I received my allotment of food stamps, $230, to feed a family of three. That's $7.60 a day–$2.53 each. Despite rationing, the Stamps are quickly spent. By week four, our diet is Top Ramen in the morning, Top Ramen in the evening. I cook for the children and have long since learned to ignore my hunger.
>
> Some days the refrigerator and the cabinets are empty. It can't be helped. The kids know that when I cook the pinto beans and take out the tortillas that we are back on rice and beans.
>
> I don't turn on the heat when we are cold. It is too expensive. Electricity. Electricity is a luxury. Restaurants,

theater, music are vague memories of the past. That was another time and I was another person.

I've lost my house, my car, clothes (which were put in storage when I was evicted and which were subsequently sold by the storage company when I couldn't pay the rental fees).

It occurred to me that I had hit bottom when I sat there at the Social Services Office signing permission slips to open the entire book of my life to every government agency imaginable.

Poverty is humiliation.

The draining of all my vitality.

It is an acute sense of longing.

Poverty is relentless . . .

Poverty is never having enough of anything.

It is gratitude for the family that anonymously sent me a turkey dinner for Thanksgiving.

Poverty is forgetting that I once enjoyed all the things I no longer have.

Judge Larson never would have allowed the jury to hear that. He would have called it inflammatory, and he would have been right. But sometimes, a fire should be lit.

∧ ∨ ∧ ∨ ∧

"JOAN," I SAID, "THERE'S BEEN SOME TESTIMONY ABOUT A TRIP THAT you made to the hospital in May of 2000. Do you remember what that was about?"

"Yes," she said. "I had very severe pain in my arm. I thought I had broken it actually. I had borrowed a friend's car because mine had been repossessed, and it had a stick shift, and I was driving it in traffic. I hurt my arm to the point that I thought I had broken it. I went to Kaiser, to the emergency room. I was treated by a doctor there who examined me and put me through some tests."

"Were you given a diagnosis by the Kaiser doctors?"

"Yes. Lateral epicondylitis."

"Were you given a treatment goal following your examination?"

"Yes," Joan said, "to get me down to a three or four on a pain scale of ten. The doctor referred to the goal as being 'tolerable living.'"

"As opposed to what?" I asked.

"The nine or ten at the hospital and the seven or eight by the time I got to physical therapy again."

"Dr. Hangarter, when you purchased this policy back in the 1980s, when the company name was Paul Revere, did anyone tell you that if you ever filed a claim because you were unable to perform your work as a chiropractor, you might not be paid if you could still do the bookkeeping part of your job?"

"No."

"Did anyone tell you that you might not be considered disabled if you could still teach a patient seminar once a month?"

"No."

Aside from some minor additional reading from various depositions, we were done.

The plaintiff rested.

∧ ∨ ∧ ∨ ∧

HAVING ALREADY QUESTIONED ITS OWN WITNESSES AS A PART OF OUR case in chief, the defense, aside from making the usual motions for a directed verdict and so on, and aside from some of its own deposition reads, was done as well.

All that remained at this point, were summations, final argument, and the judge's jury instructions.

Chapter Eleven

SOME WITH A
FOUNTAIN PEN

D RIVING HOME FOLLOWING JOAN'S TESTIMONY, I WRESTLED WITH different approaches for our closing. If only I knew what the jurors were thinking. But this was a very noncommunicative group—disturbingly so. After having spent four weeks sitting not ten feet from them, I still had no more of an idea where they were coming from than I'd had on the first day of trial.

Some arguments are best made to yourself–alone, in your car, with the windows rolled up. That this company was an outfit being run by a gang of avaricious, devious, sinister, inhumane, malevolent, amoral people was one such argument. That the jury should simply do to them what they had done to Joan–drive them into bankruptcy–was another.

True, there would be a certain poetic satisfaction in picturing a smug Ralph Mohney being hauled off his high horse, stripped of his assets, evicted from his home, and left standing, trying to preserve some sense of dignity, in donated clothing, on a food stamps line. Likewise, in picturing Chris Collins, Esq., in his battle fatigues, explaining to a bigwig stockholder how a jury of ordinary, decent folks could have chosen to consign UnumProvident to the same desperate fate as those whose lives it had destroyed.

But as personally satisfying as it might be to make those arguments, I had to do just the opposite. I had to ask the jury *not* to act out of vengeance or anger but to simply consider, in a very rational way, what it would take to deter the kind of profitable misconduct involved.

I had thought about it for months, hashing and rehashing what I was going to say when "The Moment" finally arrived. I had notes, outlines, evidence, testimony, and copies of key jury instructions all ready to be put up on the overhead.

When the morning for summation finally arrived, I got up early, drove down to the darkened courthouse, and arrived at my spot in the cafeteria long before it opened. Staring at my prepared, re-prepared, and re-re-prepared summation notes, I finally just pushed aside everything I had worked on for so long.

I wouldn't have enough time to go through it all with the jury in painstaking detail. Even if I did have time, it would be a mistake. They had already heard all the important details, some of them more than once. Instead, I thought it best to spend my allotted time talking about the broader picture.

∧ ∨ ∧ ∨ ∧

WHEN I STOOD TO ARGUE THE CASE, I ALMOST DRAGGED A CHAIR OVER in front of the jury box and sat down to just talk about what all this really meant. Whatever the jurors decided, whatever that was, they would give Provident either a green light or a red light. The company would be told to continue what it was doing, or it would be told to stop–immediately.

Disability claimants were not just numbers in a formula. They were human beings who bought policies in good faith, dutifully paid premiums, and believed that they would, as promised, receive help should they no longer be able to earn a living.

How could a company, *any* company, do what UnumProvident had done?

How could the people in charge keep their own employees in the dark, setting them up like this? How could they author memos about shredding documents, manipulating files, and not putting anything in writing? How could they develop secret plans to increase profits by terminating benefits? How could company officers and senior management willingly sacrifice the Joan Hangarters of the world to increase the value of their own stock options? How could they force disabled people with little or no income to go through years of agonizing litigation just to get what they were owed in the first place?

The most basic tenets we work so hard to teach our children are, in truth, so very simple: to be honest, to work hard, to have character, to honor commitments, to treat people decently. These are such elemental principles.

When you buy something like disability insurance, what you are paying for year in and year out is simply security–that so-often repeated phrase, "peace of mind."

The numbers were astronomical, almost impossible to fathom. So many insurance policies were in force that the most senior management didn't know how many. More than four hundred thousand claims per year–that exceeds the population of Honolulu. Managers had no ability to even estimate the number of people whose benefits were cut off annually.

They hire people like Dr. Swartz and call them "independent." They pay people like Dr. Bianchi and call them "consultants." They ask professionals for opinions and then manipulate the information given to them. They hold roundtable meetings to search for pretexts to terminate claims. They set cutoff goals without any idea of whose payments were going to be stopped in order to meet those goals.

This had to change. And the people who could change it were these jurors. If a poor person were caught ripping off a few hundred dollars from UnumProvident's petty cash, that person would be arrested, fingerprinted, hauled before a judge, and threatened with incarceration. Yet the company had taken approximately $95,000 a year from Joan Hangarter, and all we were talking about was civil damages. The jury had no power to put people in jail. But it could send a money message to the board of directors of this company–a calm, clear message written in large letters that this was unconscionable, despicable, and wrong.

∧ ∨ ∧ ∨ ∧

HORACE GREEN, IN HIS SUMMATION, DENIED THAT THE DEFENDANTS had *ever* terminated a claim to increase their profits. He denied that they had ever trained their claims adjusters to shred anything. He contended that they didn't even *have* a shredder in the claims department. He said that roundtables were not designed to deny claims. He attacked Caliri's credentials. He contended that Joan had continued to adjust patients after going on disability. He said it didn't make any difference if she treated five patients or fifty. He told the jurors that they "had seen her move her head and neck up and down and from side to side in the courtroom."

Besides, he said, Joan had not *one* occupation, chiropractic, but *two*, chiropractic and bookkeeping. Joan could shop and do laundry and write a manual for chiropractors. So why wasn't she able to do chiropractic manipulations? He accused Joan of not telling the truth in her deposition. He said it was her own fault that she was bankrupt and living on food stamps. The plaintiff's medical testimony and factual testimony? Bogus. And he did not neglect to criticize Joan's character and credibility.

He urged the jury not to forget Ralph Mohney's testimony that his philosophy was to be thorough, fair, and objective. As for Joe Sullivan, Green "didn't know a nicer guy." He claimed that Sullivan paid Joan even when he had doubts about the claim. How was that unfair? He said that Sullivan had a "field rep" deliver the news of Joan's termination to her *personally*. Was that unreasonable? Wasn't that a nice thing to do?

"Even if you disagree with the decision," said Green, "where was the fraud? Where?"

Joan Hangarter had more of a desire to sue than she had a desire to work, he contended. What this suit was about was her looking for a way to get free medical treatment because she was destitute.

He even argued that by not showing up every day at the trial, Joan demonstrated she didn't think the case was very important. Her decision not to work was her "choice."

When we took a recess following the defense summation, Alice, David, and I saw the company representatives and their lawyers giving each other high fives in the hallway.

∧ ∨ ∧ ∨ ∧

ON REBUTTAL, WE TRIED TO GO THROUGH EACH POINT GREEN HAD made by quoting from witness testimony, documents in evidence, the termination letter, and the insurance policy. We said we couldn't understand the attacks on Joan and on her character. We didn't understand how Provident could interpret the evidence in a way that would justify such positions. It takes only a few people, in positions of authority, to cause big problems.

For some reason, a line popped into my head from a tune by Woody Guthrie ("Pretty Boy Floyd") sung by Ramblin' Jack Elliott, whom I had recently seen at the Sweetwater Saloon in Mill Valley. Ramblin' Jack has been characterized by some as the first cowboy-folk rap artist; to others, he's a philosopher.

"Some steal with a six-gun," he said that night, "some with a fountain pen."

Mohney had a fountain pen.

"This company should be reasonable with people," I said. "It should conduct investigations that are thorough and honest. It should interpret information objectively, not in a one-sided way. It should select IME doctors carefully and properly and not go out and find people with offices in Las Vegas and Reno where they perform no surgeries and have no patients.

"This company should interpret its policy fairly and honestly. It should treat people with decency. It should not willingly destroy peoples' lives for their own profit.

"That's what the implied covenant of good faith and fair dealing is all about. It's why our courts read that promise into *every* insurance policy—just as if it were written right there on the front page with a big felt-tipped pen.

"Insurance companies have a 'continuing duty' to review all aspects of a claim, to review any 'new' information that it might say it was previously unaware of. In this case, with all the depositions, and even with the testimony of their own witnesses and of their own experts, UnumProvident never changed its decision. Even now, right up to this minute, it continues to deny. It continues to attack."

People can criticize our legal system—and it certainly is a long way from perfect—but I would be afraid to live in a place with a system that didn't provide a remedy for people whose lives had been destroyed like this. What else would they be forced to do if it were not for our system? Get down on their hands and knees and beg?

It was true that Joan had made some bad financial judgments and decisions. So had Provident, for that matter. Provident's bad financial judgments and decisions cost it $423 million. People make mistakes. But Joan didn't blame Provident for her bad investments or her bad choices. And she didn't want to receive any damages for the losses caused by her mistakes.

The question was why did the company kick her when she was down? If it had continued to pay the benefits it owed, she never would have been bankrupted or lost her house or been forced to turn to food stamps to feed her children.

How many other Joan Hangarters were out there? Unum-Provident had to "terminate" thousands of claims per year just to meet its profit goals.

If only I could have told the jury about others who had been cut off: the people with organic brain damage and cancer and Parkinson's disease, those with coronary artery disease and severe depression and AIDS, and the countless other victims of Unum-Provident's "initiatives" and "goals" and "roundtables" and "profiling." If only I could have told them about the facts behind all of the "confidential settlement agreements," about what really went on behind the scenes.

But I couldn't. All of that had all been ruled out of bounds.

UnumProvident argued that it paid billions of dollars in claims. But that was like Jesse James talking about all the banks he *didn't* rob. Of course, the company wasn't dumb enough to refuse to pay *all* claims. It kept its eyes on the big-picture prize.

In 1995 the prize was $60 million per year. That was before the acquisition of Paul Revere and Unum and dozens of other companies. Sixty million dollars became the proverbial tip of the iceberg. We would have to come up with an estimate for the entire iceberg. Chandler, Mohney, Fryc, Sullivan, Ryan, and the others at Unum-Provident professed to not know or not recall or they wouldn't tell. Perhaps that information was also "privileged," having been "shared with them by counsel."

This jury had a solemn responsibility here. This was one of the most important decisions these people would ever make. Like it or not, their selection as jurors in this case had thrust them into the role of serving as the conscience of the community. They had the opportunity and the responsibility to stand up and say no to the behavior of this corporation and its officials.

Dr. Feist was right. What happened to this insurance company after Chandler and Mohney took over was wrong.

Corporations could not be allowed to chew people up like this. UnumProvident simply had to be stopped–right here, and right now.

∧ ∨ ∧ ∨ ∧

JUDGE LARSON SPENT FORTY-FIVE MINUTES READING INSTRUCTIONS TO the jury. These included dozens of statements on the law that the jurors were required to follow in their deliberations: the duties of insurance companies; the covenant of good faith and fair dealing; and the plaintiff's burden of proof–"more likely than not" for the bad-faith causes of action, "clear and convincing evidence" for the punitive damages allegations. He gave an explanation of the difference between direct and circumstantial proof; gave the definitions of malice, fraud, and oppression; and ended with guidelines for the juror's deliberations.

Then suddenly it seemed they were being solemnly escorted to the jury room by the bailiff. As they filed out of court, the jurors passed to the left of both counsel tables. I couldn't see their faces as they passed behind us, in front of the defense lawyers. But as they walked by our table, not one of them turned and smiled at us or at Joan. Not one.

It was 3:25 on a Friday afternoon. Alice, David, Joan, and I went upstairs to the eighteenth-floor lounge to sit and wait. It was not the best of times for a plaintiff or her lawyers.

A number of decisions had to be made by the jury, and one of particular significance would later be in the hands of Judge Larson. The jury had to decide whether

- a breach of contract had occurred
- the company had acted in bad faith
- Joan was entitled to past benefits, and if so, how much
- she was entitled to future benefits, and if so, in what amount
- she was entitled to emotional distress damages and/or attorneys' fees, and if so, in what amount

- the plaintiff had proven "by clear and convincing evidence" that the defendants had acted with fraud, oppression, or malice
- exemplary/punitive damages would be awarded, and if so, in what amount

The long wait began. We sat and talked about the trial, speculated about the judge and jury, reconsidered what we had said and done or not said and not done, and we worried.

⌃ ⌄ ⌃ ⌄ ⌃

IN RECENT YEARS, JUROR QUESTIONNAIRES HAVE BECOME POPULAR AS a timesaving voir dire device. When prospective jurors are first called up to a particular department, they are given a five- or six-page form to fill out. Included on the form are questions concerning attitudes about the legal system.

People are asked if they feel that verdicts are too high, too low, or about right. They are asked how they feel about lawyers, judges, and the system of justice. They are asked about their attitudes concerning people who sue, emotional distress awards, and punitive and other damages.

With depressing regularity, these forms come back with statements like "awards way too high," "lawyers tend to be greedy," and "system of justice is out of whack." So when these same people say in voir dire that they can be fair and impartial, I sometimes wonder how fair and impartial.

Special interests spend vast amounts of money every year undermining public confidence in our legal system, lobbying for restrictions on punitive and general damages, advocating the acceptance of one-sided binding arbitration agreements, and contributing heavily to politicians who will press their legislative agenda. Unfortunately, lawyers with "dancing cash register" ads in the yellow pages and those who file cases against homeowners on behalf of burglar clients bitten by a family sheepdog do not help the situation.

But a few years ago, it turned out that the insurance industry itself was behind some of the negative publicity. One of the major insurers ran a full-page ad in a national magazine criticizing the civil litigation system and urging legislative reforms. The ad featured a multimillion-dollar award in a defective-highway-design lawsuit brought by a drunk driver who had plowed his careening Jaguar into a Miami Beach median divider.

The ad made great copy. A hundred television and radio news programs ran stories on it. Late-night talk-show hosts made hilarious jokes about it. Corporation presidents, upset about being sued just because they sold products that killed people, jumped on the bandwagon. A flurry of new tort reform legislation was authored proposing caps on damage awards.

The only problem was that the story in the ad was completely false. It was made up by the company behind the ad. But reporters never bothered to revisit the issue or correct the story. Why should they make themselves look foolish? The damage was done, and it made no difference that the whole story was a hoax.

I often wonder if some of the lawyers running around filing the lawsuits that we all hate are really shills for those seeking to insulate themselves from accountability. How recently was it that our nation's security laws were "reformed" to protect us from "frivolous accounting firm litigation"? How long afterward did the accounting firm of Arthur Andersen go on a confetti-manufacturing binge on behalf of Enron?

In 1990 in California, tobacco companies got a bill signed insulating them from–guess what?–liability for secondhand-smoke lawsuits. At the time, few people even knew what secondhand smoke was. Who cared?

Who cared? The same cabal of characters who stood before Congress with their pudgy little hands solemnly raised, swearing that nicotine isn't addictive and smoking doesn't cause cancer. If only we could sentence them to twenty or more years of secondhand smoke being pumped into their jail cells and then deny them medical care.

∧ ∨ ∧ ∨ ∧

SUCH ARE THE FRUSTRATIONS ONE THINKS ABOUT WHILE PACING around the eighteenth floor of the Federal Building waiting for a jury. It beats rereading, for the third time, the sports section of a two-day-old newspaper.

I pictured what UnumProvident's reaction would be to dodging the bullet. It would prove it was right, by God–right and invincible. If you spent enough money, you could get away with anything.

Late in the day, the jurors sent a message to Judge Larson, and we were all summoned to his courtroom. Judge Larson read the note. The jurors, who had been told they could go home for the weekend at five in the evening, if they hadn't reached a verdict, wanted to know if they could stay longer.

I hadn't seen that one before and had no idea what it meant. Were they close to a verdict? Hopelessly deadlocked? Just trying to avoid coming back?

Judge Larson agreed to the request, and we went back to the eighteenth floor.

Ninety minutes later, there was still no decision, so we were sent home for the weekend.

Our office looked like the world headquarters for Litterbugs Anonymous. Legal pads, scraps of paper, phone messages, drafts of motions, and instructions were everywhere. However, organizational efforts would have to wait a few more days. It was time to reintroduce myself to my family, have dinner at home, and pretend to think about the movie we went to see.

On Monday, Alice, David, and I headed back to the eighteenth floor. Entering the building, I ran into Frank Watterman. Frank, a security guard, had worked in the building for many years. He took one look at me and smiled. "Got a jury out?"

"How'd you know?" I said, thinking I must have looked sick or something.

"No briefcase today," he laughed.

At least the lounge coffee table had been restocked with a fresh supply of newspapers.

Chapter Twelve

A MESSAGE

T WO HOURS LATER, WE GOT THE CALL. "THEY HAVE A VERDICT," SAID Judge Larson's clerk.

By the time we arrived downstairs in Judge Larson's court, the defense was already in place. Many of those who had listened to the closing arguments were also back in court.

The jurors filed in. One by one, they shuffled down the two narrow aisles in the jury box and settled quietly into their seats—blank stares, no outward emotion, no eye contact, nothing.

I glanced at Joan. She was sitting with her ankles crossed, fidgeting with a paper clip. Dark circles ringed her eyes. She appeared as if she hadn't been getting much sleep. She looked isolated, worried, lonely, and completely drained.

I could tell she was thinking the same questions I was: Why wasn't there even a hint from the jurors? Not a sympathetic smile? Not a reassuring nod? Not the slightest positive sign of any kind? It was as though we were completely invisible to them.

"I'm told you have a verdict," said Judge Larson.

"We do," said the jury foreman, Jeffrey Goldfine.

"Please hand it to the clerk," the judge said.

Goldfine handed the three-page, stapled verdict form to Wings Hom, who carried it to the bench.

Judge Larson silently read the pages, checking to make sure that everything had been filled out correctly. Then he handed the form back to Hom to read aloud.

> We the Jury in the above-entitled action unanimously find the following special verdict on the questions submitted to us.

Question No. 1: Do you find that after May 21, 1999, the date her benefits were terminated by the defendant, plaintiff was unable to perform the substantial and material duties of her own occupation in the usual and customary way with reasonable continuity? Answer "yes" or "no."

Answer: Yes.

I breathed a sigh of relief. At least I knew that the jurors' blank expressions were not a sign of utter rejection and repudiation.

If you answered Question No. 1 "yes," then:

A. Is plaintiff entitled to recover the value of her past benefits up to the present day as a result of defendant breach of contract? Answer "yes" or "no."

Answer: Yes.

If you answered "yes," then:

1. What is the value of plaintiff's past disability benefits, up to the present day?

Answer: $320,849.

Question No. 2: Did defendants' breach the duty of good faith and fair dealing to plaintiff? Answer "yes" or "no."

Answer: Yes.

If you answered "yes," then:

A. Is plaintiff entitled to recover the present value of her future policy benefits as a result of defendants' breach? Answer "yes" or "no."

Answer: Yes.

If you answered "yes," then:

1. What is the present value of plaintiff's future disability benefits?

Answer: $1,200,000.

B. Did plaintiff suffer mental and emotional damages as a result of defendants' unreasonable conduct? Answer "yes" or "no."

Answer: Yes.

If you answered "yes," then:

1. What is the amount of damages that will fairly compensate plaintiff for her mental and emotional distress?

Answer: $400,000.

C. Is plaintiff entitled to recover her reasonable attorneys' fees and costs incurred in obtaining the benefits owed under her policy? Answer "yes or "no."

Answer: Yes.

If you answered "yes," then:

1. What is the amount you wish to award plaintiff in her attorneys' fees and costs?

Answer: $750,000.

Question No. 3: Did defendants act with oppression, fraud, or malice in handling plaintiff's claim and denying her benefits? Answer "yes" or "no."

Answer: Yes.

That was it. That was the biggie—the most important question.

If you answered "yes," then:

1. What is the amount you wish to award in punitive damages?

Answer: $5,000,000.

Joan's dark circles suddenly vanished. Gone was the look of exhaustion. Gone was the fear. Joan was smiling. She was vindicated. No, the jurors didn't think she was a liar and a fraud. No, they didn't conclude that she had somehow made this up. No, they didn't buy UnumProvident's denials and excuses and smooth, prepared, professional-sounding witnesses. They didn't buy Mohney and Sullivan and Fryc and Swartz and Bishoff and Peymani and Corey and Bianchi.

With all of Provident's money and power, the company hadn't pulled the wool over the jurors' impartial eyes. By clear and convincing evidence, Paul Revere/UnumProvident had been found guilty of malice, fraud, or oppression. The jury was unanimous.

"Would either side like the jury polled?" asked Judge Larson. The defense said it would.

One by one the jurors were asked if they agreed with the verdict. One by one they responded, "Yes."

After being thanked for their service and excused by Judge Larson, the jurors were told that they were now free to discuss the case and that they could stay and talk to the lawyers if they wished to do so.

An Associated Press reporter and some local media representatives cornered members of the jury to get their perspectives and insights. As I stood listening, it soon became clear that little doubt existed as to the verdict from the very beginning of deliberations. Most of the time it took to reach a verdict had been spent discussing damage amounts. Several jurors said they had wanted to award much higher punitive damages. The only reason, they said, that they didn't was that they didn't want the shock to be that great to Joan. They were concerned that whenever the award was finalized she not go from being destitute to having $20 to $30 million overnight.

Although I was certainly heartened and happy with the verdict, I was somewhat concerned, given the huge numbers motivating the company in the first place, that the exemplary damage amount wasn't large enough to change UnumProvident's corporate practices. Eventually, I wondered how much of an impact the verdict would really have.

Little did I know how right my concerns were.

∧ ∨ ∧ ∨ ∧

THE NEXT DAY, STORIES WERE CARRIED BY AP, THE *SAN FRANCISCO Chronicle,* the *Examiner*, and in other California newspapers, as well as in broadcast reports on radio and television. Chris Collins was quoted, complaining that all the verdict demonstrated was that insurance companies couldn't get a fair trial. He claimed that Joan's own doctor had said she was not disabled, which was, of course, not correct. He also claimed that Joan had been "treated by a friend"– again this was inaccurate.

While I considered this a typical Collins knee-jerk response, it was nonetheless infuriating. How could it be viewed as anything but an insult to the jury, the judge, the plaintiff–to everyone associated with the case? How many depositions would it take? How many motions? How many rulings? How many court orders? How many before the message got through to this guy?

∧ ∨ ∧ ∨ ∧

THE NEXT THING WE KNEW, UNUMPROVIDENT ADDED A NEW LAYER OF lawyers to its team: Evan Trager and Christopher Wang of the DC law firm of Mayer, Brown, Rowe & Maw. They came on board to file posttrial motions for a "judgment as a matter of law." They were asking that the verdict be disregarded and a judgment be entered for the defendants or, in the alternative, that a new trial be ordered.

The record, said Trager, was "insufficient" to support the plain-tiff's claims of breach of contract, much less bad faith. Evidence had been admitted that should have been excluded and had been excluded that should have been admitted. The court should have done this and did not. It should not have done that but it did. Neither the emotional distress nor the punitive damage amounts were supported by law, and even if they were, the amounts awarded were excessive. The plaintiff's contentions were predicated on "unsupported assertions and outright distortions of the record."

One certainly got the impression from reading his work that Trager found little to approve of in the transcript. As part of Trager's "excessive verdict" argument, he stated that even the California Department of Insurance had never issued a $5 million fine. To prove it, he prepared an exhaustive list of company violations and fines issued by the DOI from 1991 to 1996. Scanning the list, I saw that the most common penalties hovered in the $5,000 to $25,000 range. The names of the companies that had been fined read like a membership roster for Insurance Anonymous: Anthem Life, American States, Midland Risk, Principal Mutual Life Insurance, IDS Life

Insurance Company of New York. It was obvious that no insurance commissioners were going to be called on the carpet by the Big Boys over the likes of this.

I thought about the stereotype of Washington, DC, law firms as boring sophisticates being paid enormous sums of money merely to delay the implementation of federal regulations or to get administrative agencies to drag their feet in any of a thousand ways. I knew next to nothing about the Mayer, Brown firm, but if they were cut from a similar cloth as other DC firms, they certainly understood how watchdog agencies were routinely turned into house pets. It was hard to believe they even bought into their own arguments. It was harder still to believe they thought a smart judge like Larson would fall for it.

He didn't.

The hearing on the defendants' motions was held on June 5, 2002. Since virtually all the issues raised by UnumProvident's Washington lawyers had been raised previously, and repeatedly, by its California attorneys, the hearing yielded few surprises. UnumProvident was given the opportunity to present its views "on the record" once again. But the old dog still wouldn't hunt.

Judge Larson denied all defense motions except for a minor issue involving the amount of the jury's award for costs and fees.

But the shoe that had yet to drop was the big one–the one that could really make a difference. That shoe was California Business and Professions Code Section 17200.

∧ ∨ ∧ ∨ ∧

ONE OF THE LEGAL THEORIES SET FORTH FROM THE OUTSET IN OUR lawsuit on behalf of Joan was that UnumProvident's conduct not only constituted bad faith and fraud but also violated a California law outlawing unfair business practices. Such violations permitted a judge to issue an injunction against the company.

Until 17200 was amended by a ballot initiative funded by big corporations in November 2004, the statute permitted law enforcement actions to be filed by individual citizens acting to protect the public from "immoral, unethical, oppressive, unscrupulous, or injurious commercial activities." The initiative that put an end to the private enforcement of 17200 narrowly succeeded by misrepresenting to the public that 17200 was being used to file "frivolous lawsuits." The truth of the matter is that 17200 could be used to outlaw wrongful conduct or order the disgorgement of unlawfully gained profits.

In this case, following the verdict, Judge Larson directed both sides to submit what are known as "proposed findings of fact and conclusions of law" for his 17200 ruling. The two sides were told to exchange their initial papers simultaneously. They were then allotted ten days to respond to the other's brief.

Our proposed findings ran some twenty-three pages, plus several hundred pages of attached testimony and exhibits.

We reviewed the evidence, quoted from the policy, cited Provident's own witnesses and documents, and went over key testimony. We pointed out that in their termination letter, the defendants had lied not only about Joan's total disability benefits but about her residual, rehabilitation, and recovery benefits as well. On top of that, they tried to deceive her by saying her claim was preempted by ERISA.

We reiterated that the company realized the people authorized to terminate claims still did not know what they were doing. We pointed out that the defendants' own claims managers said they would have to seek legal advice on the meaning of policy provisions that they expected laypeople to figure out on their own. We talked about the risk profiles, targeting, termination goals, and formulas. We discussed the shredding, file manipulation, IME approach, and surveillance. We hammered the point that if what UnumProvident was doing did not qualify as unfair business practices, very little short of stun-gun torture would. These practices should not be ignored. We asked that they be stopped.

UnumProvident presented a different take on all of this. It was just a company doing its best, paying a lot of claims, and operating under a banner of fairness. The company deftly sidestepped the testimony and danced around the evidence, focusing on the self-serving pronouncements and proclamations of Mohney and his customer care managers. It cast aside our arguments with a casual wave of the hand and opposed our 17200 papers, pretending that they were all much ado about nothing.

The big concern here was that unless Judge Larson lowered the boom on it in the 17200 case, UnumProvident would go right back to business as usual. Within a year, a new batch of brain-damaged, heart-diseased, or other disabled claimants would be holding their termination letters. And most of them would wind up unable to do a thing about it.

At the time of oral argument on the posttrial motions, Judge Larson indicated that he would notify the parties if he wished to hear oral argument on the 17200 claim.

All we could do, once again, was wait.

∧ ∨ ∧ ∨ ∧

IN ADDITION TO THE INITIAL PRESS COVERAGE OF THE VERDICT, THE print and broadcast media started to take a deeper look at what was going on with UnumProvident. It started with an editorial in the *San Francisco Examiner*, headlined "From Welfare to Windfall."

> Joan Hangarter lost her livelihood. She lost her home and her peace of mind when her insurance company, the mighty UnumProvident, decided she wasn't disabled anymore. She nearly lost her children.
>
> On Monday, a federal jury said the insurer was wrong and awarded Hangarter $7.7 million. Very Wrong: The punishment part of the Award was $5 million.
>
> Cause for her to celebrate, but wait . . .
>
> She has no idea when she'll see any money, and until she does . . . she'll be standing in line for her $230 in food stamps . . .
>
> Dot-coms fail, big corporations spew millions in debts, and it starts to seem like it's all a paper trail with no connection to reality. But people have to live here and now. They need to feed and shelter themselves, and their children . . .
>
> It's a paper victory for now, but we hope it's soon a real win for the Marin County resident.

One day, a few weeks after the trial, I received a telephone call from one of *60 Minutes'* top producers. He wanted to explore the possibility of doing a story. Was it true this company was denying claims involving people with heart disease, brain damage, cancer? Was it true what they had heard about these memos? Would Dr. Hangarter talk on camera? Would Dr. Gluck? Would Susan McGregor? Did we have videotaped depositions of Chandler? Of Mohney?

Two days after receiving the *60 Minutes* call, I saw Joan. She invited me to a small party she had put together for a few friends. The theme of the party, she said, was "Celebration of Life."

I wondered how she had made it through all of this. It was one thing to talk about it in a conference room or to hear evidence presented in the pristine, rational, protective, almost-supportive atmosphere of a federal courtroom. It was another to endure what she had.

Joan was a remarkable and courageous woman. How long she was going to have to wait before she saw any money remained to be seen. As the *Examiner* pointed out, the day after the verdict she was back to being a welfare mother. It was incredible to think that after UnumProvident representatives had seen and heard all the evidence and testimony about what she had gone through, they were still holding back the benefits they owed.

I thought about the memo we found in the four-thousand-document file that talked about the company having to implement security measures to deal with disgruntled claimants. I wondered how long it would be before some cheated policyholder or his son, daughter, or spouse simply said, "The hell with all the lawyers, the hell with all the litigation, the hell with all of this," and took matters into his or her own hands.

When would someone's frustration level reach that point? When would the helplessness, powerlessness, humiliation, pain, sense of injustice, and rage simply take over?

I went to Joan's party. The food was delicious—it was donated.

Chapter Thirteen

LIAR'S DICE

MICHAEL KARZIS FLEW TO SAN FRANCISCO ON A WEDNESDAY AFTER-
noon. Karzis, though young, had managed to land a job as an
assistant producer with the best investigative news program in television history, *60 Minutes*. Talking with him, I soon realized why.

Several weeks before, Karzis and his senior producer, David Gelber,
had asked us to send them copies of depositions, trial transcripts,
motions, court orders, and other documents from our various cases
against UnumProvident. This involved thousands of pages. I'd doubted
that anyone could possibly read, much less process, all the stuff we'd
sent—certainly not within a matter of weeks.

But by the time Karzis showed up at our office, it was obvious he'd
absorbed the material in its entirety. He knew the facts from every
angle. He could quote witnesses verbatim and cite documentary evidence by the exhibit number. It was incredible. He wanted more.

Karzis asked questions I'd never heard *anyone* ask before. He
was meticulous, serious, and very bright.

He talked to Alice, David, Susan McGregor, Dr. Stuart Gluck,
Joan Hangarter, Judge Alfred Chiantelli, and California Insurance
Commissioner John Garamendi. He talked to paralegals, to secre-
taries, to other lawyers, and to God knows who else. He would arrive
early, go through files, disappear for hours, and return with more
information and more questions.

After a week or so, David Gelber arrived. Gelber, who had produced some of the most incisive pieces to ever air on *60 Minutes*, was
legendary.

In addition to *60 Minutes*, Alice and I were contacted by a producer from NBC's *Dateline* about doing a story. At last, I thought,
after almost a decade of carrying out its "claims initiatives" in virtual

secrecy, UnumProvident was about to find itself facing national media scrutiny from two major network news teams with budgets and resources that were forces to contend with.

After Gelber and Karzis completed their work in San Francisco, Ed Bradley came out to interview Joan, Susan, Stuart, Alice and me, Judge Chiantelli, Garamendi, and others. I assumed that Bradley, Gelber, and Karzis then moved on to Chattanooga or New York to interview the folks from UnumProvident.

Whatever came of those discussions, the next thing I knew, Unum-Provident suddenly posted a notice to stock analysts and shareholders warning them that the company was about to receive "some negative national publicity." UnumProvident had decided, said the notice, to take a proactive approach to the anticipated publicity. This approach consisted of hiring not one, not two, but three well-connected public relations firms to neutralize the expected charges before they were aired.

To some, it might have seemed that UnumProvident was willing to spend more money on PR trying to explain the terminations of claims than it would have spent if it had paid the claims honestly in the first place. But this was not the case. What the company was really fighting for was the preservation of its system and the ability to continue doing business as it had been. UnumProvident didn't want to change and was willing to fight claimants, judges, insurance commissioners, lawyers, the media, and everyone else in a desperate effort to avoid having to do so.

The company's proactive strike consisted of an attack on what it called "tabloid" journalism and "certain" lawyers. UnumProvident, said a company notice, paid hundreds of thousand of claims—more than $3 billion in benefits—per year. So what if a few weren't handled 100 percent correctly? Everybody makes mistakes once in awhile. What was the big deal?

Of course, UnumProvident's senior managers knew very well what the "big deal" was. They knew that most of the hundreds of thousands of claims being paid were for short-term disabilities, those sprains and pains with small payouts and speedy recoveries. The "big deal" centered on the long-term benefit claims.

They also knew that its "mistakes" argument was bogus. Even if some initial terminations could be called mere "mistakes," the problem went far beyond that. It went beyond a mistake when the company continued to refuse to pay a legitimate claim for years following the initial cutoff. Time after time, and in case after case, that was exactly what UnumProvident did. Likewise, company memos revealed intentional, not inadvertent, conduct.

As far as blaming it on the lawyers was concerned, lawyers wouldn't be needed if policyholders didn't have to sue to get what they had paid their premiums for in the first place.

Despite all this, it was surprising to see how many newspapers simply printed the press release arguments that UnumProvident was cranking out in Chattanooga and Worcester without the slightest attempt to analyze them. If we were going to force UnumProvident to change its practices, we were going to have to fight them on the PR front as well.

∧ ∨ ∧ ∨ ∧

BEFORE EITHER OF THE NETWORK PIECES AIRED, CAROLYN SAID WROTE a front-page investigative report on UnumProvident for the *San Francisco Chronicle*. Said included interviews with Gluck, Hangarter, and McGregor. Jamie Court, executive director of the Foundation for Taxpayer and Consumer Rights, a Santa Monica nonprofit, characterized the situation as "a real tragedy because these are people who bought insurance believing it would be there if they got sick, and instead the promise was broken."

The *Chronicle* article quoted from numerous company documents, including Mohney's "$60 million memo." Company spokesman Tom White, vice president for corporate relations, claimed that this memo "referred to saving costs by consolidating claims management in a central location." Company spokespeople also accused two former employees who were speaking out against the company—Dr. Feist and Dr. Patrick McSharry—of being nothing more than "disruptive."

It was a powerful story, made more so by Said pointing out that Joan Hangarter had not received any money—not even her policy benefits—because UnumProvident was appealing. "Based on the award," wrote Said, "she borrowed money, which allowed her to buy a car and rent a nice house in Novato. That money will run out in another couple of months."

∧ ∨ ∧ ∨ ∧

NBC'S *DATELINE* SEGMENT AIRED OCTOBER 16, 2002. IT CONTAINED several extremely shocking stories. One concerned John Montano of Albuquerque, New Mexico, the victim of a serious car accident that left him paralyzed.

> Unable to work to support his family, Montano faced losing everything. But like millions of Americans, he had prepared for just such a disaster. He had paid $59 a month for disability insurance which promised that if he was ever too sick or too injured to keep working, it would help replace his lost income. The checks began arriving as promised, but after two years he got a shocking letter. His disability benefits were being cut off. . . .
>
> "I was frightened,' said Montano. "I go, well there's got to be a mistake."
>
> But there was no mistake. Montano's insurance company had decided that despite his paralysis, he was no longer deserving benefits.
>
> So what was going on? Sources tell *Dateline* that what happened to John Montano may have been part of something much larger. A *Dateline* investigation into whether the largest disability carrier in the United States–UnumProvident–launched a companywide effort to cut costs aggressively, and in the process, unfairly denied benefits, selling out people it promised to protect.

The *Dateline* piece went on to describe letters sent to Unum-Provident by Montano's doctor, Jonathan Burg, telling the company in no uncertain terms that Montano was a quadriplegic. Montano contacted the company himself and offered to take any test it wanted him to, but the company ignored him.

As he spiraled toward bankruptcy, Montano's wife divorced him. Facing the prospect of losing his home and children, he became suicidal.

Dateline interviewed three former UnumProvident employees, who talked about the pressure on them to terminate claims. One described the almost bizarre atmosphere of pizza and ice cream parties to celebrate claims closings. Another described the roundtable meetings as intended to identify and target large, long-term claims.

> And they are not the only ones saying this, [said *Dateline*]. In all, ten UnumProvident employees agreed to speak with *Dateline*, but only if we promised not to reveal their names. . . . Their jobs range from claims representatives all the way up to vice presidents.
>
> Some left the company on their own, some were fired, and some still work at UnumProvident. But all have described the same atmosphere—one of intense pressure coming from management down to employees—pressure to cut off benefits to policyholders.

Using the documents Alice and I had obtained, *Dateline* showed the memos that talked about "terminated claims" having "reached a record level." An internal email from 2001 alerted a group of adjusters that it had one week to close eighteen more claims to meet its projections. Company employees told *Dateline* that if they didn't meet their projections, they'd have what they called "fire drills," intensive efforts to find claims to close.

UnumProvident wouldn't agree to an on-camera interview. As usual, it vehemently denied setting goals to terminate claims. In a letter to *Dateline*, the company trotted out its knee-jerk defense, that it estimates claims results to "project a business plan into the future" and that it was paying more than $3 billion in benefits per year.

Dateline also interviewed Rosemary Wright.

> Once a healthy, vibrant schoolteacher from Illinois, Rosemary Wright began suffering from a progressive fatal form of emphysema. Even the smallest activity can leave her gasping for breath.

Her doctors say the kind of emphysema Wright has is genetic, it's not from smoking. The same disease has already killed her younger brother, and now it's killing her.

When Wright became too sick to teach, UnumProvident began paying her disability benefits. But two years later, just as in John Montano's case, the company cut her off.

Like Montano, Wright believed that it must have been a mistake. But it wasn't. UnumProvident had based its decision on the opinion of a staff doctor who not only had never examined Wright but also disregarded the opinions of her two doctors, both lung specialists who had examined her and found her to be totally and completely disabled.

After UnumProvident ended her disability payments, Rosemary Wright says she was forced to begin spending money she had saved for a lung transplant just to cover living expenses. Wright sued UnumProvident, which suddenly reversed itself, reimbursed her back benefits and began paying her again. But Wright has not dropped her lawsuit and says stress took its toll.

UnumProvident says it regrets how it handled the cases of Wright and Montano, but says they are exceptions. . . . Yet in the eyes of at least one insurance commissioner it may be more than an occasional mistake.

"There are some substantial problem areas," says Georgia Insurance Commissioner John Oxendine.

UnumProvident says any problems in Georgia represent a small percentage of their overall claims, and it will do what is necessary to correct those issues. . . .

"It's like stealing," says John Montano. "They should be held accountable for that."

While UnumProvident's PR team was continuing to put out its "Who, us?" yarn, Judge Larson was putting the finishing touches on his ruling and order on our Business and Professions Code Section 17200 case. Given the overwhelming evidence presented and the unanimity of the Hangarter verdict, Alice, David, and I were astonished that the company hadn't tried to settle both the bad-faith and 17200 cases. Although it's a presumptuous and dangerous business to try to predict what a federal judge is going to do, we didn't see how Judge Larson would not rule in our favor.

On numerous occasions, we had approached UnumProvident representatives and asked them to reform their claims-handling practices, set up a system for reviewing closed claims, and settle *Hangarter*, *McGregor*, and other cases in our office. We never got a response.

I don't know whether they thought they were somehow going to prevail with Judge Larson on the 17200 case or whether they simply didn't care what his ruling was in the context of the revenue they were deriving from continuing to handle claims as they were. Whatever the reasons, they ignored us. Once again, we worried that somehow they knew something that we didn't. As it turned out, that was not the case.

When it was suddenly issued on November 12, 2002, Judge Larson's "Findings of Fact, Conclusions of Law and Order" was a painstakingly footnoted and strongly worded decision. It was aptly characterized by the legal press as a "62-page hand grenade."

Citing, by page and line number, the testimony of every key witness, Larson scrutinized the evidence presented, applicable legal standards, and the facts and the contentions of the parties.

He specifically found that UnumProvident had "targeted claims for termination when they met a certain profile," that claims were taken to the roundtable "where they were examined for ways to terminate them," and that the defendant "had sent Plaintiff to a biased medical exam." He noted that Dr. Feist testified that "before Chandler and Mohney came to Provident claims were handled in a fair and aboveboard way, but that after their arrival, standards slid to those that were not ethical for an insurance company."

Judge Larson noted admissions from the defendants' own witnesses that they didn't know the proper definition of "disability," had admitted to the destruction of original medical reports from examining physicians, had adopted a policy of failing to document claims processes in the file, had failed to advise insureds of covered benefits, had failed to settle claims when liability was clear, and had forced insureds to litigate in order to obtain benefits.

"The court," wrote Judge Larson, "hereby adopts the factual finding of the jury that the Defendants acted in bad faith in denying Plaintiff's claim and further finds that the Defendants' multiple acts of bad faith constitute violations of the California Unfair Competition Act."

Judge Larson proceeded to issue an injunction ordering UnumProvident "to obey the law" and enjoining the defendants "from future violations, including but not limited to targeting categories of claims or claimants, employing biased medical examiners, destroying medical reports, and withholding from claimants information about their benefits."

∧ ∨ ∧ ∨ ∧

SHORTLY AFTER JUDGE LARSON MADE HIS RULING, THE *LOS ANGELES Times* weighed in with a front-page story by staff writer Lisa Girion. In the story, a UnumProvident executive said, "The company was proud of its claims management practices." It was unbelievable!

Incoming Insurance Commissioner John Garamendi told Girion that he had reviewed the cases and documents and that it appeared clear to him that UnumProvident was engaged in a conspiracy to defraud individuals.

Then *60 Minutes* aired its report. Instead of broadcasting the interviews that Ed Bradley had conducted in California, the segment featured numerous UnumProvident claims adjusters, supervisors, and managers–including a number of individuals who had resigned from the company in disgust. They told Bradley of pressure from upper management to cut off people's benefits and to close claims, regardless of the validity or severity of a person's disabilities, in order to increase revenues. They told of financial incentives given to company claims officials and of promotions suddenly materializing following someone's termination of a large, long-term claim. Apparently, *60 Minutes* had found so many insiders and whistle-blowers willing to lower the boom on UnumProvident that there wasn't enough time to put them all on the air.

In no time, newspapers in Miami, Chattanooga, Portland, and other cities all over the country were reporting the allegations of local residents.

When UnumProvident put out yet another press release with Chandler denying any wrongdoing and blaming lawyers, claimants, the media, judges, disgruntled employees, and everyone other than itself for what was happening, Alice and I decided we had to respond. We released our own statement calling UnumProvident's responses "complete nonsense" and saying that we were now convinced that the only way change could happen would be for heads to roll "at the highest levels" within the company.

"The problem," we pointed out, "was that senior executives were being insulated from personal financial accountability. They don't have to pay judgments out of their own pockets. That money, instead, came directly or indirectly from the stockholders. If someone walked into UnumProvident's headquarters in Chattanooga and stole a computer, that person would be hauled off to jail. At the same time, Company officials who drove claimants into bankruptcy, caused them to be evicted from their homes, and led them to the brink of suicide were getting off scot-free.

"Insurance Companies had to be held to a higher standard than other corporate wrongdoers. What they were selling, in the first place, was peace of mind."

∧ ∨ ∧ ∨ ∧

THE BATTLE CONTINUED. UNUMPROVIDENT FILED ITS NOTICES OF appeal in *McGregor* and *Hangarter*. We responded by retaining Daniel U. Smith, a well-known and highly respected appellate attorney with an unmatched track record for upholding trial court verdicts in both state and federal appellate courts. Appeals were a very different matter from trials. Trial courts were focused on the particular case, the particular plaintiff. Appellate courts were more concerned with the precedents being set—the overall public policies that were being established. Dan had excellent judgment and the ability to see and fully comprehend both the broad picture and the subtle details of a case. He also had a work ethic that would shame Horatio Alger.

As the fight escalated, I wondered where it would all end. Joan and her children were still living on welfare. And although she was willing to stand by while her case ran its course, she hoped she wouldn't have to wait forever for some kind of ultimate resolution. She was told that there were companies that would advance her money against the verdict without any kind of security other than the verdict itself. But the price for such an advance was high. If she lost the appeal, she would owe nothing, but if she won, she would have to pay back double the amount that had been advanced to her. It wasn't a hard decision for Joan. She wanted to get off food stamps as soon as possible. So she applied for an advance, ultimately borrowing tens of thousands of dollars to live on while the appeal ran its course.

As far as Alice and I were concerned, other claimants were lining up in various stages of desperation and despair. We found ourselves suddenly limiting our practice to own-occupation disability insurance bad-faith cases against UnumProvident/Paul Revere and various subsidiaries. Beyond this, a multistate task force was being organized to investigate UnumProvident. In addition, John Garamendi was preparing to launch his investigation in California. Articles continued to be written. People continued to be outraged. News commentators continued to do stories.

∧ ∨ ∧ ∨ ∧

DAYS AND WEEKS ROLLED BY. FOR A TIME, UNUMPROVIDENT'S STOCK dropped sharply, then it simply leveled off. One of the company's large institutional investors grumbled that it was better for the company not to pay claims that it should than for it to be paying claims that it shouldn't. Disabled UnumProvident policyholders, shaking their heads in disbelief, kept calling and contacting us for help–people from all over the country–with horror story after horror story.

Despite all that had happened, little really seemed to be changing in the way UnumProvident was doing business. Company decision-makers gave us the impression that they were neither concerned, impressed, nor moved by what had happened. If anything, they appeared emboldened. I imagined a small cadre of hunched-over, egocentric, tough-guy, senior-level insiders slithering into a meeting room at the mammoth UnumProvident headquarters in Chattanooga to "educate" their PR teams and to reinforce each other's rationalizations as they retrenched and fortified themselves for their next round of intransigence–soldiers bound together by their common bonds against common enemies.

∧ ∨ ∧ ∨ ∧

I HAD OCCASION TO SPEAK WITH EUGENE ANDERSON, A FORMER FEDERAL prosecutor and a savvy, thoughtful, kind man who had formed a New York law firm that specialized in prosecuting insurance companies that were cheating their policyholders. An icon and role model for insurance practice litigators throughout the country, Anderson was a man for whom I had the highest personal respect. He was in San Francisco for a conference and we had dinner at Piperade, a wonderful Basque restaurant, with a first-rate wine cellar. When I told him I was writing this book, he responded immediately.

Anderson's firm is a treasure trove of information on every major insurance company in the country. When it comes to this industry, not only does he know where the bodies are buried, he has the dental records to prove it.

"Ray," he said in his slow, thoughtful way, "I'll tell you what I think. I think that even though it's illegal in most states, insurance companies like these guys may have found a way to buy insurance, or reinsurance, to cover *themselves* against punitive damages verdicts so that they can slash their exposure even when we have uncovered clear and convincing evidence of malice, fraud, or oppression.

"Not only that, but, to the extent that they haven't insured for it, I think they actually write off punitive damages on their tax returns, treating them as a 'business expense.'"

I was stunned. This would be the coup de grâce. The companies were telling policyholders to work in pain, take pennies on the dollar for a policy buyout, or sue. And if you sue, we'll dump all the ERISA claims along with those from the no-remedy states, remove most of the rest to federal court, and either undersettle or "roll the dice." The only real exposure left would be from unanimous high verdicts that couldn't be wiped out in posttrial motions, subsequently lowballed, or successfully appealed. Then, as to those, insure them or deduct them. If Anderson was right, US taxpayers were subsidizing

UnumProvident for exemplary damages awards levied against it based on the company's fraudulent or malicious conduct.

All of a sudden, I remembered how Mohney looked at me after completing his testimony in Joan's case. I saw that expression just as sharply and clearly as though Mohney were sitting there smirking with the quiet assurance of someone who was beyond accountability, beyond reach.

This was what he must have known all along, the reason UnumProvident and its operatives had such an arrogant attitude. To their way of thinking, none of what we had accomplished would make any difference in the end—not the unanimous verdicts, not the punitive damages, not the bad publicity, not the short-term stock losses.

The whole system was so tilted in their favor that nothing could force them to change the way they were doing business. Destitute claimants had *no* power.

Publicity would be countered. Injunctions would be attacked, buried, or ignored. Stock price dips would be reversed as long as the bottom line was protected.

In the end, the initiatives were all that mattered. They were the only parts of all this that meant anything, that were sacred, and would endure.

No matter who said or did what, a few thousand net terminations per year, worth an average of $40,000 to $50,000 each, compounded over ten years, would still add up to hundreds of millions and billions of dollars.

Judges, juries, lawyers, claimants, *60 Minutes*, *Dateline*, the Associated Press, insurance departments, and everyone else could just get used to it, learn to live with it, or go to hell.

The company could do whatever it wanted to do. That was all that any of this had proved, nothing more.

∧ ∨ ∧ ∨ ∧

ABOUT THIS TIME, THE ERISA POT REACHED A SIMMER. I RECEIVED CALLS from Julie Appleby, a reporter for *USA Today*, from Lisa Girion of the *Los Angeles Times*, and from Chris Oster of the *Wall Street Journal.* All three were interested in pursuing the issue of ERISA preemption.

How many Americans, they wanted to know, were subject to the immunities provided to insurance companies through ERISA-governed policies? Was it true that these people had lost all their rights to recover any damages for insurer fraud? Why was Congress permitting this? Why were our courts doing nothing about it? Could we provide some examples of the human suffering resulting from this? Would the victims be willing to talk on the record? Was there anything–anything at all–that was being done about it?

Given that only a tiny percentage of the nation's employers–and even fewer American employees–had the slightest idea that insurance purchased at work gave immunity to carriers engaging in fraudulent practices, I came up with the idea of demanding that state insurance commissioners issue a disclosure to be signed by everyone buying one of these policies. The disclosure would inform purchasers that ERISA-governed insurance policies stripped them of all their rights under the unfair claims practices laws and insurance regulations of their state. This, I believed, would cause at least some people to pause. More importantly, it would also result in some carriers offering competitively priced group policies that were *not* ERISA preempted.

∧ ∨ ∧ ∨ ∧

MEANWHILE, UNUMPROVIDENT WAS EXPERIENCING PROBLEMS ON other fronts. The Securities and Exchange Commission opened an investigation into the company's accounting practices and was apparently questioning how UnumProvident had been reporting certain financial matters to regulators. Several class actions were filed against UnumProvident charging that the company had been withholding crucial financial information from its shareholders. More claimants filed more lawsuits, including several alleging that the company was guilty of engaging in various racketeering (RICO) activities.

UnumProvident stock took another slide. One day it plummeted 36 percent; the next day, 25 percent. Then it recovered a bit. Up it went, down it went, back and forth with the opinions of analysts and rating agencies and with the ebb and flow of the markets.

I wondered about all of this in the broader picture of America's corporate practices environment. Would the UnumProvident situation be the one that would finally make a difference? Was the Unum-Provident situation going to establish a true turning point? Would it, along with the Enron, WorldCom, American Tobacco, Merrill Lynch, and other scandals, create a groundswell demand for sharp, systematic, institutional changes? Were companies that were manufacturing and selling drugs known to cause severe injuries and cars known to cause rollover deaths going to be forced to stop destroying people in order to increase profits? Or was it all simply going to wind up being crushed by the lumbering tanks of our nation's powerful economic machine?

One evening, after a particularly difficult and frustrating day, I turned to Alice and David and asked them for their take on this question. Looking drawn and in desperate need for a strong shot of hope, Alice smiled weakly and shrugged. "I don't know," she said. "I think it will really depend on how America and our leaders and institutions react to all of this. Are we going to respond effectively to what is going on or not?"

Chapter Fourteen

FRIENDS IN
HIGH PLACES

Alice didn't have to wait long for an answer. On April 7, 2003, white-collar crime was given its biggest boost in history. Corporate swindlers, con artists, scammers, thieves, and killers had found an ally in a very unlikely place: the Supreme Court of the United States. In *State Farm Mutual Automobile Insurance Company v. Campbell*, our nation's highest court slapped down the rights of states to sanction the awarding of punitive damages at a level sufficient to deter outrageous fraud.

Big exemplary damage awards, said the court, were "unfair." The thieves were "not on notice" for what could happen to them if they were caught robbing the bank. Punitive damages, said the court, had to have a "single digit" relationship with the actual (compensatory) damages awarded. If the compensatory damages were, say, $200,000 or $300,000, exemplary damages should not be more than about $2 million or so.

This arbitrary standard, which was simply made up by the justices signing off on this ruling, would obviously do nothing to deter a company focused on increasing profits by hundreds of millions or billions of dollars. If anything, the ruling would reward the biggest crooks from the biggest gangs in the land. The more a company could steal, the less the percentage of the loot it would have to cough up. States with exemplary damages laws that took into account the amount necessary to deter the conduct in question were dismissed with a wave of the hand. "Here's your hat," said the Supreme Court. "What's your hurry?"

It's interesting to note that constitutional conservatives who had spent lifetimes arguing for "states' rights"–the rights of states to fashion their own standards and laws without having to bow before federal authorities–did a sudden about-face and were no longer in favor of any such ruling. States' rights had met their doom at the altar of the Almighty Buck.

At the same time that states' rights were going down, the Supreme Court's conservative majority was reevaluating its philosophical disdain for judicial activism. Maybe the notion of rewriting laws before interpreting them wasn't such a bad idea after all.

Meanwhile, back in Congress, key leaders from the Republican majority were busy figuring out how to take their own whack at the concept of corporate accountability. Assured by the certainty of fat special-interest payoffs, these legislators, all of them strong opponents of restricting campaign contributions, were busy at work developing big ideas for restricting jury verdicts. Rather than searching for ways to reduce fraud, they went on a treasure hunt for new ways to reduce litigation against it.

They wanted to cap whatever they could, cut whatever they couldn't cap, limit whatever they couldn't cut, and tax whatever was left.

At one point (perhaps following a marathon round of pricey wine-and-cheese fund-raisers), Senators Jon Kyl (R-AR), Lamar Alexander (R-TN), John Cornyn (R-TX), and John Ensign (R-NV) came up with the idea of levying an excise tax on attorneys' fees in cases involving corporate misconduct. In other words, these were the cases where cheated, injured, maimed, or bankrupted consumers were daring to sue the corporations who had ruined their lives.

The idea of going after attorneys as a way of protecting fat-cat, crooked contributors was, of course, nothing new. Long ago, politicians discovered that trial lawyers were easy targets. A fast talker could get voters to support dumping boiling oil over innocent people as long as an attorney would get splattered in the process. Many lawyers were hardly innocent bystanders. The ones with ruby pinkie rings and dancing cash-register ads helped paint the entire trial bar as sleazy charlatans. In spite of this, the excise tax idea bit the dust.

While this was going on, a front-page story appeared in the *New York Times*. The story, though it had nothing to do directly with

UnumProvident, did have to do with disability insurance. "The Bush Administration," it said, "was planning major changes in Medicare that would make it more difficult for beneficiaries to appeal benefit denials." In thousands of recent cases, administration officials complained, federal judges had ruled that frail elderly people with severe illnesses had been improperly denied coverage. This was unacceptable to President Bush, so he proposed new federal rules that would limit the independence of the judges and even allow for their replacement. Tommy Thompson, President Bush's then secretary of Health and Human Services, said the proposed changes would make the system "more effective and efficient."

Not long before these changes were proposed, top Unum-Provident officials had testified before a House subcommittee on the subject of how the Social Security Administration "could learn" from the way UnumProvident handled claims. Right, I thought, perhaps the Social Security Administration's claims functions should be privatized and taken over by UnumProvident.

∧ ∨ ∧ ∨ ∧

JUST WHEN I THOUGHT NOTHING WOULD EVER HAPPEN TO SHAKE UP the senior management at UnumProvident, word came over the newswires that on March 31, 2003, Harold Chandler had been fired. It was not the usual retirement announcement associated with the dignified departure of a respected corporate leader. Nothing was said about his wanting to spend more time with the family or about his having decided to pursue other interests. Chandler was simply given the boot.

This was a signal, I thought, to all within earshot.

And so it first seemed. All the work, all the effort had finally paid off. Heads *were* going to roll. UnumProvident *was* going to clean house.

I couldn't have been more wrong. It turned out that Chandler was the only one being dumped. Mohney remained. The legal department remained. The senior management remained. Not only that, but Chandler's longtime protégé, Tom Watjen–a guy who had been in the thick of things for years–was named interim president and CEO.

Moreover, the defrocked Chandler was given what might be called a nice go-away gift: $17 million. Whether this was hush money or whether any express or implied nondisparagement agreement was entered into, no one seemed to know, or at least no one was saying.

I thought that perhaps we would eventually find out—in the discovery phase of one of the many individual or class action suits that were continuing against the company. But the insight came from a different source—Chandler himself—when he joined the ranks of those suing UnumProvident by filing an action of his own against his former company for breach of contract. If it wasn't so indescribably ludicrous, this twist would have been thoroughly hilarious.

∧ ∨ ∧ ∨ ∧

BY JUNE 2003, JUDGE LARSON'S INJUNCTION HAD BEEN IN EFFECT FOR seven months. Despite this, we kept seeing case after case where it appeared that UnumProvident was ignoring the order. Other attorneys reported the same observation.

This was curious. The rule on injunctions issued by a federal judge is that unless a "stay" is obtained, an injunction remains in full force and effect even if an appeal is filed.

On that basis, we filed an Order to Show Cause (OSC) seeking to have UnumProvident held in contempt of court. A party seeking such a ruling has a heavy burden of proof. Contempt-of-court orders are serious business.

The judge who issues an injunction retains jurisdiction over proceedings concerning it. And so our OSC was filed in Judge Larson's court.

In our moving papers, we filed sworn affidavits signed by numerous lawyers and claimants. These included the following cases.

Laurie Hindiyeh, a comptroller and accountant with a real estate firm. Laurie had bilateral Ménière's disease, rhinitis, sinusitis, chronic vertigo, headaches, nausea, and exhausting fatigue. She had undergone five unsuccessful surgeries for her condition. Her doctors all confirmed her condition. In the usual pattern, after paying for some time, on April 25, 2002, UnumProvident cut off her benefits. Despite the company's "continuing duty" to pay claims that are due and despite Laurie's repeated pleas for reinstatement, UnumProvident refused to pay.

Eugene Molfino, formerly a warehouseman with Thomas J. Lipton Inc. Eugene also suffered from Ménière's disease. He had severe hearing loss, chronic vertigo, constant ringing in both ears, and excruciating headaches. He experienced extreme convulsive episodes, was repeatedly hospitalized, and was treated with intravenous injections. His condition was so severe that his doctors, who again were unanimous in their confirmation of his disability, reported that he often had extended bouts of severe vomiting. Molfino underwent three surgeries for his condition. None were successful. When he appealed UnumProvident's September 26, 2002, termination of his benefits, the company failed to acknowledge or respond to his appeal.

Julie Guyton, a 911 operator for the city of Gilroy, California. Julie had Crohn's disease, endometriosis, ankylosing spondylitis, irritable bowel syndrome, interstitial cystitis, and urinary incontinence. UnumProvident refused to pay benefits, lied to her about the policy being ERISA preempted, and misrepresented her policy coverage–until we accepted her non-ERISA preempted case. At that point, UnumProvident–with no additional medical information–reversed itself and put her on claim, paying her past benefits in the process.

Michael Baldwin was a former dentist with multiple spinal injuries confirmed by MRIs. Some days, he was unable to move his head. At other times, he was unable to walk. He was treated with spinal injection and morphine. For two years, his UnumProvident claim was ignored. Again, when we notified the company of our representation, checks started to arrive.

UnumProvident's new strategy appeared to be to shoot first and wait for a reaction. How many disabled people gave up without returning fire may never be known.

Margaret Santana, a former nurse who could barely walk, suffered from fibromatosis and neurofibromatosis. Her condition was so severe that her doctors wanted to amputate one of her deformed feet. She had five surgeries on her right foot and two on the left for tumors that grew back. In addition, Margaret had palmar fibromatosis on her hands. She couldn't even hold a telephone receiver without assistance. After initially paying her claim, UnumProvident cut her off. She appealed, and UnumProvident denied her appeal.

She appealed again; again UnumProvident denied. Margaret lost her home, was constantly late paying bills, and finally was forced to hire lawyers to fight for her.

Dr. Gary Brazina was a former orthopedic surgeon who suffered from bulging discs at C5-6 and C6-7. He had permanent radiculopathy with permanent numbness and muscle loss over his dominant right extremity. Three positive nerve conduction studies and positive MRIs confirmed his injuries. Following unsuccessful surgery, his doctors recommended a double-level fusion in which portions of his spine would be basically welded together to reduce the types of movements that caused him pain. Unfortunately, such a fusion could result in even greater disability and pain.

UnumProvident didn't see the case in quite the same way as his physicians. As far as the company was concerned, he simply wasn't disabled.

Maria Ecker, a former claims investigator for American International Group, a large, multinational insurance company headquartered in New York, suffered from debilitating back injuries that were so clear that even UnumProvident's doctors confirmed her disability. That must have come as a surprise to UnumProvident, but where there's a will, there's a way. The company offered to buy out her policy. It would pay $50,000 in return for her surrendering her policy to the company with a release of all further liability.

At first blush, $50,000 cash might sound like a pretty good deal. Maria could pay off some large bills and put a few dollars in the bank. Besides, she was told, her case was ERISA preempted, and she had no right to accelerated payments or to consequential, compensatory, general, or punitive damages. Like so many others, she almost accepted the deal. Thankfully, she didn't.

The problem with UnumProvident's $50,000 offer was that the actual value of Maria's policy—the amount she was actually entitled to—was over $580,000. If she had taken the deal, UnumProvident would have pocketed a fast half million plus.

In response, and after having paid her claim for more than two years, UnumProvident simply cut off her benefits. She appealed. Reinstatement was refused. And on May 15, 2003, six months after Judge Larson's injunction had been issued, UnumProvident refused to reconsider, again affirming its decision.

Another client, whose real name is being withheld for privacy, was a feature film producer suffering from severe psychotic manic depression and other bipolar disorders. He attempted suicide twice and was institutionalized in a psychiatric hospital when UnumProvident rejected his pleas for payment.

∧ ∨ ∧ ∨ ∧

IN ADDITION TO THESE CASES, OUR CONTEMPT MOTION INCLUDED AFFI-davits from Thornton Davidson, Teresa Renaker, Jeffrey Metzger, Melvin Silver, and Ruth Taube. These people were all attorneys, all specialists in handling disability claims—all supporting the request for a contempt order based on their experiences in thirty or forty additional denials or refusals to pay since Judge Larson's November 12 ruling.

We knew it would be an uphill battle, but as part of our OSC, we were asking the court to order UnumProvident to reopen all ERISA and non-ERISA denials, terminations, and refusals to pay subsequent to the injunction. We asked for sanctions, the disgorgement of ill-gotten revenues, the establishment of a claims-review procedure, and the setting aside of a fund to pay the claimants.

In August 2003, our OSC was dismissed. His injunction, ruled Judge Larson, was intended to apply only to Joan Hangarter and her case, not to UnumProvident's conduct in other cases. It was back to square one as far as the broad picture was concerned.

And because the math is still the math, and the dollars at stake are enormous, I believed the battle would continue. But no matter what happened, a company—any company in America today—has time on its side. Not only time, but the money, the leverage, the regulatory process, and just about everything else. It has the directors' and officers' liability insurance policies and the indemnity agreements and the golden parachutes and the "business expense" deductions and perhaps even the offshore punitive damages policies.

Companies that have decided to increase revenues by cheating people have even more going for them than that. Contacts. Through their multimillion-dollar-per-year individual, corporate, or trade group organizations, they bestow millions of dollars a year in campaign "contributions" to every mover and shaker in Washington. In fact, if you want to have a little fun, by talking to some name-brand politician, all you have to do is fib to the assistant about who is on the line. Look up the name of a Chair of some Platinum Club member and prepare to exchange pleasantries. Unless they have installed a voice-recognition system you'll get the guy on the phone, in person, in less than no time. Just call whomever you want. Explain that you want to chat for a bit, one to one, about fund-raising. Bingo. Political analyst Dick Tuck told me several years ago, "Payoffs used to be illegal. So they legalized them."

Hey, what are friends for?

Chapter Fifteen

KICK IN
THE ASSETS

Years after UnumProvident had filed its appeals in *McGregor* and *Hangarter* to the Ninth Circuit, and months after oral argument, two different three-judge panels issued rulings in both cases. The first ruling came in *McGregor* on January 15, 2004. The panel unanimously affirmed the trial court's verdict, finding UnumProvident guilty of bad faith. Following a futile attempt to obtain an *en banc* hearing (involving a panel of twelve judges) from the entire circuit, UnumProvident finally gave up and paid the judgment. It really had no choice but to do so. The only additional appeal it had left was to petition the US Supreme Court, and the types of cases accepted by the court are almost always restricted to matters involving major constitutional or first impression issues or cases involving conflicting decisions among the circuit courts.

A few months later on June 25, 2004, the *Hangarter* panel also ruled. Again the decision was unanimous. Again, the ruling affirmed the trial court's verdict (disagreeing only as to Judge Larson's injunction on the technical grounds that a Section 17200 case has to be brought in state, not federal, court). Again, following its usual feeble grumbling and after using what seemed like every delaying device imaginable to put off paying for as long as possible, UnumProvident threw in the towel.

Susan and Joan would finally get their money. And they were both thrilled beyond words. For them and a few hundred others, this battle had been worthwhile. We had made our point. We had kicked UnumProvident right in its corporate assets. We had forced it to pay. For claimants living in California or in the handful of other states with decent bad-faith laws on the books, the situation might improve somewhat. Our firm, along with the few others that had the evidence, experience, tenacity, track record, and war chest necessary to get UnumProvident's attention, might be able to get some respectable settlements in the future on behalf of our relatively small number of clients.

But what about all the others? What about the insureds from states with no meaningful bad-faith protections? What about the policy-holders who know nothing about their rights? What about those who were simply too disabled, too meek, or too tired to fight? What about all of those claimants whose policies are ERISA preempted? All of these folks and their claims added up to a pile of money.

What would happen to them?

The answer to this question came from an unlikely source. At about the same time the Ninth Circuit was deciding *Hangarter*, I received a phone call from Daniel Feldman, a deputy state attorney general (AG) in New York. Feldman's office had collected hundreds of millions of dollars in fines from Merrill Lynch and other securities firms for engaging in activities such as issuing flawed "buy" recommendations to customers, releasing bogus stock research, and engaging in late trading to increase company profits at the expense of clients. Feldman informed me that he was investigating UnumProvident for its claims-handling practices. He wanted me to help by providing information from our firm's own investigations of UnumProvident and from the deposition and trial testimony obtained in our cases.

One of the concerns expressed by Feldman was related to a multistate market conduct investigation that had been launched by the insurance departments of Massachusetts (the home base of Paul Revere), Maine (the home base of UnumProvident), and Tennessee (the home base of Provident). The concern was that this investigation would whitewash the entire UnumProvident scandal and that other states would be asked to ratify the Maine, Massachusetts, and Tennessee findings and conclusions—thus effectively concluding the state DOI investigative aspects.

Believing that Feldman's office would light a fire under any lapdog regulators working to gloss over UnumProvident's conduct, I provided him with the information he was requesting. From talking to colleagues who were also involved in UnumProvident's bad-faith litigation, I learned that they had also been contacted by him.

Although I didn't know exactly what Feldman had in mind, I assumed that his investigation would result in written findings against UnumProvident, a specific agreement to provide third-party oversight for the reopening of hundreds of thousands of denied claims, a large fine (like those in his securities cases), and the forced replacement of the top UnumProvident officials who had been involved in the wrongdoing. It was therefore shocking to me that none of these occurred.

On November 18, 2004, a multistate settlement with Unum-Provident was announced with the New York AG signing on. First, the agreement, negotiated with some of the very people at Unum-Provident who were up to their ears in the scandal, provided for the reopening of 215,000 previously denied claims–but with no third-party oversight whatsoever. In other words, UnumProvident would get to investigate its own wrongdoing. Second, claimants who had been financially destroyed by the company would have to waive the right to recover damages for having lost everything as a precondition to receiving a dime in compensation for their wrongfully terminated claims. Third, an "agreed to" fine would be paid by UnumProvident with no admission of wrongdoing. The fine ($15 million) was not even a fraction of the revenues generated by the claims initiatives that had been launched by the company and in place for over ten years.

If Mohney's original projections in his "$60 million memo" were correct–and they were probably low given the mergers, acquisitions, and expansions that had occurred after the issuance of that memo–the compounded money generated by the company could well have been in excess of a billion dollars. Fifteen million dollars wasn't even a slap on the wrist. A tweak on the pinkie would be a more accurate description. And although the settlement permitted the imposition of higher fines in the future–in the event that Unum-Provident failed to live up to the agreement–it was clear that that would never happen.

No resignations were demanded. No findings were issued. That was it.

Wall Street's reaction confirmed that the settlement was bogus. The day after it was announced, UnumProvident stock jumped 11 percent. Joseph Belth, professor emeritus of insurance at Indiana University's School of Business and editor of the *Insurance Forum*, described the settlement as "a victory for the Companies" that would "offer significant help to very few of the claimants who have been victimized by the disability claims practices . . . and may offer little improvement for the benefit of future claimants." Professor Belth noted that the agreement did not even call for the reopening of undersettled claims–claims on which the company had used the threat of termination to pay pennies on the dollar. In his deliberative academic style, and with classic understatement, Belth called it "regrettable" that the New York AG had signed on at all.

Former federal prosecutor Gene Anderson (one of the people to whom this book is dedicated) took it a step further. Noting that Massachusetts was the center of UnumProvident's targeted abuse of mentally ill disabled people, he characterized putting this investigation in the hands of its insurance department as akin to putting a pack of wolves in charge of the chickens. He noted that although a large portion of the companies' business came from the acquisition of blocks from John Hancock, Equitable, MetLife, and others, the settlement was carefully defined to include only Unum, Provident, and Paul Revere. Thus, noted Anderson, the agreement was a free ride for up to 50 percent of this total business.

∧ ∨ ∧ ∨ ∧

ON DECEMBER 8, 2004, OUR FIRM WROTE A LETTER TO EACH OF THE forty-seven state insurance commissioners who were being asked to endorse the Maine-Massachusetts-Tennessee agreement.

UnumProvident had set aside reserves of only $80 million for its projection of the amount that would be necessary to pay settlements on the reevaluated claims. Given that it had targeted high-dollar claimants for terminations in the first place, this meant its reserves estimate assumed that only a tiny fraction of the 215,000 claimants would wind up being paid. Either that, I thought, or the company wasn't planning on offering much per claim.

In our letter we asked the forty-seven state insurance commissioners to reject the proposed agreement on the grounds previously mentioned: that it provided for no outside compliance monitoring; that it permitted the same claims officials who had made the denial decisions in the first place to investigate their own actions; that it contained no provisions to address the problem of undersettlements; that the proposed fine was inadequate; that it failed to cover UnumProvident claims denials on policies originally written by John Hancock, Equitable, General American, New York Life, MetLife, National Life, Vermont Life, and other companies; and that it failed to require the resignations of any top UnumProvident officials.

We hoped that if the settlement in its proposed form was rejected, commissioners from other states would be able to force UnumProvident and its DOI friends in Maine, Massachusetts, and Tennessee to make important improvements in the agreement. Given the approach of most insurance regulators and the fact that the public didn't have a clue of what was going on with any of this, we knew we were in for an uphill battle.

Two insurance departments took action. California's insurance commissioner, John Garamendi, rejected the proposed settlement. Citing concerns with oversight, the amount of the fine, and other problems, Garamendi advised David Leslie, the attorney for the multistate taskforce, that it "would not be in the best interests of California to sign on to the . . . settlement." Instead, Garamendi entered into negotiations with UnumProvident aimed at crafting a separate agreement covering California policyholders. The insurance commissioner of Montana also refused to sign on.

The rest of the nation's insurance watchdogs wagged their tails, rolled over, and went back to sleep. None of them even bothered to respond to our letter. One by one, they signed on to the multistate agreement in late 2004 and early 2005, thus ratifying the settlement by February 2005.

UnumProvident then started sending out its reevaluation letters. Unfortunately, this created yet another problem. The fine print in the company's notice vaguely implied that claimants receiving any offer of payment at all under the reevaluation program would have to waive their right to any additional compensation, including "extracontractual" damages. Thus, a cheated insured who was offered $10,000 on a policy benefit worth $500,000 would–by virtue of having requested the review–lose the right to recover anything more. This was so regardless of how much the company owed under the policy, regardless of any additional losses suffered by the claimant beyond the policy benefits, and regardless of whether the claimant accepted the reassessment offer or not. There was no right to appeal.

When I read UnumProvident's letter I was amazed. The incredible thing about this company, I thought, was that its audacity knew no bounds. It was one thing to turn lemons into lemonade–but quite another to mold horse manure into platinum. UnumProvident always seemed to go for the latter.

We asked the California DOI to send out its own notice clarifying the situation, advising it that we intended to file a class action in state court against UnumProvident based on the allegation that its notice to consumers fraudulently misrepresented the terms of the multistate settlement agreement. The problem was that two weeks before, on February 18, 2005, President Bush had proudly signed legislation that he had personally proposed, effectively banning most state court class actions by forcing them to be filed in federal court. He favored this bill, he grinned, because it protects us from "frivolous litigation."

Chapter Sixteen

BACK TO THE FUTURE: MATTHEW BOURHIS'S UPDATE

As mentioned, it has been over ten years since the Hangarter and McGregor trials. The Ninth Circuit unanimously confirmed the Hangarter judgment, and the National Association of Insurance Commissioners, the California Department of Insurance, and other regulators levied seven-figure fines on the insurance companies. In addition, Harold Chandler was fired, Unum was ordered to reopen and reevaluate thousands of previously denied claims, and news outlets such as *60 Minutes*, NBC's *Dateline*, *USA Today*, and the *Wall Street Journal* shined a national spotlight on this historically overlooked area of the law.

It was astonishing to see how much public awareness was being garnered around the fraudulent conduct of disability insurance companies. This trend seemed to be ushering in an era of justice in the cloaked world of the insurance industry. Yet one could not help but wonder what the moral of the story was. Would punitive damages, big verdicts, and disgraceful press coverage really teach insurance companies a lesson? Based on my experience with subsequent cases, I would have to say no.

My dad once told me that he had posed a similar question years ago to Marvin Lewis Sr., a highly accomplished and storied San Francisco trial lawyer. My dad, a newly minted lawyer himself, attended one of Lewis's speaking engagements. He spoke with Lewis afterward and asked his opinion as to whether big verdicts and punitive damage awards against insurance companies would eventually doom bad faith as a specialty.

Lewis laughed and said, "Ray, you don't have to worry about that. Insurance companies make so much money cheating their policyholders that no amount of punitive damages will deter them from doing that."

Years later, Lewis's observation proved truer than expected. After the Hangarter case, my dad met with the legal counsel of the California Department of Insurance to discuss broader insurance reform. They talked about bad-faith conduct and what it would take to straighten the companies out. The DOI lawyer correctly observed that to effectively deter unfair claims-handling practices, the DOI would need to issue such huge fines that doing so would trigger major backlash.

The companies would fight back by filing lawsuits, threatening to increase premiums, laying off employees, and launching a campaign to curtail the department's power and limit its authority. Thousands of people would lose their jobs, the price of insurance coverage would rise, and ordinary individuals who need insurance would suddenly find themselves uninsurable. All of this confirmed what Marvin Lewis had said years before: "There is simply no amount of money that can get insurance companies to abide by their obligations under the law."

Unfortunately, my experience confirms this. Here are just a few examples of what the industry continues to do.

Dr. Kama

Dr. Kama was the client in my first big case. I was fresh out of law school when I first spoke with him. Dr. Kama was a general anesthesiologist when he was diagnosed with prostate cancer in December 2016. He underwent a radical prostatectomy with lymph node resection, resulting in significant blood loss, anemia, and permanent damage to his bladder. As his condition worsened, he filed disability claims with his two insurance companies, whose identities we are required to keep confidential.

In June 2017, Dr. Kama's oncologist found that his cancer had metastasized and that he needed to undergo a repeat robotic laparoscopic surgery. Over the course of eight weeks, he had forty radiation treatments and hormone therapy, which quite literally resulted in the transformation of his gender. He had chronic fatigue, muscle wasting, lower extremity weakness, and substantial mental health changes. Due to his injured bladder, he had to use the restroom every thirty minutes. The urge to urinate was often precipitated by stress, especially during high acuity procedures or emergencies. His treatment lasted until December 2018, by which time his health issues made it impossible for him to practice anesthesiology. He went from administering the full slate of anesthetics to mostly performing administrative tasks and occasional low-level operations. Because he was unable to perform his specialty in the usual and customary manner and with reasonable continuity, he clearly qualified for total disability benefits under California law. Nevertheless, his insurers denied his claims. One even demanded reimbursement of a prior partial disability payment of $25,000, which it claimed had been paid in error.

Insurance representatives then started calling Dr. Kama, harassing him for money while he was going through radiation therapy. The nonpayment of his benefits forced Dr. Kama to continue working despite the advice of his treating physicians and colleagues.

I remember being in awe of his strength and resilience. While so many things in his life were spiraling out of control, he was able to persevere. People in his situation often quit work, run away to travel, and spend their remaining time they have left checking off as much as possible from their bucket list. Dr. Kama didn't do that. Although he lived a fulfilling life, he did not let doing so overshadow the fact that his family was relying on him. He did not want them to be left in the lurch. He knew that if his insurance companies got away with cheating him out of his benefits, his loved ones would be the ones who suffered. Dr. Kama was not going to let that happen. He was going to pursue his claims, gather the pertinent documentation, get his doctors to fill out the necessary paperwork, submit to the insurance companies' investigations, put up with their accusations, and, if necessary, file a lawsuit, hire expert witnesses, give depositions, and take his case to trial.

It takes persistence to do this. And many people don't follow through. They settle for pennies on the dollar or even give up entirely. That is just fine with the insurance companies. They save money by not paying claims and wind up with zero accountability.

I would love to know how many legitimate claims insurance companies actually deny. But, of course, there is no way of finding out.

In Dr. Kama's case, faced with the possibility of a lawsuit for wrongful death if they persisted in their actions, the insurers blinked. The case settled for $1.565 million. Even at that, the insurance companies made out very well. If the bad-faith case had gone to trial, they might well have been hit for much more than that.

Dr. Gally

Like Dr. Kama, another client, Dr. Gally (real name withheld), dealt with similar abuse from his insurer. Dr. Gally's case centered around a mental health disability. Mental illness is a killing field when it comes to disability insurance. Denials and underpayments are extremely common due to both public attitudes regarding the subject and the particular vulnerability of the victims. I hope that this situation will change as people develop a greater awareness of the issues.

Dr. Gally was a neuroradiologist. His occupation entailed interpreting MRI scans and functional imagining results of patients' brains and spines. At first, this sounded to me like a rather sedentary occupation with minimal patient interaction in a low-stress environment. But as I gained a greater understanding of the occupation, I soon realized how demanding Dr. Gally's work was.

His role was central to the operation of urgent and emergency neurological care. Patients' lives depended on his ability to focus on very complex radiology tests and quickly render decisive opinions. He alone was responsible for identifying aneurysms, tumors, and other medical conditions that, if undetected, could kill a patient within minutes. Dr. Gally regularly worked over twelve hours a day, and without him, neurosurgeons would basically be blindfolded during their operations. The unrelenting stress of his occupation caused very serious mental health issues.

He sought psychiatric help and was diagnosed with major depressive disorder, severe obsessive-compulsive disorder, attention deficit hyperactivity disorder, debilitating contamination fears, crippling anxiety, insomnia, and posttraumatic stress syndrome. Unable to continue working, he resigned, walked away from his extensive training, and gave up his prestigious position and large salary at a very young age. The work was simply killing him. The fact of the matter is that medical doctors have the highest rate of suicide of all professions in the United States. Dr. Gally at least had the foresight to realize this and to do something about it.

He filed a total disability claim, which was denied on the basis that he was still capable of doing research and therefore was only partially disabled. That stance concerning a neuroradiologist is about as persuasive as saying that if Lebron James tore his Achilles heel, he would not be considered disabled if he could sit on the bench. Dr. Gally's insurer mischaracterized the nature of own-occupation coverage. Dr. Galley purchased this policy to protect himself in the event he became unable to perform his clinical duties.

Dr. Gally spent years going back and forth with his insurance company. His insurer argued that if his mental health improved, he might be able to return to neuroradiology–ignoring the obvious fact that his work is what caused the problem in the first place–and it disregarded his treating doctor's insistence that it would be dangerous for him to attempt to return to his prior occupation. His insurer tried to intimidate him, asserting that if he did any work at all, even research, it would reduce his benefits. The insurer pulled out every trick in the book, knowing that he was already suffering from severe anxiety, fear, and depression and banking on the expectation that it could intimidate him into giving up and ignoring his doctor's advice. The insurer guessed wrong. Dr. Gally stood up for himself and we settled his case for $1.5 million–but only after he had been pushed far beyond the point of reasonable treatment.

Dr. Lala

Dr. Lala (real name withheld) encountered one of the most dangerous pitfalls of our justice system: the statute of limitations.

Dr. Lala, an orthopedic spine surgeon, practiced in a small town. His occupation was very demanding. It often required him to stand for hours on end, hunching over his patient, focusing on fine maneuvers where a minor slip could result in the patient's paralysis or death. It required physical stamina and a high level of focus. When he became disabled with severe osteoarthritis of his knees and feet, it was obvious that he could no longer endure the demands of spine surgery. It would put the health and safety of his patients in jeopardy. So he retired and filed a claim with his disability carrier.

Given his medical condition and the demands of his occupation, Dr. Lala expected his disability claim to be approved without resistance. Unfortunately, his insurance policy, like most policies, was riddled with fine print that served no purpose but to give his insurer an escape hatch from having to pay a legitimate claim. In this case, the fine print dealt with what is called a "regular medical care" requirement. This requirement, if fairly interpreted, has the legitimate purpose of requiring a claimant to obtain appropriate treatment from a physician other than the insured for an impairment. It is a common provision contained in most policies. The purpose of a regular medical care provision is twofold. First, by requiring the policyholder to undergo regular medical care with a doctor, the insurance company has a witness who can verify the disability. Second, it provides a monitor to track the condition in case the impairment eventually resolves as a result of medical care. When that happens, the insurer can sometimes terminate the claim.

Dr. Lala underwent regular medical care for severe osteoarthritis, but he was treated by a colleague in the small rural town where he was living. Their doctor-patient relationship was informal: there was no exchange of payment, no health insurance was involved, no written medical records were kept, and prescription medications were provided from the treating doctor's sample supply inventory provided to most doctors by drug manufacturers. Dr. Lala received medical treatment as a professional courtesy. This is a common practice between doctors. Nothing about it is illegal or violated any of the terms of Dr. Lala's insurance policy. Nevertheless, Dr. Lala's insurer, while it did not contest that he was disabled, denied his claim on the basis that he failed to satisfy the regular medical care requirement in the policy.

The law on this issue is clear. An insurance company cannot deny a claim on specious, technical grounds like this. It cannot circumvent the purpose of the policy. No one argued that Dr. Lala was not totally disabled—it was obvious. However, because the treating doctor did not maintain contemporaneous records, the insurance company refused to honor the claim. It did this despite the fact that no provision of the policy was violated and that the treating physician wrote to the company and informed it that he had diagnosed Dr. Lala with arthritis, prescribed him medication, advised him to stop practicing surgery, and declared him permanently disabled. The insurer ignored all of this and delayed paying the claim for years. Unbeknownst to Dr. Lala, the statute of limitations was running while the insurer was delaying. He didn't have an attorney at that point and was unaware that time was running out for him to sue.

When he came to us for help, we filed suit immediately. We were well aware that the insurer was going to make a motion to dismiss our case on the basis that the statute of limitations had expired. The reason we have statutes of limitations is to avoid problems with recall, the disappearance of witnesses, and the destruction of records and evidence. None of these were issues in this case, but for a claimant to survive this motion, the judge would have to accept somewhat tenuous legal theories such as equitable tolling and estoppel, which "stop the clock" on the statute of limitations. The judge has considerable latitude and discretion regarding this decision. It is a difficult and unpredictable situation, and even if the facts are otherwise compelling, the law can be unforgiving when a plaintiff has slept on his or her rights. If Dr. Lala lost the statute of limitations argument, he would recover nothing.

Therefore, Dr. Lala decided to settle his claim with the insurer for $350,000–less than the "present value" of the insurance benefits.

∧ ∨ ∧ ∨ ∧

THE PURPOSE OF THESE EXAMPLES–INSURANCE COMPANY MISREPRESENTA-tion, unfair policy interpretation, unreasonable delay, harassment, and intimidation–is simply to show that occasional verdicts, exposés, and publicity have almost no effect on even the most egregious of insurer misconduct.

As Joan Hangarter said in her note at the beginning of this book, the insurance industry has a heavy hand on the scales of justice. It has money, power, leverage, lobbyists, lawyers, and friends in high places all on its side. It writes policies that are not negotiable. And all of its costs and expenses associated with claims handling are tax deductible. For policyholders, the pursuit of justice is impossibly difficult, time-consuming, expensive, and unpredictable. The public needs to understand how the insurance industry works and demand change. Unless that happens, the problem will only get worse. Every year, the insurance industry becomes richer, more powerful, and more sophisticated than ever before. The rate at which insurance companies are brought to justice is much smaller than the rate at which they limit their liability–not by refraining from bad faith, but by finding better ways to cover it up.

As you may have gathered, I am very concerned by the power of insurance companies. However, I believe justice will ultimately find its way into the insurance industry. This area of the law is unique in that every case starts with an insurance company biting the hands that are feeding it. That is not a sustainable business model. From an economic, ethical, and legal standpoint, it is fundamentally unfair. Our justice system may fall short too often, but the collective power of people can change that. The ability of people to discern right from wrong is the timeless power of humanity, and it is unstoppable.

Conclusion

CLAIMS GAMES

A COLD WIND CUT ACROSS THE FLAT EXPANSE OF THE MARINA GREEN. In the distance stood the majestic Golden Gate and beyond it, the green hills of bucolic southern Marin County. Evening rush-hour traffic was snaking its way up Highway 101, car after car filled with tired, hardworking, mask-carrying commuters inching their way back to Larkspur and Corte Madera, Mill Valley and Kentfield. Across the country, drivers in Chicago and Miami, Indianapolis and Philadelphia, Boston and Atlanta were doing the same thing. As they listened to their radios or talked to their loved ones, their thoughts likely ranged from their child's seventh-grade science project to dinner plans to what movie to check out for the weekend. The second to last thing on their minds was the subject of corporate integrity. In dead last place was the topic of insurance.

As I gazed at the Marin headlands, the deep blue sky and undulating sea stretched out for a hundred miles or more before my pensive eyes. The world I was gazing at was such a different place from the one I'd grown up in—not because of new gadgets or styles, not due to advances in technology or communications, but as a result of changes far more important, far more basic, far more revealing than any such trappings of progress.

I thought about something a lawyer friend had recently said to me—an insurance defense lawyer as a matter of fact. "When I was growing up," he said, "my grandfather cared a great deal about being successful. It meant a lot to him and he worked hard at it. It was a source of pride. It made him feel good about himself. He wanted to *be* somebody.

"But to him, integrity was everything. Honesty defined who and what he was all about. It was at the core of his very being. It made him the person he was. People looked up to him because of it. Everybody did.

"He would never have cheated anyone out of anything. He'd never have used tricks or excuses to rationalize destroying another person's life. To have done such a thing would have been an act of self-destruction. It would have been completely self-defeating. It would have stripped him of the very goal he was striving for–of what he was working so hard to achieve. It would have made him feel worthless. He wouldn't have felt like a hero, not to others and not to himself. No amount of money, no big payoff, would have changed that fact."

A huge cargo ship, bound, undoubtedly, for the Far East, made its way under the Golden Gate, toward the open ocean, past the stately mansions of Seacliff–homes housing the corporate barons of the Bay Area. These ten-thousand-square-foot, multimillion dollar residential prizes had housekeepers and servants, Rolls Royces and Chagalls. I used to wonder who lived in such houses, not just here but in counterpart mansions all over the county. Who were these people? What did they do?

I thought about Harold Chandler and his $17 million good-bye. I contrasted his confident, manicured image with thoughts about Joan and Susan, Gary and Margaret, Julie and Stuart, Michael and Laurie, and the countless others.

It's important for the people of a nation to feel a bond, a connection, a sense of unity–a sense of "we." We need to have the idea that despite all our daily struggles and challenges, we are still somehow bound together as part of a bigger, more important picture.

Somewhere along the line in our country, it seems that this notion got lost. Something in the very fabric of our society had changed, something in the ethical underpinnings that define who we are and what we are about as a people. It became common practice for successful business leaders to steal from customers, competitors, and employees–as long as the financial incentives were high enough. When this happened, everything changed.

The question is whether or not it can change back.

Exhibit 1

Hungry
Vultures...

Exhibit 2

Your Job Isn't Dangerous. You Make A Lot Of Money. So Why Should You Care About Disability Income Insurance?

Many professionals think that when it comes to getting seriously sick or injured, they just don't face the same dangers as people in blue collar jobs.

That's true.

The fact is, because you've invested so much to reach your present position—and are earning an impressive income—you stand to lose a *lot more* than they do if you can't work.

Think about it. If disability forces you off the job, how will you pay your bills? Will you be able to maintain your current lifestyle?

Will You Become Disabled?

CHANCES OF BECOMING DISABLED FOR THREE MONTHS OR LONGER BEFORE AGE 65

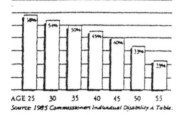

AGE 25   30   35   40   45   50   55
Source: 1985 Commissioners Individual Disability A Table.

As you can see, it's quite possible you'll become disabled. And if you do, it can take a long time to recover...

AVERAGE DURATION OF DISABILITY
WHICH LASTS OVER 90 DAYS:

At Age	Duration	At Age	Duration
25	2.1 years	45	3.2 years
30	2.5 years	50	3.1 years
35	2.8 years	55	2.6 years
40	3.1 years		

Source: 1980 Commissioners Ordinary Table.

Falling Income Plus Rising Expenses Equals Trouble.

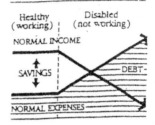

What You Stand To Lose.

Ever heard it said that your health is your wealth? How true it is...

YOUR POTENTIAL EARNINGS TO AGE 65.

AGE	ANNUAL INCOME				
	$24,000	$36,000	$48,000	$85,000	$200,000
30	840,000	1,260,000	1,680,000	2,975,000	7,000,000
35	720,000	1,080,000	1,440,000	2,550,000	6,000,000
40	600,000	900,000	1,200,000	2,125,000	5,000,000
45	480,000	720,000	960,000	1,700,000	4,000,000
50	360,000	540,000	720,000	1,275,000	3,000,000
55	240,000	360,000	480,000	850,000	2,000,000

Exhibit 3

SECURITIES AND EXCHANGE COMMISSION
Washington, D.C. 20549
FORM 10-K/A
AMENDMENT No. 1

ANNUAL REPORT PURSUANT TO SECTION 13 OR 15(d)
OF THE SECURITIES EXCHANGE ACT OF 1934

For the fiscal year ended December 31, 1993   Commission file number 000-19383

PROVIDENT LIFE AND ACCIDENT INSURANCE COMPANY OF AMERICA
(Exact name of registrant as specified in its charter)

Tennessee	62-1321664
(State or other jurisdiction of incorporation or organization)	(I.R.S. Employer Identification No.)

One Fountain Square Chattanooga, Tennessee	37402
(Address of principal executive offices)	(Zip Code)

Registrant's telephone number, including area code   (615) 755-1011
Securities registered pursuant to Section 12(b) of the Act: None
Securities registered pursuant to Section 12(g) of the Act:

Class A Common Stock, par value $1.00 per share
(Title of Class)

Class B Common Stock, par value $1.00 per share
(Title of Class)

8.10% Cumulative Preferred Stock, liquidation value $150 per share
(Title of Class)

Indicate by check mark whether the registrant (1) has filed all reports required to be filed by Section 13 or 15(d) of the Securities Exchange Act of 1934 during the preceding 12 months (or for such shorter period that the registrant was required to file such reports), and (2) has been subject to such filing requirements for the past 90 days.   Yes X No ___.

As of February 28, 1994, there were 8,547,066 shares of the registrant's Class A Common Stock, 36,725,585 shares of the registrant's Class B Common Stock, and 1,041,667 shares of the registrant's 8.10% Cumulative Preferred Stock outstanding. The aggregate market value of such shares based on the closing price of those shares on the New York Stock Exchange held by non-affiliates was approximately $94.4 million and $475.6 million respectively.

Selected material from the Annual Report to Stockholders for the year ended December 31, 1993 and Proxy Statement for the Annual Meeting of Stockholders scheduled for May 4, 1994, have been incorporated by reference into parts I, II, and III of this Form 10-K.

Indicate by check mark if disclosure of delinquent filers pursuant to Item 405 of Regulation S-K is not contained herein, and will not be contained, to the best of registrant's knowledge, in definitive proxy or information statements incorporated by reference in Part III of this Form 10-K or any amendment to this Form 10-K. [ ]

Total of sequentially numbered pages: 70
Index of Exhibits: Page 69

**Sales of group life insurance can vary from year to year depending on the number of groups to whom cases are sold, the size of the groups, the participation of employees in the plans, and the amounts of insurance provided and/or elected.

Disability Operations

Revenue in the Disability Operations segment increased 17.0 percent in 1993 to $862.1 million from $737.0 million in 1992. Premium income grew 12.1 percent to $617.3 million in 1993, resulting from higher premium levels in both the individual disability income line and group long-term disability line. In addition, net investment income was 31.1 percent higher in 1993, totaling $241.8 million compared to $184.4 million in 1992. Revenue in this segment was affected positively by the assumption of a block of individual disability income business from John Hancock Mutual Life Insurance Company effective August 1, 1992. This block generated $51.1 million of revenue in 1993.

In 1992, revenue grew 17.1 percent to $737.0 million, primarily due to higher levels of individual disability income premiums. Acquired blocks of individual disability income business boosted revenue in 1992. The block acquired from Provident Mutual Life Insurance Company on July 1, 1991 added $25.2 million in 1992, while the John Hancock block added $21.8 million in 1992.

During 1992, this segment experienced higher levels of claim payments and additions to reserves in the individual disability income business, as well as higher levels of claims in the group long-term disability business. Claim payments and reserves were higher in the individual disability income business in 1992 because of the general economic recession that affected white collar workers in greater numbers than was the case in other recent recessions, regional increases in claims for certain types of disabilities, and past competition for this product that resulted in underwriting and policy terms more liberal than those that exist today. As a result, income for the segment declined 28.8 percent in 1992 to $5.2 million from $7.3 million in 1991.

This segment reported a loss of $422.0 million in 1993 compared to income of $5.2 million in 1992. The loss was the result of a special charge of $423.0 million before-taxes taken in the third quarter of 1993, relating to the Company's block of individual disability income business. The special charge recorded the estimated future losses from this block of business and was required after the Company completed a loss recognition study as of September 30, 1993. This charge was recorded as an increase in "policy and contract benefits" and "change in reserves for future policy and contract benefits." The increase in reserves was required primarily as a result of a significant decline in interest rates and higher claim experience.

The Company considers its individual disability income business to be one block or line of business for purposes of conducting a loss recognition study. The individual disability income business is analyzed on an on-going basis to determine particular geographic areas, occupations, policy provisions, etc. which may be a factor in the results being experienced. Such reviews have shown that policies written for residents of California and south Florida are more likely to result in claims than those written in other areas of the United States or Canada. Additionally, policies written during the period 1983 through 1989 have a higher claim rate than those policies written before or after this time period. The Company, in intense competition with other companies in

6

this line of business during this time period, liberalized underwriting standards and policy provisions without a corresponding increase in premium rates to offset the increased risk undertaken. Since 1989, however, the Company has been strengthening its underwriting and policy provisions and adjusting the price on its new business written to reflect the risks in this product.

Because individual disability income policies are long-term contracts (with typical effective terms of five to forty years, depending upon the age of the insured at the time of issue), assumptions as to interest rates and morbidity, as well as expenses, lapse rates and other variables, used to price the product and to calculate policyholder liabilities during the term of the contracts, must be made with a long-term perspective. Fluctuations in actual experience from such assumptions are normal, especially since these assumptions are a long-term prediction of future events and conditions. These assumptions are long-term averages of the experience that the Company expects to realize over the duration of the policies and do not attempt to predict each short-term rise or decline in interest rates, morbidity, or other factors. Variations between actual experience and such long-term averages are monitored through a variety of on-going statistical studies. Such variations over a one or two year period do not necessarily indicate that a change in the long-term assumptions is necessary or that higher or lower reserves are required. Normally, such fluctuations between actual experience and assumed experience are included in income or loss in the current year. However, when these deviations occur in a magnitude and/or over a time period such that if they continued the sufficiency of reserves and the recoverability of deferred policy acquisition costs is questionable, it is prudent to perform a loss recognition study.

In a loss recognition study, the Company uses its best estimates as to future experience with regard to interest rates, morbidity rates, lapse rates, expenses and other factors to update its assumptions. These revised assumptions are then used to determine if reserves currently held plus the present value of future cash inflows (primarily from premiums and investment income) are projected to be sufficient to meet the present value of future cash outflows (primarily for benefits and expenses) and the amortization of deferred policy acquisition costs. If they are not sufficient, an additional provision must be recorded either as a reduction of deferred policy acquisition costs or as an increase in reserve liabilities.

While claims were higher and interest rates generally lower in 1991 than in previous years, at that time the Company believed these fluctuations to be short-term and acceptable variations from the assumptions underlying these long-term policies. However, in light of a continuing decline in interest rates and deterioration of morbidity experience during 1992, the Company began such a loss recognition study on its individual disability income business in December, 1992 to determine whether or not a loss recognition deficiency existed at December 31, 1992. An independent actuarial consulting firm was engaged to assist in the development of a gross premium valuation model appropriate to the Company's business, to review the reasonableness of the assumptions used by the Company at the time of the study, and to work with Company employees in the actual performance of the calculations. The loss recognition study completed in February, 1993 showed that no loss recognition deficiency existed at December 31, 1992, using the assumptions with respect to morbidity, interest rates, and expenses that reflected management's best estimates as of that date. Although there is always uncertainty as to the direction of future morbidity experience and interest rates, the Company believed the results of the study indicated that reserves were sufficient as of that date. The Company also believed at that time that, under its "most likely case" scenario, interest rates would rise in 1993 and morbidity rates would do no worse than remain at 1988-1992 levels.

Through the first half of 1993, however, the interest rates continued to decline, and the Company experienced further morbidity deterioration related to this business. As a result, reserves were increased during the first two quarters of 1993. Also, as part of its normal on-going reserve analysis, the Company performs several detailed actuarial studies, including measuring morbidity experience over a run-off period of several years. Increased claim activity experienced in the first two quarters of 1993 and studies performed in the second and third quarters of 1993, which reflected 1992 morbidity experience, caused management to revise its December 31, 1992 estimate of long-term morbidity rates. At the same time, the portfolio of assets related to this line of business experienced a significant decline in long-term interest rates combined with increased prepayment of fixed maturity securities, resulting in a significant decline in the portfolio's future investment returns. The yields on assets supporting the individual disability business declined to 9.32 percent at the end of the first quarter and to 9.17 percent at the end of the second quarter, compared to an aggregate yield of 9.57 percent at the end of 1992.

Because of these developments during the first half of 1993, the Company again evaluated the sufficiency of reserves and the recoverability of deferred policy acquisition costs. Although a loss recognition study had been scheduled for year-end 1993 as a follow-up to the study at December 31, 1992, the deviations between actual experience and assumptions were widening rapidly enough to warrant accelerating the study to the third quarter of 1993 to determine if reserves continued to be sufficient in light of these fluctuations.

The specific conditions that precipitated the third quarter 1993 loss recognition study were.

1   A sharp drop in interest rates as evidenced by the decline in the rate on 10-year U.S. Treasury Notes from 6.93 percent in December, 1992 to 5.23 percent in September, 1993. This drop of 170 basis points was a 25 percent decline in nine months.

2   Prepayment of many fixed maturity securities during this nine-month period, brought about primarily by the lower interest rate levels, caused the yield on the portfolio supporting the individual disability income business to decline 59 basis points in only nine months.

3   Morbidity studies covering the first and second quarters of 1993 reflected further deterioration in morbidity experience during this part of 1993 compared with previous morbidity experience.

The September 30, 1993 loss recognition study followed the same principles as the study performed as of December 31, 1992. The independent actuarial consulting firm, which assisted in conducting the December 31, 1992 study, served in a review capacity (rather than as an active participant) in the performance of the study. Based upon the revised assumptions, which represented management's best estimates at the time of the study, a loss recognition deficiency of $423.0 million on a pre-tax basis was required to be recognized under generally accepted accounting principles. Management believes that the required charge taken in the third quarter was a prompt and appropriate response to these previously unforeseen changes.

8

The following table shows the portfolio yield interest rate assumptions used in the December 31, 1992 and September 30, 1993 loss recognition studies. The interest rate assumptions in each of the loss recognition studies represented management's best estimates at the time the studies were performed.

	December 31, 1992	September 30, 1993
1993	9 38%	
1994	9.33	8 57%
1995	9 27	8 46
1996	9 24	8 43
1997	9 21	8 45
1998	9 18	8 42
1999	9 16	8.31
2000	9 14	8.23
Ultimate	8 92	7 13
Equivalent Level Rate	9 27	7 91

Interest rates at which new money was invested for the individual disability income business for the year 1992 and the first nine months of 1993 were 8 82 percent and 7 59 percent, respectively. The overall portfolio yields for invested assets supporting the individual disability income business were 9 57 percent and 8 98 percent as of December 31, 1992 and September 30, 1993, respectively. The September 30, 1993 loss recognition study projected that morbidity would improve as a result of improved claim handling procedures (consisting of centralization of the claim paying function in the home office and the availability of additional technical resources), the effects of anti-selection wearing off over time, and general improvement in the economy.

In performing a loss recognition study the Company is required to use its best estimates with regard to assumptions used in the calculation. Using "best estimates" means that no provision for adverse deviation is included in the assumptions and the expectation is for a break-even outcome, that is, there is about an even chance that experience will be better than or worse than the assumptions. If future experience conforms to assumptions used in the loss recognition study, no gain or loss would be expected from the line of business other than (i) investment income relative to the capital and surplus allocated to that line, and (ii) profit from new individual disability income policies. If actual experience in a future period is worse than assumed and is expected to continue, an additional loss would have to be recognized. If actual experience is better than assumed, the resulting gain will be recognized over future years as it is actually realized.

On a pre-tax basis, approximately 51 percent of the difference between the results of the December 31, 1992 and September 30, 1993 loss recognition studies related to the effects of rapidly declining interest rates during 1993, including prepayment of fixed maturity securities as well as lower portfolio yields on both new and reinvested money. Approximately 26 percent of the difference related to higher morbidity costs and the associated claim administration expenses. Approximately 11 percent of the difference was related to the inclusion in the September 30, 1993 loss recognition study of guaranteed increases in coverage on existing policies. The remaining amount was primarily attributable to differences in assumptions with respect to expenses, other than claim administration expenses, and to persistency.

9

Exhibit 4

Provident Internal Memorandum

To: Harold Chandler

From: Ralph Mohney

Date: May 22, 1995

Re: Revised 1995 Budget - Individual Disability Claims

To support our vision of becoming the "best in industry" individual disability claim operation, a number of claim improvement initiatives have been identified and are currently being implemented.

Broadly, these initiatives (summarized in Attachment 1) are designed to move Provident from a claim payment to a claim management approach. The keys to this transition are (1) more intensive claim investigation and (2) skill development to maximize effectiveness. While developed internally, these initiatives have been validated and are supported by the LeBoeuf review.

Due to the significant financial leverage associated with individual disability claims, the return on these claim improvement initiatives is expected to be substantial. A 1% decrease in benefit costs due to more effective claim management translates to approximately $6 million in annual savings. We believe that aggregate improvements in the 5% - 10% ($30 million - $60 million annually) range are possible - once the initiatives have been fully implemented. This range of potential savings is consistent with the recently completed Tillinghast study.

However, to achieve these results, significant investment will be required. Attachment 2 summarizes expense and manpower requirements associated with our recently revised 1995 budget. As shown in the attachment, 1995 expense is projected to grow 13% ($1.3 million) over the original 1995 budget and 57% ($3.8 million) over actual 1994 expense - on a comparable basis.

The substantial increase in expense is driven predominately by higher staffing levels. Compared to the original 1995 budget, staffing is up 41 positions. Attachment 3 provides a breakdown of the staffing changes.

This memorandum represents a request for formal approval of the manpower and expense additions necessary to fully implement our claim improvement initiatives. We believe that these additions are necessary and in the best interests of the company.

Achievement of our "best in industry" vision is inherently a long term proposition. However, it begins with continued support for our claim initiatives. We are convinced that these initiatives will far exceed the costs - even during 1995.

Please let me know what additional information is needed.

RWMair

cc: Tom Heys
    Al Morales

Exhibit 5

The IME

REASONS TO ORDER ONE

- TO CHALLENGE THE IMPAIRMENT/DISABILITY FINDINGS

- TO RULE OUT OR IDENTIFY OTHER TREATABLE PROBLEMS WHICH COULD EXPLAIN THE IMPAIRMENT, AND IF TREATED, WOULD REMOVE THE IMPAIRMENT

- TO CONFIRM THAT THERE IS IMPAIRMENT, THUS AVOIDING UNNECESSARY ADDITIONAL CLAIM COSTS, ALLOWING CONSIDERATION OF A VOCATIONAL SPECIALIST TO ASSIST, OR OPENING THE DOOR FOR CLAIM SETTLEMENT

WHEN TO ORDER AN IME

- EARLY IN THE CLAIM OR BEFORE THE CLAIM IS ACCEPTED OR AT ANY POINT THE IMPAIRMENTS ARE QUESTIONED

- AT A POINT IN THE CLAIM WHERE THERE IS A QUESTION OF IMPROPER CARE BEING ORDERED

DRAWBACKS TO THE IME

- UNEXPECTED IMPAIRMENTS ARE IDENTIFIED

- THE QUALITY IS POOR

- THE IME DOCTOR PROVIDES UNSOLICITED, DAMAGING INFORMATION

- IT IS AN UNNECESSARY CLAIM COST AS THE RATIONALE FOR ORDERING IT WAS NOT FULLY EVALUATED IN ADVANCE AND CORRECT QUESTIONS WERE NOT CREATED

- THE IME WAS NOT HANDLED WELL ONCE RECEIVED... IT SAT IN THE FILE

WHEN NOT TO ORDER AN IME

- WHEN THERE IS NO EXPERT

- WHEN THE FACT GATHERING IS NOT COMPLETE   IME

Exhibit 6

May 21, 1999

Dr. Joan Hangarter

Claim #01-02424291-003
   #01-02140404-003
   #01-02424292-003

Dear Dr. Hangarter:

Thank you for the courtesies that you extended to our Field Claim Representative, Mr. Ken Seaman, during his recent visit. We have received his report and are writing this letter as a follow-up to his visit.

Dr. Hangarter, you are claiming Total Disability as of July 4, 1997. The conditions listed on your most recent Progress Report are, "lateral epicondylitis, IVD Cervical spine, chronic traumatic arm strain". You have indicated that you are unable to treat patients as a result of your conditions.

Your file was first reviewed by our in-house orthopedic consultant, Dr. John Bianchi, on December 10, 1997. At that time, Dr. Bianchi felt that your conditions would have resolved or improved and that you should be able to return to work. Dr. Bianchi recommended an Independent Medical Examination, if the claim continued.

As we advised you in our December 8, 1998 letter, your file was again reviewed by Dr. Bianchi. This review took place on December 2, 1998. Dr. Bianchi stated, "Difficult to assess any significant limitations bases (based) on available medical reports." In addition, "Last reviewed 12-10-97 and felt that her neck pain, lateral epicondylitis, and partial rotator cuff tear should reasonably be expected to resolve with conservative treatment over time. M.R.I. of the cervical spine was normal." Dr. Bianchi recommended an Independent Medical Examination.

When we wrote to you on December 8, 1998, in addition to advising you of the recent medical review, we requested an "Occupational Description" form to clarify your current duties at your business. You indicated on this form that you were working 6-8 hours a week at your business. You indicated that your duties included meeting with staff, paying bills, payroll, and problem solving. You also indicated, "performance of my job as a chiropractor has been restricted. Have not been able to treat patients."

3

As you may recall, you first met with our Field Claim Representative, Mr. Ken Seaman, on May 27, 1998. You advised Mr. Seaman that you continued to work 20 to 30 hours a week in your office at that time.

Your file was again referred to Mr. Seaman, on February 19, 1999. The purpose of this referral, in part, was to further clarify your current occupational duties. During your meeting, you confirmed that your current duties are the same duties that you had prior to claim, but you indicated that you are no longer able to treat patients. In addition, you advised Mr. Seaman that in some months you do take a draw from your business of between $300 and $1000. You indicated, however, that you felt you would still qualify for Total Disability benefits.

We then received the report of the Independent Medical Examination that you attended with Dr. Aubrey A. Swartz on March 11, 1999. Dr. Swartz indicated, "There were no valid objective findings in my examination to support Dr. Hangarter's subjective report of pain or impairment." In addition, "I am unable to find impairment with respect to Dr. Hangarter's ability to provide chiropractic care. Dr. Hangarter claims that she would not be able to perform manipulative or adjustment procedures on more than two patients per day. Dr. Hangarter would be capable of providing full chiropractic treatment techniques to at least two patients per hour, or one every 30 minutes, over an 8-hour day."

The Independent Medical Examination was then reviewed by Dr. Bianchi on March 26, 1999. Dr. Bianchi indicated that he agreed with the assessment of the Independent Medical Examination regarding your ability to return to work.

As a courtesy, we will forward a copy of the Independent Medical Examination to your attending physician, Dr. Berry. This will be done in the near future.

Policy #01-02424291, which is your Disability Income policy, contains a Total Disability benefit. This policy states, "'Total Disability' means that because of Injury or Sickness:

    a. You are unable to perform the important duties of Your Occupation; and

    b. You are not engaged in any other gainful occupation; and

    c. You are under the regular and personal care of a Physician."

This policy also contains a Residual Disability benefit. "'Residual Disability', prior to the Commencement Date, means that due to Injury or Sickness:

a. (1) You are unable to perform one or more of the important duties of Your Occupation; or

(2) You are unable to perform the important duties of Your Occupation for more than 80% of the time normally required to perform them; and

b. Your Loss of Earnings is equal to at least 20% of Your Prior Earnings while You are engaged in Your Occupation or another occupation; and

c. You are under the regular and personal care of a Physician.

As of the Commencement Date, Residual Disability means that due to the continuation of that Injury or Sickness:

a. Your Loss of Earnings is equal to at least 20% of Your Prior Earnings while You are engaged in Your Occupation or another occupation; and

b. You are under the regular and personal care of a Physician.

Residual Disability must follow right after a period of Total Disability that lasts at least as long as the Qualification Period, if any."

Policy #01-02424292 is one of your Business Overhead Expense policies. This policy states, "'Total Disability' means that because of Injury or Sickness:

a. You are unable to perform the important duties of Your Occupation; and

b. You are under the regular and personal care of a Physician."

This policy also contains a Partial Disability benefit. This benefit states, "'Partial Disability' means that because of Injury or Sickness:

a. You are:

(1) Unable to perform one or more of the important duties of Your Occupation; or

(2) Unable to perform the important duties of Your Occupation for more than 80% of the time normally required to perform them; and

b. You are under the regular and personal care of a Physician.

Partial Disability must follow right after a period of Total Disability for which benefits were payable."

Based on all of the information currently in your file, it does not appear that you would be Totally Disabled under the terms of your contracts. As such, we are unable to consider additional Total Disability benefits at this time.

We would also like to remind you that the definition of Total Disability under your Disability Income policy states, in part, "You are not engaged in any other gainful occupation;" As we stated above, it appears that you continued to work in your business and did take a draw from the business. Therefore, regardless of the extent of your impairment, you would not qualify for Total Disability benefits, under the terms of this contract.

As you may recall, you again met with our Field Claim Representative, Mr. Ken Seaman, on April 30, 1999. Mr. Seaman met with you to provide our position regarding your claims. At that time, you advised that you have now sold your business.

Since you have now sold your business, and are not working, you would not qualify for additional Overhead Expense benefits under Claim #01-02424292-003, nor would you qualify for Residual Disability benefits under Claim #01-02424291-003. Once again, this is regardless of the extent of your impairment.

Policy #01-02140404 is your other Business Overhead Expense policy. This policy has a maximum benefit period of 15 months or a maximum total benefit of $90,000. As you know, as of December 1, 1998, we paid the maximum total benefit of $90,000 under Claim #01-02140404-003.

Although we have had ongoing concerns about the extent of your impairment, we have provided a total of $146,700 in benefits under claim #01-02424291-003, a total of $90,000 under #01-02140404-003 and a total of $100,808.15 under #01-02424292-003. This was done in good faith, in an effort to be of financial assistance to you, while we continued to assess the extent of your impairment.

It appears that your policy coverage is governed by the Employee Retirement Income Security Act ("ERISA"). Accordingly, if you disagree with our determination you may submit an appeal which must be in writing and accompanied by any records, tests, reports, or documents that you feel support your claim for benefits.

Your appeal must be received by this office within 90 days of the date of this correspondence. Your appeal period can be extended for a valid reason if you write to us requesting the extension and informing us of the reasons for the extension within the initial 90 day appeal period.

Section 2695.7 (b)(3) of the California Fair Claims Settlement Practices Regulations requires that our company advise you that if you believe your claim has been wrongfully denied or rejected, you may have the matter reviewed by the California Department of Insurance at:

> California Department of Insurance Claims Services Bureau
> 300 South Spring Street, 11th Floor
> Los Angeles, CA 90013
> (800)927-4357 or (213)897-8921

If you should have any questions, please do not hesitate to contact us.

> Very truly yours,

> Joseph F. Sullivan, ALHC
> Senior Claim Representative
> The Paul Revere Life Insurance Company

JFS
cc 193-69556

Exhibit 7

PRIVILEGED

Provident Internal Memorandum

To: *IDC Management Group*
Glenn Felton

From: *Jeff McCall*

Date: *October 2, 1995*

Re: *ERISA*

A task force has recently been established to promote the identification of policies covered by ERISA and to initiate active measures to get new and existing policies covered by ERISA. The advantages of ERISA coverage in litigious situations are enormous: state law is preempted by federal law, there are no jury trials, there are no compensatory or punitive damages, relief is usually limited to the amount of benefit in question, and claims administrators may receive a deferential standard of review. The economic impact on Provident from having policies covered by ERISA could be significant. As an example, Glenn Felton identified 12 claim situations where we settled for $7.8 million in the aggregate. If these 12 cases had been covered by ERISA, our liability would have been between zero and $0.5 million.

In order to take advantage of ERISA protection, we need to be diligent and thorough in determining whether a policy is covered. Accordingly, I have attached a rough draft of questions that should be asked in our claim investigation process. I recommend that it be used for all claims. The key for determining the applicability of ERISA is whether or not the employer "sponsors" or "endorses" the plan. If the employer pays the premium, the policy would usually, but not always, be considered to be governed by ERISA. Salary allotment or payroll deduction arrangements, by themselves, do not necessarily mean that a policy is subject to ERISA. While our objective is to pay all valid claims and deny invalid claims, there are gray areas, and ERISA applicability may influence our course of action.

Another requirement needed in order to take advantage of the protection offered by ERISA, is to establish a formal appeal process for ERISA situations. When we deny a claim, we must include language in our letter that informs the claimant of the right to appeal our decision within 60 days. I have attached a copy of sample language. The appeal must be in writing and should be reviewed by a panel specifically established to review ERISA appeals. I recommend that the panel be composed of Chris Kinback, Bob Parks, Becky Absher, Tom Timpanaro and me.

We will be modifying the salary allotment agreements used at the point of sale to include endorsement language.

I am interested in any comments or feedback you may have on this issue.

JM:ajr

Exhibit 8

FILE COPY

To: Tom Heys

From: Ralph Mohney

Date: April 17, 1996

Re: Individual Disability Claims - Monthly Report

Claim Results

As reflected in the attached Exhibit I, claim results were highly favorable in March. New claims moderated, reopens remained low and terminations reached a surprisingly high level.

Strong results in March largely offset the unfavorable results in January and February. Exhibit II compares first quarter 1996 results with the previous four quarters. First quarter results are shown both before reserve factor changes (to allow comparison with the previous four quarters) and after reserve factor changes.

On a before factor change basis:

- New claims of $126.6 million were $10.7 million (9.2%) above the previous four quarter average. Higher claim size (due principally to larger monthly indemnities) accounted for the increase, as the number of claims grew less than one percent. Exhibit V reflects a profile of new claims for 1996 vs. 1995.

- Re-opens totaled $28.0 million down $8.8 million (23.9%) from the previous four quarter average. As a percentage of terminations, first quarter re-opens were 19% compared to 28% in 1995. The improvement in re-open ratio reflects a higher quality of claim terminations.

- Terminations reached the second highest level ever at $147.2 million, up $15.1 million (11.4%) from the previous four quarter average. While terminations were down slightly from the fourth quarter of 1995, it was expected that the low level of new claims in the fourth quarter of 1995 would translate (after an approximately three month lag) to lower termination levels in the first quarter.

- Before factor changes, the tabular change moderated somewhat from the fourth quarter level but remained $4.4 million (7.4%) above the previous four month average. After factor changes, the tabular change decreased sharply.

Overall, we are highly pleased with first quarter results. Before factor changes, the net termination ratio (terminations minus re-opens divided by new claims) reached 94% compared to 47% in the first quarter of 1995 and 82% for the entire year of 1995. When applied to first quarter new claims, the twelve percentage point improvement in net termination ratio from the 1995 average, translates to $15.9 million of lower reserves for the quarter. This result demonstrates that the investments in claim effectiveness over the last eighteen months are beginning to pay substantial dividends.

637

Exhibit 9

Provident Internal Memorandum

To: Tom Heys

From: Ralph Monney

Date: November 7, 1995

Re: Individual Disability Claims - Monthly Report

Claim Results

As reflected in the attached Exhibit I, claim results were highly favorable in October:

- New claims dropped to $34.1 million - the lowest level this year and 11% below the previous twelve month average. Smaller monthly indemnities were responsible for the decline as the number of new claims remained stable.

- Reopens increased for the second consecutive month reaching $14.7 million - 29% above the previous twelve month average. We have asked Internal Audit to review claims reopening in September and October in an attempt to gain better insights into the causes of reopens. Preliminary findings are expected by the end of this week.

- Termination's reached $45.1 million - the highest level ever for non-scrub months and 9% above the average of the previous twelve months. Both the number and size of terminations were high - particularly for the first month in a quarter.

- The tabular change moderated somewhat at $21.3 million but remained 16% above the average of the previous twelve months.

Aggregate October results are the best of any non-scrub month since January 1994. These results as well as expected lower than normal new claims in November and December (due to seasonality) bode well for fourth quarter results. At this early stage, it is reasonable to expect aggregate results comparable to the second quarter.

Key Activities

The attached Exhibit II summarizes activities related to our claim improvement initiatives since our last report.

During an off-site planning retreat in October, the objectives and action items associated with our "Top 10" initiatives were reviewed and updated. By year-end we expect that four of the ten initiatives will have been substantially accomplished:

- Effectively manage MNDA claims.
- Audit financial aspects of Residual claims.
- Increase staffing.
- Introduce rehabilitation capabilities.

551

Exhibit 10

Memo

To: Ralph Mohney
From: Steve Harmon
Date: July 14, 1995
Re: "Institutionalizing the Scrub"

The Northern Unit met on Thursday, July 13, 1995 to brainstorm ideas that will insure we are effectively managing our claims. Based on our meeting, we have agreed to institute the following procedures on a permanent basis immediately:

1. "Top 10 List" -- Each adjuster will maintain a list of ten claimants where intensive effort will lead to successful resolution of the claim. As one name drops off, another name will be added.

2. Vocational Rehabilitation Resources -- Each adjuster will identify 3 files per quarter to refer to Rehab. Issues concerning the file can range anywhere from assistance with occupational analysis to full rehabilitation of the claimant into another occupation. If three good opportunities are not present though, this standard can be relaxed somewhat. We're looking for quality here, not quantity.

3. Identification of Files for the Special Handling Unit -- Instituting this step in our procedures will free up more time and resources to devote to claims in the investigative stage. Consultants will be signing off on any file prior to shipment to review for settlement possibilities.

4. List of All Claims in Investigative Stage -- Each adjuster will maintaining a list of all claims on their CICS system where the first payment has not been paid. Periodic review of the list will insure that we are moving the investigation along. This will not only lead to quicker claim resolution, but also provide the claimant better service.

5. Field Referrals -- A minimum of 10 files will be referred to the field per month. This number can be less or more based on the volume of new claims. Again, we want quality field referrals, not quantity. With the number of new claims in our Unit though, reaching the minimum should be no problem.

6. Claims Over 2 Years Old -- Each adjuster will do an in-depth review of 2 files per week in this category of claims. As issues surface, the adjuster will work with the consultant to find resolutions.

01032

GSCONF 41.1

7. Claims Reaching the 6-Month Mark -- Using the attached audit worksheet, each adjuster will review their claims six months from the date of disability. Why let Quality Assurance have all the fun?

8. Roundtable Discussions -- Based on the auditing efforts of #6 and #7, each adjuster will identify two files per quarter for this forum. The adjuster will then work with the consultant to develop the issues and actions for the case.

9. Lists -- Periodically, we will request lists from Systems to review certain categories of claims. These can be coding error lists, over 60-day lists, impairment code lists, etc.

While the above actions will increase workloads somewhat initially, everybody in attendance at our meeting agreed that their efforts will be more than compensated by spreading the work over the entire period rather than the third month of the quarter. Of course, if additional effort at quarter end is needed, we are more than equal to the task.

abs/SH

cc: Steve Korshoff
          Paul Douglass
          Andrea Barrett
          Roger Coulter
          Anne Davis
          Joy Gaston
          Judy Hahn
          Cindy Garland
          Pam Killough
          Kim Simmons
          Clayton Smith
          Charlene Stamey
          Anne Talley
          Dolly Vinci

GSCONF 41.2

Exhibit 11

Outline for "INFORMATION MANAGEMENT"

(Presented by the Law Department of Provident Life & Accident Insurance Co.)

Protecting your Company's confidential information and following Company guidelines for document retention is an important part of your job. The Company's success in managing legal and business information depends in part on how you and others handle or manage this information. Doing your part means following three simple rules:

(1) Think before you speak or write;

(2) Keep private documents and conversations private; and

(3) Follow your Department's document retention and destruction rules.

These rules and some of the other important points illustrated by the video are summarized in this outline.

I. <u>Think Before you Speak or Write.</u>

A. Answer three questions before speaking or writing about sensitive or confidential Company information.

1. Is the information private?

2. Does the person I'm speaking or writing to <u>need</u> to know it?

3. By disclosing it, am I putting the Company at risk legally or financially?

B. Make it a habit to weigh your words carefully <u>before</u> you write or speak and trim out the incautious language when you revise.

1. Do not confuse facts and your opinions. Facts are what people usually want to hear. Uninvited opinions and "off the cuff" remarks should be kept out of print.

2. Be clear and precise, and do not make sweeping generalizations or exaggerate for effect.

3. Imagine how your words would sound to an "outsider" in the event your communication is later brought up in court.

4. For matters that are especially sensitive or confidential, consider conducting most of your communication in person, not on paper. If you do write something that's sensitive, be cautious. Say only what's necessary, and copy only those who need to know.

C. If you are dealing with a legal issue, get some legal advice before you write, -- that's what the Company attorneys are here for. <u>Do not conduct your own legal investigations.</u>

1. If a task-force is organized for the issue you're dealing with, include one of the Company attorneys.

GSCONF 3920

2. Any memo announcing a legal investigation should come from the Law Department or a high level manager following consultation with the Law Department. The memo should be sent only to those employees who need to be involved and should remind them of the need to keep it and all matters concerning the investigation confidential.

3. Any status memos, non-attorney notes, or other documents generated during a legal investigation should be retained by or as instructed by the Law Department. Copies should not be retained unless you are otherwise informed.

D. In a nutshell, when you're writing for the Company or about the Company, keep it straight, keep it right -- and, most importantly, keep it ethical - keep it legal!

II. Keep Private Documents and Conversations Private.

A. If your communications about Company legal matters have been discussed only with attorneys and other Company personnel with a need to know, then you have the right to keep these communications private (and to avoid having to testify about them in court).

B. You and the Company may lose this right if the communications are disclosed to persons inside or outside the Company who do not have a legal need to know.

C. Company information should be protected just as any other type of Company property.

1. Do not give out confidential document identification numbers or computer passwords.

2. Do not leave computer workstations logged on and unattended.

3. Take steps to avoid eavesdropping situations with speakerphones, open doors, conversations in hallways and other public places.

4. Do not leave sensitive documents on desks or in plain view.

5. See that any visitors to your Department are properly escorted.

6. When a sensitive legal document is sent to you, do not copy it, post it on a bulletin board, forward it to others, or otherwise discuss it's contents without first getting clearance from the Law Department. After getting clearance, make sure the documents are marked "Privileged and Confidential" if appropriate.

7. Use the "Mark-Message-Private" and Special Delivery features of PhoneMail for confidential messages.

8. Avoid sending written memos about sensitive subjects when a phone call or face-to-face discussion will suffice.

9. Shred all sensitive papers that will not be needed for business purposes. Generally, when copies of certain legal type documents are sent to you for informational purposes only, these documents should be shredded after you have read them. These may include:

a) documents prepared for lawsuits, and reports of investigations or legal audits;

b) memos, responses or reports from the Law Department involving actual facts about Company business or legal situations;

c) Any copies of legal document drafts, especially when the drafts contain handwritten notes or comments in the margins (these documents should be kept by the Law Department).

III. Follow Your Department's Document Retention and Destruction Rules.

A. Learn the document retention and destruction requirements for your own area. If you do not know, ask your manager. You should also review the attached memo from the Records Management Department titled "RECORDS AND INFORMATION MANAGEMENT - a Policy Statement" for additional information about records retention matters.

B. Retain only those documents needed for operations, legal compliance, and official archives.

C. When finished with a project, destroy temporary drafts, reminder notes, worksheets, personal memos, duplicate copies and the like.

D. Set up a plan for managing your own records. At least once each year you should identify important records to be retained and properly destroy the rest.

E. When documents are due to be destroyed, usually after retaining them for seven years for legal purposes, go ahead and destroy them! Do not be a "pack rat" who saves them "just in case."

F. Destroy chronological files or series of old, unnecessary documents wholesale instead of selectively purging "unfavorable" documents and creating suspicious "gaps in the record."

G. Do not forget computer records! They should be saved or destroyed according to the same principles as paper records.

H. Do not print SYSM messages unless they contain information needed in the file.

I. And last, but not least, if you get a legal directive to suspend your regular document destruction program, take it seriously! Such directives are usually a sign that legal action is on the horizon. It is important to follow instructions in these situations. In fact, if you are in doubt about any of the legal aspects of document retention, check first with the Law Department.

Conclusion: This video and outline have covered many situations and rules. No one can be expected to memorize all of these points, so we hope that this handout will serve as a useful reference and reminder. More importantly, we hope both the video and outline will help you recognize situations where you can better protect the Company's confidential information. If you have questions concerning a particular situation, please contact the Law Department.

RCA\1210a01

GSCONF 3922

Exhibit 12

20 Reasons Why Paul Revere,
A National Leader In The Disability Income Industry,
Is Best For You . . . The Preferred Professional

1. Your coverage is non-cancellable and guaranteed continuable to age 65 — as long as the premium is paid on time, we cannot change your policy or its premium rate until the first premium due date after your 65th birthday.

2. If you continue to be actively and regularly employed on a full-time basis beyond age 65, you have the option to continue your coverage for life at the Company's then applicable premium rate. The maximum benefit period will be 24 months to age 75 and 12 months thereafter.

3. You have the option when you cease to be employed after age 65 to continue the policy for your lifetime as a "hospital confinement" benefit of $100 per day for up to 6 months per disability.

4. Ten-day free look after receipt of your policy.

5. Preferred definitions of injury and sickness:
    — "accidental bodily injury"
    — "sickness which first manifests itself while the policy is in force"

6. Covered in "your occupation" for the maximum benefit period you select — when total disability occurs you are protected in your occupation. It is your election whether to work or not in another occupation.

7. Residual Disability Benefits are paid on a proportionate basis for the benefit period selected if you go back to work so long as prior to age 65 you:

    — satisfy the qualification period, if any
    — have a 20% or more loss in earnings due to your injury or sickness
    — are under the regular and personal care of a physician
    — are unable to perform one or more important duties or cannot work for more than 80% of the normal time. However, no "time or duties" loss is required once the elimination period has been satisfied

    And, if your earnings are 20% or less of prior earnings we will pay the Total Disability benefit.

    During the first six months of a Residual Disability, each monthly benefit will not be less than 50% of your benefit for Total Disability.

8. Recovery Benefit — This benefit allows you to return to work on a full-time basis and still receive benefits. If you received total or residual disability benefits and continue to suffer an income loss of at least 20%, we will pay a proportionate benefit for up to four months. No physician's care required.

9. Favorable Prior Earnings Definition for computation of Residual or Recovery Benefits. You have the choice of (a) your average monthly earnings for the six months prior to disability, or (b) your highest average monthly earnings for any two consecutive years out of the last five

    An inflation adjustment will be made to your Prior Earnings after each year of continuing disability. We will increase your Prior Earnings by the annual compounded changes in the Consumer Price Index, but not less than 7% (simple rate) of Prior Earnings, regardless of the CPI.

10. Automatic Increase Benefit — This built-in feature provides automatic increases to your monthly benefit each year, for a five year term. You can choose up to a 5% (simple) annual increase. At the end of each term, if you are under age 60, you can apply for additional automatic increases.

2

GLOSSARY

adjuster–A representative of an insurance company who handles claims. The adjuster can be either an employee of the insurance company or an outside representative hired by the company. The adjuster is never a representative of the policyholder. Adjusters must always follow the procedures and directives of the company.

agent–A person or organization licensed to sell insurance for an insurance company. The two basic types of agents are captive and independent. Captive agents work for and sell the policies of one insurance company only. Independent agents may work with and sell policies for many different insurance companies.

alternative dispute resolution (ADR)–A method of resolving disputes between a policyholder and the insurance company without going to court. An ADR provision in a policy may require appraisal, mediation, or arbitration. Although ADR can be cheaper and faster than filing a lawsuit, ADR provisions are always written by the insurance company and therefore favor its interests. Virtually all ADR provisions require the insured to waive, or give up, important legal rights.

anastomosis–A natural communication between two blood vessels or other tabular structures.

arbitration–A proceeding whereby a supposedly neutral third party is empowered to decide disputes between a policyholder and the insurance company. Arbitration provisions are usually created within the terms of a contract–such as an insurance policy. Depending on the procedure set forth in the policy, arbitration can be either binding or nonbinding. Binding arbitration decisions are usually not appealable.

bad faith–"Unreasonable" or "unfair" conduct. Where an insurance company has acted in bad faith in denying an insurance claim, the claimant (depending on the state in which he or she lives) may be able to take steps to recover compensation for the damages he or she was caused as a result of the insurer's conduct.

broker–A licensed person hired by a policyholder to look for insurance on the policyholder's behalf. A broker is usually considered the representative of the policyholder.

cancellation–The termination of insurance coverage during the policy period. A policyholder can cancel the insurance policy at any time. The insurance company can cancel the policy only if the policyholder made a material misrepresentation or failed to pay the premiums.

chart review–A review of the clinical data relating to a patient's case.

claim–A request to the insurance company for the payment of benefits payable under an insurance policy.

claimant–A person who makes the claim on an insurance policy.

COLA–Cost of living adjustment. Provisions in the policy that raise benefits to keep pace with inflation. COLAs can vary widely. Read the fine print very carefully.

conditions–Terms that set forth what the policyholder must do in the event of a loss. For example, the claimant must give prompt notice of a loss and file certain documents if asked to do so.

cooperation clause–A clause in an insurance contract that states the policyholder's duty to cooperate with the insurance company concerning a claim. The policyholder should return phone calls, appear at appointments, answer questions related to a claim, and provide information necessary to investigate a claim. Breaching the duty to cooperate can provide a carrier with a basis for the denial of a claim.

coverage–The portion of a policy that explains what types of losses are insured by the policy.

coverage opinion–The opinion of an insurance lawyer, usually given to an insurance company, concerning the proper interpretation or meaning of provisions in an insurance policy. A coverage opinion is usually sought when the company is considering whether to deny a claim or not. Coverage opinions are not always correct.

declarations–A section of a policy that usually contains information concerning the various types and amounts of the benefits provided, the premiums to be charged, and other similar information.

declaratory relief–A lawsuit filed by an insurance company against its policyholder that seeks a court decision about coverage.

deductible–The amount of the loss that the policyholder must pay before the insurance company is obligated to pay benefits.

definitions section–The section of an insurance policy that defines certain words and phrases used in the policy. The insurance company is bound by these definitions, and any ambiguity must be interpreted in the policyholder's favor.

delinquency–The failure of a policyholder to make a premium payment on time.

disability insurance–Coverage that provides benefits if an insured should become unable to work because of a sickness or injury covered by the policy.

discounts–Ways to reduce your premium payments. For example, insurance companies may offer discounts on automobile insurance for good drivers, senior citizens, safety features, antitheft features, good grades, or carpooling.

effective date–The date coverage under the insurance policy commences. Generally, the policy goes into effect when it is delivered to the policyholder. However, the insurance company may agree to cover the policyholder while the policy is being written.

endorsements–Extra paragraphs or pages added to a policy to increase or reduce the coverage. Endorsements are often referred to as "riders."

ERISA–The Employment Retirement Income Security Act. A law passed by Congress to protect working people that has since been twisted into having the opposite effect. Watch out for "ERISA-preempted" policies. These policies are provided through employers. Under such policies, policyholders have virtually no rights or leverage against unscrupulous or fraudulent conduct.

examination under oath–An interrogation by an insurance company lawyer, with a court reporter transcribing everything that is said, usually takes place when a claim is being disputed by the insurance company.

exclusions–That portion of a policy explaining the causes and conditions of loss for which the insurance company does not have to pay for damage or injury.

expiration date–The date the insurance policy ends.

incontestability clause–A policy provision in which the company has agreed not to contest the validity of the contract after it has been in force for a certain period of time, usually two or three years.

indemnity–(1) A security against loss or damage. (2) The obligation or duty resting on one person to make good any loss or damage another has incurred or may incur by acting on one's request or for his or her benefit. (3) The right that the person suffering the loss or damage is entitled to claim. (4) An assurance or contract by one party to compensate for the damage caused by another. (5) Reference to a total shifting of the economic loss to the party chiefly or primarily responsible for that loss.

independent medical examination (IME)–Also called an insurance medical evaluation, the examination of a claimant by a doctor of the insurance company's choosing, who comments on the insured's disability.

insurance contract–A contract between the policyholder and the insurance company stating the terms and conditions of coverage. Generally, the policyholder agrees to pay a fee in return for protection against risks associated with either owning a home, owning or driving an automobile, or owning a business. In addition, the policyholder may obtain insurance to pay for expenses if the policyholder becomes ill or disabled.

insureds or additional insureds–The people or entities covered under a policy, such as residents of a household or children away at school. It is often possible to add specific people as insureds.

investigator–A person hired by an insurance company to determine the facts surrounding a claim. Investigators may take surveillance videos from behind trees and from inside darkened vans, record conversations, contact former spouses and disgruntled former colleagues, and otherwise search for "interesting" information.

iontophoresis–Therapy that uses a local electric current to introduce medicine into tissues; used as a means of getting medicine into tissues without injecting it.

Jamar dynamometer test–A test to assess gripping strength.

lapse–A termination of coverage that occurs when the policyholder fails to pay premiums. If the premium payment is late, the insurance company may decide to reinstate the policyholder, but the insurance company does not have to pay for claims that arose during the lapse period.

lateral epicondylitis–A condition commonly known as "tennis elbow," an infection of the lateral side of the distal end of the bone.

liability coverage–A type of protection available in homeowner's insurance or automobile insurance. Not only does it pay the victim's damages when the policyholder is responsible for an accident, but if a lawsuit is filed against the policyholder, liability insurance also pays the cost of the policyholder's defense (lawyers and other expenses) and indemnity (payment for the settlement or judgment).

long-term disability–Coverage that becomes effective after the short-term disability benefits are exhausted; generally covers employees to age sixty-five or through their lives.

lowballing–The practice of offering an unreasonably low payment to settle an insurance claim.

material misrepresentation–A situation that occurs when a policyholder/applicant makes a false statement or omits an important fact on the application. The insurance company may be able to rescind the insurance contract if the policyholder makes a material misrepresentation.

mediation–A private, informal dispute resolution process in which a neutral third person (mediator) helps disputing parties to reach an agreement.

misquote–An incorrect estimate of the insurance premium.

myofascial releases–A release relating to the fascia surrounding and separating muscle tissue.

notice of claim–Notice to the insurance company by a policyholder that he or she is seeking benefits under the policy.

notice of loss–The informing of the insurance company by a policyholder within a specific period of time that a loss has occurred.

own-occupation (own-occ)–In the context of insurance disability policies, the occupation in which the insured was engaged at the time he or she became disabled. If a person is unable to perform his or her normal duties in the usual and customary way and with reasonable continuity, the person is considered disabled from his or her own occupation.

policyholder–The person insured under a policy.

policy surrender–The sale of a policy back to the insurance company, often for much less than it's worth.

policy term–The period in which the policy continues in effect.

premium–The amount of money an insurance company charges for insurance coverage.

prompt notice of the loss–The informing of the insurance company by a policyholder within a specific period of time that a loss has occurred.

quote–An estimate of how much it will cost to provide a specific insurance policy.

radial humeral bursitis–An injury or complication involving the forearm and upper arm.

radiculopathy–A disorder of the spinal nerve roots.

reinstatement–The restoring of a lapsed policy to full force and effect. The reinstatement may be effective after the cancellation date, creating a lapse of coverage. Some companies require evidence of insurability and payment of past premiums due plus interest before they will reinstate a policyholder.

repetitive stress disabilities–A disability resulting from overuse and noted by numbness, chronic pain, weakness, and even depression due to pain.

rescission–A remedy sought by one of the parties to a contract that will allow the party to void the contract or treat it as if it never existed. This remedy is usually sought by the insurance company if a policyholder made misrepresentations of facts on the insurance application. It may be sought even after the policyholder has paid premiums for years.

reservation of rights–The act of an insurance company in which it agrees to defend a liability suit against an insured, but it says that it does not have to pay for any settlement or verdict in the case. This is called a defense with a reservation of rights.

short-term disability–Generally a provision in employer-sponsored group plans covering the first sixty days an employee is unable to work.

Spurling test–A test often used by insurance company doctors to confirm cervical spine (neck) injuries.

stenosis–The narrowing of a passage.

underwriting–The practice of assessing risk before the insurance company agrees to insure someone or something.

unearned premium–The portion of the premium that must be returned to the policyholder when an insurance contract is canceled before the anniversary date of the policy.

waiver–The act of giving up one's legal rights, usually in exchange for some payment or consideration.

NOTES

INTRODUCTION–CORPORATE AMERICA

xiii   GORDON GEKKO CLAIMS: Oliver Stone, dir. *Wall Street*, directed by Oliver Stone (Twentieth Century Fox, 1987).

xiv   IN THE UNITED STATES ALONE, WE SPEND: Center for Medicare and Medicaid Services, "Health Care Spending Reaches $1.6 Trillion in 2002," press release, US. Department of Health and Human Services, January 8, 2004, http://www.cms.gov/newsroom-press-release-health -care-spending-reaches-16trillion-2002.

CHAPTER ONE–FALSE PROFITS

3   A FEW YEARS EARLIER, JOAN HANGARTER: Joan Hangarter, meeting with R. Bourhis, September 1999, San Francisco, CA.

5   THE BABYLONIANS DEVELOPED AN INTERESTING VARIATION: John Hare, "The Omnipotent Warranty: England v the World" (paper presented at the International Marine Insurance Conference, University of Antwerp, November 1999), nn. 4-5.

5   A CATASTROPHIC OCCURRENCE: London Fire and Emergency Planning Authority, "London Fire Brigade," http://www.london-fire.gov.uk /about_us/our_history/key_dates.asp (site discontinued).

6   ONE HUNDRED YEARS LATER: Ben Franklin Busybody, "Benjamin Franklin Facts," http://www.franklinbusybody.com/facts.asp (site discontinued); see also Charles D. Barber, "Historic Insurer to Exit the Business," *Philadelphia Business Journal*, December 15, 2004, http:// philadelphia.bizjournals.com/philadelphia/stories/2004/12/13 /daily19.html.

6   OTTO BISMARCK INSTITUTED A SOCIAL INSURANCE IN GERMANY: Social Security Administration, "Social Security History: Otto van Bismarck," http://www.ssa.gov/history/ottob.html.

7   BETWEEN 1983 AND 1989: Tom Heys, Provident Life & Accident Insurance Company, memo to Harold Chandler, September 29, 1994.

9   ENTER J. HAROLD CHANDLER: "Insurer Won't Instantly Find Replacement CEO," *Chattanooga Times Free Press*, April 10, 2003.

11   "THE . . . SPREAD OF SHAREHOLDING: Senate Committee on Banking, Housing, and Urban Affairs, *Federal Reserve Board's Semiannual Monetary Policy Report to Congress*, testimony of Alan Greenspan,

Federal Reserve Board's Semiannual Monetary Policy Report to Congress, 107th Cong., 2d sess., July 16, 2002.

11 IN THE CASE OF ENRON: Frank Rich, "The Two-Enron System," Opinion, *New York Times*, February 16, 2002.

12 THOUGH MODERN CHIROPRACTIC: American Chiropractic Association, "History of Chiropractic Care," http://www.amerchiro.org/media /whatis/history_chiro.shtml (site discontinued).

12 TODAY, AN ESTIMATED THIRTY-FIVE MILLION PEOPLE: American Chropractic Association, "The Chiropractic Profession: Key Facts and Figures," 2019, http://www.acatoday.org/portals/60/About/Key_Facts_ Figures_2019.pdf

13 DESPITE BEING PUT IN CHARGE: *Hangarter v. Provident Life and Accident Ins. Co.*, 373 F.3d 998 (9th Cir. 2004), trial transcript vol. 7, pp. 1170-1171.

14 AS A RESULT OF THE PROFITABILITY: Peter R. Donker, "Revere Merger May Cost 400 Jobs," *Worcester Telegram and Gazette,* December 12, 1996, sec. B.

14 BY 1999 IT WOULD GOBBLE UP UNUM: "Unum, Provident Merger Approved," *Journal of Commerce*, July 6, 1999.

CHAPTER TWO–LICENSED TO STEAL

15 "THE PROCEDURES ARE VERY SPECIFIC": *Hangarter v. Provident Life and Accident Ins. Co.*, vol. 3, p. 390.

16 "SOMETIMES," SHE SAID: *Hangarter v. Provident Life and Accident Ins. Co.*, vol. 3, p. 446.

16 "THEY WORKED ON MY NECK . . .": *Hangarter v. Provident Life and Accident Ins. Co.*, vol. 3, pp. 422-423.

17 J. HAROLD CHANDLER HAILED THE MOVE: Business Wire, "UnumProvident Merger Final: Merger Is Consummated Following Shareholder Votes Today," June 30, 1999; BestWire, "Unum, Provident Complete Merger," July 1, 1999. http://www.apdigitalnews.com /bestwire.html (site discontinued).

18 PROVIDENT, SEAMAN SAID: *Joan Hangarter v. Provident Life & Accident Ins. Co. et al.*, 236 F. Supp. 2d 1069 (2002), deposition of Joan Hangarter, pp. 278-280, June 6, 2001; trial transcript vol. 9, pp. 1600-1606, 1638-1642, and 1655-1658.

18 DR. SUGARMAN DEFAULTED ON HIS NOTE: *Hangarter v. Provident Life and Accident Ins. Co.*, deposition of Joan Hangarter, pp. 213-220, June 6, 2001; trial transcript vol. 3, pp. 448-449 and 454.

18 THEN WEXLER BECAME PHYSICALLY ABUSIVE: *Hangarter v. Provident Life and Accident Ins. Co.*, vol. 3, p. 456.

18 THERE SHE, AS SHE PUT IT: *Hangarter v. Provident Life and Accident Ins. Co.*, vol. 3, p. 457.

20   IN 1945, AS A RESULT OF INSURANCE INDUSTRY "URGING": *McCarran-Ferguson Act*, 15 U.S.C.S. § 1011 et seq. (1945).

22   WHEN CALIFORNIA'S PROPOSITION 103: California Department of Insurance, "Proposition 103 Fact Sheet," http://www.insurance.ca.gov/docs/Factsheet/Prop_103_Fact_Sheet.html (site discontinued).

22   THE WHISTLE ON QUACKENBUSH WAS BLOWN: B. Drummund Ayers Jr., "Scandal Involving Earthquake Victims Hits California Insurance Commissioner's Office," *New York Times*, June 18, 2000.

23   INSTEAD OF FINISHING UP HIS TERM: Todd S. Purdum, "Investigation Leads Official to Step Down in California," *New York Times*, June 29, 2000.

24   IN AN OPINION WRITTEN IN THE CASE: *Pilot Life Ins. Co. v. Dedeaux*, 481 U.S. 41, 107 S. Ct. 1549 (1987).

CHAPTER THREE–SO SUE ME

30   SULLIVAN DEPOSITION: *Joan Hangarter v. Provident Life & Accident Ins. Co. et al.*, deposition of Joseph F. Sullivan, pp. 38-39, 51, 73, 119-122, 124, 138, 140, 146, 172, 201, 205, 213, 215-220, 229, 236-240, and 327, April 25, 2001.

35   FRYC TESTIMONY: *Joan Hangarter v. Provident Life & Accident Ins. Co. et al.*, vol. 6, pp. 929-1021, January 25, 2002.

36   BIANCHI DEPOSITION: *Joan Hangarter v. Provident Life & Accident Ins. Co. et al.*, deposition of John L. Bianchi, MD, pp. 4-6, 13-15, 22, 55-56, 148-149, and 153-154, April 26, 2001.

38   RYAN DEPOSITION: *Joan Hangarter v. Provident Life & Accident Ins. Co. et al.*, deposition of Christopher Ryan, pp. 50, 60, and 68, April 26, 2001.

41   "YOU KNOW, LORI,": Lori Bernard, private conversation with R. Bourhis, June 6, 2001.

41   THE JOB ENTAILED ACCURATELY TRANSCRIBING COURT PROCEEDINGS: California Business and Professions Code §8020; *McGregor v. Paul Revere Life Ins. Co. et al.*, 369 F.3d 1099 (2004), trial transcript vol. 7, p. 1183.

42   CHIANTELLI SAID THAT SHE WAS THE BEST COURT: *McGregor v. Paul Revere Life Ins. Co. et al.*, vol. 5, pp. 773-774.

42   IT WAS ONLY AFTER SUSAN'S LAWSUIT: *McGregor v. Paul Revere Life Ins. Co. et al.*, vol. 7, pp. 1133-1136.

44   UNUMPROVIDENT STARTED OUT BY SIMPLY: Attorneys' correspondence in *McGregor v. Paul Revere Life Ins. Co. et al.* between Francis J. Torrence and Eric R. McDonough for the Defendant and Raymond Bourhis, Alice J. Wolfson, and Margo Barg for the Plaintiff.

44   RUBENSTEIN TESTIMONY: *McGregor v. Paul Revere Life Ins. Co. et al.*, vol. 10, pp. 1953-1957 and 2000-2004.

46   "AND HE NEVER GAVE IT TO YOU BEFORE?": *McGregor v. Paul Revere Life Ins. Co. et al.*, vol. 10, pp. 1953-1957 and 2000-2004.

1999. deposition of Dr. William Feist, pp. 9-12, 25, 50, 98-100, 124-125, 131, 147-148, 152-153, 156-157, 183-194, and 457-458.

CHAPTER NINE–CUSTOMER CARE

115   FRYC TESTIMONY: *Joan Hangarter v. Provident Life & Accident Ins. Co. et al.*, vol. 6, pp. 929-1021, January 25, 2002.

117   COREY TESTIMONY: *Joan Hangarter v. Provident Life & Accident Ins. Co. et al.*, vol. 6, pp. 1029 and 1051-1053, January 25, 2002.

118   PEYMANI TESTIMONY: *Joan Hangarter v. Provident Life & Accident Ins. Co. et al.*, vol. 6, pp. 1086-1127, January 25, 2002.

122   MOHNEY TESTIMONY: *Joan Hangarter v. Provident Life & Accident Ins. Co. et al.*, vol. 7, pp. 1140-1141, 1143-1144, 1146-1147, 1150-1152, 1158, 1160, 1162, 1163-1166, 1168-1169, 1171-1173, 1176, 1178-1179, 1199-1201, 1212-1214, and 1215-1220, January 28, 2002.

123   DR. STUART GLUCK, A WONDERFUL: *Gluck v. Provident Life and Accident Ins. Co.*, Superior Court of California, San Francisco County, Case No. 323492, August 6, 2001.

124   AS OF THAT DATE, UNUMPROVIDENT WAS AWARE: Gluck's medications included Serostim, Deca Durabolin, Ritonivir, Fortovase, Zerit, Serzone, Neurontin, Diflucan, Ethambutol, Bactrim, Zithromax, Lomotil, Oxandrin, Nandrolone, Valium, Benadryl, and Somatropin.

133   SULLIVAN TESTIMONY: *Joan Hangarter v. Provident Life & Accident Ins. Co. et al.*, vol. 7-8, pp. 1224-1227, 1230-1231, 1335, 1346, and 1450, January 28-29, 2002.

135   SWARTZ TESTIMONY: *Joan Hangarter v. Provident Life & Accident Ins. Co. et al.*, vol. 9, pp. 1598, 1611-1612, 1614-1620, 1634-1635, 1647-1649, 1652, 1658-1661, and 1669-1671, January 30, 2002.

CHAPTER TEN–FACT OR FICTION

140   BISHOFF TESTIMONY: *Joan Hangarter v. Provident Life & Accident Ins. Co. et al.*, vol. 7, pp. 1409, 1418-1419, 1421-1426, 1428-1440, and 1442-1443, January 28, 2002

145   "CALL ME BACK IN THIRTY MINUTES": Edward Katz, private conversation with R. Bourhis, January 29, 2002.

146   KATZ REBUTTAL: *Joan Hangarter v. Provident Life & Accident Ins. Co. et al.*, vol. 9, pp. 1692-1695 and 1697-1698, January 30, 2002.

149   WE NEED FOOD AS WELL AS LIGHT BULBS: Joan Hangarter, "It's Tough to Be Poor, Even Tougher in Marin," *San Francisco Examiner*, December 19, 2001.

150   HANGARTER REBUTTAL: *Joan Hangarter v. Provident Life & Accident Ins. Co. et al.*, vol. 9, pp. 1730-1732, January 30, 2002.

CHAPTER ELEVEN–SOME WITH A FOUNTAIN PEN

CHAPTER TWELVE–A MESSAGE

CHAPTER THIRTEEN–LIAR'S DICE

CHAPTER FOURTEEN–FRIENDS IN HIGH PLACES

187 BIG EXEMPLARY DAMAGE AWARDS: *State Farm Mutual Automobile Ins. Co. v Campbell*, 538 U.S. 408, 123 S. Ct. 1513 (2003).

189 "THE BUSH ADMINISTRATION," IT SAID: Robin Toner and Robert Pear, "Bush Proposes Major Changes in Health Plans," *New York Times*, February 24, 2003.

189 NOT LONG BEFORE THESE CHANGES WERE PROPOSED: Federal News Service, *Hearing of the Social Security Subcommittee of the House and Ways and Means Committee*, July 11, 2002.

190 MOREOVER, THE DEFROCKED CHANDLER: "Week in Review," *Portland Press Herald* (Maine), April 6, 2003.

190 BUT THE INSIGHT CAME FROM A DIFFERENT SOURCE: Mike Pare, "UnumProvident Will Pay CEO under Old Agreement," *Chattanooga Times Free Press*, October 1, 2003.

190 ON THAT BASIS, WE FILED AN ORDER TO SHOW CAUSE: *Hangarter v. Paul Revere Life Ins. Co. et al.*, Order to Show Cause, U.S. District Ct., N. District of CA, 2003. *Hangarter v. Paul Revere Life Ins. Co. et al.*, 289 F. Supp. 2d 1105, N.D. Cal., 2003.

194 POLITICAL ANALYST DICK TUCK: Dick Tuck, personal communication with R. Bourhis, 1990, Malibu, CA.

CHAPTER FIFTEEN–KICK IN THE ASSETS

195 THE FIRST RULING CAME IN MCGREGOR: *McGregor v. Paul Revere Life Ins. Co.*; Procter Hug Jr., Senior Circuit Judge; Betty Binns Fletcher, Senior Circuit Judge; A. Wallace Tashima, Senior Circuit Judge.

195 A FEW MONTHS LATER: *Hangarter v. Provident Life and Accident Ins. Co.*; Alfred T. Goodwin, Senior Circuit Judge; A. Wallace Tashima, Senior Circuit Judge; Richard R. Clifton, Circuit Judge.

196 FELDMAN'S OFFICE HAD COLLECTED HUNDREDS OF MILLIONS OF DOLLARS:Vytenis Didziulis, "U.S. Insurance Scandal's Effect Spreading," United Press International, October 22, 2004; Senate Governmental Affairs Committee, Subcommitee on Financial Management for the Budget and International Security, *Insurance Broker and Regulation Practices*, testimony of Eliot Spitzer, 108th Cong., 2d sess., November 16, 2004.

197 ON NOVEMBER 18, 2004: Roberto Ceniceros, "UnumProvident's Problems Not Solved with Settlement," *Business Insurance*, December 6, 2004.

197 THIRD, AN "AGREED TO" FINE: Fair Disclosure Wire, "Event Brief of UnumProvident Conference Call to Announce Settlement of Multistate Market Conduct Examination–Final," November 19, 2004.

198 JOSEPH BELTH, PROFESSOR EMERITUS: Joseph Belth, letter to Eliot Spitzer, *The Insurance Forum*, November 22, 2004.

198   FORMER FEDERAL PROSECUTOR GENE ANDERSON: Eugene Anderson, letter to author and various state departments of insurance, November 29, 2004.

199   CITING CONCERNS WITH OVERSIGHT: John Garamendi, letter to J. David Leslie, December 17, 2004.

CHAPTER SIXTEEN–BACK TO THE FUTURE

202   ALL OF THIS CONFIRMED: Marvin Lewis, personal communication with R. Bourhis, 1980, San Francisco.

BIBLIOGRAPHY

American Chiropractic Association. "History of Chiropractic Care." http://www.amerchiro.org/media/whatis/history_chiro.shtml (site discontinued).

Anderson, Eugene. Letter to author and various state departments of insurance, November 29, 2004.

Ayers, B. Drummond, Jr. "Scandal Involving Earthquake Victims Hits California Insurance Commissioner's Office." *New York Times*, June 18, 2000.

Barber, Charles D. "Historic Insurer to Exit the Business." *Philadelphia Business Journal*, December 15, 2004. http://philadelphia.bizjournals.com/philadelphia/stories/2004/12/13/daily19.html.

Belth, Joseph. Letter to Eliot Spitzer. *The Insurance Forum*, November 22, 2004.

Ben Franklin Busybody. "Benjamin Franklin Facts." http://www.franklinbusybody.com/facts.asp (site discontinued).

BestWire. "Unum, Provident Complete Merger." July 1, 1999, http://www.apdigitalnews.com/bestwire.html (site discontinued).

Bradley, Ed. "Did Insurer Cheat Disabled Clients?" *60 Minutes*, November 21, 2002.

Business Wire. "UnumProvident Merger Final: Merger Is Consummated Following Shareholder Votes Today." June 30, 1999.

California Business and Professions Code §8020.

California Department of Insurance. "Proposition 103 Fact Sheet." http://www.insurance.ca.gov/docs/Factsheet/Prop_103_Fact_Sheet.html (site discontinued).

Ceniceros, Roberto. "UnumProvident's Problems Not Solved with Settlement." *Business Insurance*, December 6, 2004.

Center for Medicare and Medicaid Services. "Health Care Spending Reaches $1.6 Trillion in 2002." Press release, US Department of Health and Human Services, January 8, 2004. http://www.cms.gov/newsroom-press-releases-health-care-spending-reaches-16-trillion-2002.

Collins, Chris. KCBS Radio, February 5, 2002.

Coulter, Ian B., et al. "Chiropractic in the United States: Training, Practice, and Research." Niagara Chiropractic Society, http://www.neschiropractic.com/ahepr/part4.htm (site discontinued).

Didzius, Vytenis. "U.S. Insurance Scandal's Effect Spreading." United Press International. October 22, 2004.

Donker, Peter R. "Revere Merger May Cost 400 Jobs." *Worcester Telegram and Gazette,* December 12, 1996, sec. B.

Editorial. "From Welfare to Windfall," *San Francisco Examiner,* February 6, 2002.

Fair Disclosure Wire. "Event Brief of UnumProvident Conference Call to Announce Settlement of Multistate Market Conduct Examination–Final." November 19, 2004.

Federal News Service. *Hearing of the Social Security Subcommittee of the House and Ways and Means Committee.* July 11, 2002.

Garamendi, John. Letter to J. David Leslie, December 17, 2004.

Girion, Lisa. "Insurer's Tactics Rebuked." *Los Angeles Times,* November 15, 2002.

Gluck v. Provident Life and Accident Ins. Co., Superior Court of California, San Francisco County, Case No. 323492, August 6, 2001.

Hangarter, Joan. "It's Tough to Be Poor, Even Tougher in Marin." *San Francisco Examiner,* December 19, 2001.

Hangarter v. Paul Revere Life Ins. Co. et al. Order to Show Cause, U.S. District Ct., N. District of CA, 2003.

Hangarter v. Provident Life and Accident Ins. Co. 373 F.3d 998 (9th Cir. 2004). Depositions of Joan Hangarter (June 6, 2001) and Ralph Mohney (August 22, 2001). Trial transcript vol. 3, 6, 7.

Hare, John. "The Omnipotent Warranty: England v the World." Paper presented at the International Marine Insurance Conference, University of Antwerp, November 1999, http://www.oralchelation.com/calcium/DegenerativeKneeJoint/p101.htm.

Hays, Tom. Provident Life & Accident Insurance Company. Memo to Harold Chandler, September 29, 1994.

Hoppin, Jason. "More Heat for Insurer on Hot Seat." *Recorder,* November 15, 2002.

"Insurer Won't Instantly Find Replacement CEO." *Chattanooga Times Free Press,* April 10, 2003.

Joan Hangarter v. Provident Life & Accident Ins. Co. et al. 236 F. Supp. 2d 1069 (2002). Depositions of Joseph F. Sullivan (April 25, 2001), John L. Bianchi (April 26, 2001), Christopher Ryan (April 26, 2001), and Joan Hangarter (June 6, 2001). Trial transcript vol. 1-4 and 6-10.

Larson, John. "Benefit of the Doubt." *Dateline,* October 13, 2002.

London Fire and Emergency Planning Authority. "London Fire Brigade." http://www.london-fire.gov.uk/about_us/our_history/key_dates.asp (site discontinued).

Lumet, Sydney, dir. *Network.* 1976: Warner Studios.

McCarran-Ferguson Act. 15 U.S.C.S. § 1011 et seq. (1945).

McGregor v. Paul Revere Life Ins. Co. et al. 369 F.3d 1099 (2004). Trial transcript vol. 5, 7, and 10.

McGregor v. Paul Revere Life Ins. Co. et al. 369 F.3d 1099 (2004). Attorneys' correspondence between Francis J. Torrence and Eric R. McDonough for the

Defendant and Raymond Bourhis, Alice J. Wolfson, and Margo Barg for the Plaintiff.

McGregor v. Paul Revere Life Ins. Co. et al., 369 F.3rd 1099 (2004), 2004 WL 68692 (9th Cir. (Cal.)).

Murphy, Edward D. "Unum Goes on Offensive: UnumProvident Begins a PR Campaign over a '60 Minutes' Segment That It Calls a 'Misrepresentation of the Facts.'" *Portland Press Herald* (Maine), October 3, 2002.

Nixon Peabody LLP, http://www.nixonpeabody.com/linked_media/publications /CAA_11112003.pdf (site discontinued).

Pare, Mike. "UnumProvident Will Pay CEO under Old Agreement." *Chattanooga Times Free Press*, October 1, 2003, sec. C.

Pilot Life Ins. Co. v. Dedeaux. 481 U.S. 41, 107 S. Ct. 1549 (1987).

Purdum, Todd S. "Investigation Leads Official to Step Down in California." *New York Times*, June 29, 2000.

Ramblin' Jack Elliot. "Pretty Boy Floyd." *Jack Elliot Sings the Songs of Woody Guthrie.* Fantasy Records, compact disc. Originally released in 1960.

Rich, Frank. "The Two-Enron System." Opinion. *New York Times*, February 16, 2002.

Said, Carolyn. "Disability Insurer Is under Fire, Legitimate Claims Denied, Suit Says." *San Francisco Chronicle*, October 6, 2002.

Social Security Administration. "Social Security History: Otto van Bismarck." http://www.ssa.gov/history/ottob.html.

State Farm Mutual Automobile Ins. Co. v Campbell. 538 U.S. 408, 123 S. Ct. 1513 (2003).

Stone, Oliver, dir. *Wall Street.* Written by Stanley Weiser and Oliver Stone. Twentieth Century Fox, 1987.

Toner, Robin, and Robert Pear. "Bush Proposes Major Changes in Health Plans." *New York Times*, February 24, 2003.

United Policyholders, Wesley Evans, and Dr. Joseph Ellis v. Provident Life & Accident Ins. Co., Baybrook Medical Group, Inc., and UnumProvident Corp., case number 815688-2, November 19, 1999. Deposition of Dr. William Feist, pp. 9-12, 25, 50, 98-100, 124-125, 131, 147-148, 152-153, 156-157, 183-194, 457-458.

"Unum, Provident Merger Approved." *Journal of Commerce*, July 6, 1999.

U.S. Congress. Senate. Committee on Banking, Housing, and Urban Affairs. *Federal Reserve Board's Semiannual Monetary Policy Report to Congress.* Testimony of Alan Greenspan. 107th Cong., 2d. sess. July 16, 2002.

U.S. Congress. Senate. Governmental Affairs Committee, Subcommittee on Financial Management for the Budget and International Security. *Insurance Broker and Regulation Practices.* Testimony of Eliot Spitzer. 108th Cong., 2d sess. November 16, 2004.

"Week in Review." *Portland Press Herald* (Maine), April 6, 2003.

FURTHER READING

CHAPTER ONE

Dawson, William Harbutt. *Bismarck and State Socialism: An Exposition of the Social and Economic Legislation of Germany since 1870.* London: S. Sonnenschien, 1891.

Egan v. Mutual Of Omaha Ins. Co., et al 24 Cal. 3d 809 (1979).

Hanson, Neil, *The Great Fire of London: In That Apocalyptic Year, 1666.* Hoboken, NJ: John Wiley & Sons, 2002.

Homer, Sidney, and Richard Sylla. *A History of Interest Rates.* 3rd ed. New Brunswick, NJ: Rutgers University Press, 1996.

Insurance Education Foundation. http://uipi.org/2001/resources/history.htm (site discontinued).

Jerry, Robert H., II. *Understanding Insurance Law.* 3rd ed. LexisNexis, 2002.

Moore v. American United Life Ins. Co. 150 Cal. App. 3d 610 (1984).

Pearson, Robin. "Mutuality Tested: The Rise and Fall of Mutual Fire Insurance Offices in Eighteenth-Century London." *Business History* 44, no. 4 (October 1, 2002).

CHAPTER TWO

Cohen, Michael. "No Faith in Bad Faith" *Hastings Law Journal* 41, no. 201 (1990).

Law, Sylvia J. "Do We Still Need a Federal Patients' Bill of Rights?" *Yale Journal of Health Policy, Law, and Ethics* 3, no. 1 (2003).

Panko, Ron. "Moving On: Several Former Insurance Commissioners Have Parlayed Their Experience into New Opportunities; Industry Strategies." *Best's Review* 102, no. 11 (March 1, 2002): 36.

Paredes, Troy. "Stop-Loss Insurance, State Regulation, and ERISA: Defining the Scope of Federal Preemption," *Harvard Journal on Legislation* 34 (1997): 233.

US Newswire. "Consumer Groups, Insurance Commissioner Denounce Federal Attack on California's Landmark Insurance Reform Prop 103." March 31, 2004.

CHAPTER FIVE

Kressel, Neil J., and Dorit F. Kressel. *Stack and Sway: The New Science of Jury Consulting.* New York: Westview Press, 2001.

CHAPTER NINE

Cole, Lance. "Revoking Our Privileges: Federal Law Enforcement's Multi-Front Assault on the Attorney-Client Privilege (And Why It Is Misguided)" *Villanova Law Review* 48, no. 469 (2003).

Hatfield, Christine. "The Privilege Doctrines: Are They Just Another Discovery Tool Utilized by the Tobacco Industry to Conceal Damaging Information?" *Pace Law Review* 16, no. 525 (1996).

Plitt, Steven. "The Elastic Contours of Attorney-Client Privilege and Waiver in the Context of Insurance Company Bad Faith: There's a Chill in the Air." *Seton Hall Law Review* 34, no. 513 (2004).

CHAPTER THIRTEEN

Best's News. "Unum Posts First-Quarter Loss, Says It's Restructuring." April 25, 2003.

Pare, Mike. "Insurer Launches Ad Blitz, UnumProvident Stresses Positives." *Chattanooga Times Free Press*, June 5, 2003.

Pare, Mike. "Insurer Seeks Chief, Fresh Capital Despite Chandler's Ouster, His Plan Remains Strategy for UnumProvident." *Chattanooga Times Free Press*, April 1, 2003.

CHAPTER FOURTEEN

Belluck, Pam. "Governors Unite in Fight Against Medicaid Cuts." *New York Times*, National Desk, December 26, 2004.

Capitol Hill Hearing Testimony Senate Governmental Affairs Insurance Brokerage and Regulation Practices; Testimony of Eliot Spitzer November 16, 2004.

Kelleher, Ellen. "Settlement Lifts Shares in Unum." *London Financial Times*, March 26, 2003.

Pear, Robert. "A Watchdog Sees Flaws in Bush Ads on Medicare." *New York Times*, March 11, 2004.

GENERAL READING

Bakan, Joel. *The Corporation: The Pathological Pursuit of Profit and Power*. New York: Free Press, 2004.

Bebchuk, Lucian and Jesse Fried. *Pay without Performance: The Unfulfilled Promise of Executive Compensation*. Cambridge, MA: Harvard University Press, 2004.

Glasbeek, Harry. *Wealth By Stealth: Corporate Crime, Corporate Law, and the Perversion of Democracy*. Toronto: Between the Lines, 2003.

Greider, William. *The Soul of Capitalism: Opening Paths to a Moral Economy*. New York: Simon and Schuster, 2003.

Grieder, William. *Who Will Tell the People? The Betrayal of American Democracy.* New York: Simon and Schuster, 1993.

Huffington, Arianna. *Pigs at the Trough: How Corporate Greed and Political Corruption Are Undermining America.* New York: Crown Books, 2003.

Jeter, Lynne W. *Disconnected: Deceit and Betrayal at WorldCom.* 1st ed. Hoboken, NJ: Wiley, 2003.

Krugman, Paul. *The Great Unraveling: Losing Our Way in the New Century.* New York: W. W. Norton, 2003.

Marchand, Roland. *Creating the Corporate Soul: The Rise of Public Relations and Corporate Imagery in American Big Business.* Berkeley: University of California Press, 2001.

Mitchell, Lawrence E. *Corporate Irresponsibility: America's Newest Export.* New Haven: Yale University Press, 2001.

Monks, Robert A. G. and Nell Minow. *Corporate Governance.* 3rd ed. Oxford: Blackwell Publishers, 2004.

Moore, Michael. *Dude, Where's My Country?* New York: Warner Books, 2003.

Moore, Michael. *Stupid White Men . . . And Other Sorry Excuses for the State of the Nation!* New York: Regan Books, 2002.

Myers, Kenneth D. *False Security: Greed and Deception in America's Multibillion-Dollar Insurance Industry.* Amherst, NY: Prometheus Books, 1995.

O'Sullivan, Julie R. *Federal White Collar Crime: Cases and Materials.* Fagan, MN: West Group, 2003.

Rosoff, Stephen M., Henry N. Pontell, and Robert H. Tillman. *Profit without Honor: White-Collar Crime and the Looting of America.* 3rd ed. New York: Prentice Hall, 2003.

Salinger, Lawrence M., ed. *Encyclopedia of White-Collar and Corporate Crime.* London: Sage Publications, 2004.

Schwartz, Mimi and Sherron Watkins. *Power Failure: The Inside Story of the Enron Collapse.* 1st ed. New York: Doubleday, 2003.

Shover, Neal and John Paul Wright, eds. *Crimes of Privilege: Readings in White-Collar Crime.* New York: Oxford University Press, 2000.

Tillman, Robert. *Global Pirates: Fraud in the Offshore Insurance Industry.* Boston: Northeastern University Press, 2001.

Weaver, Paul H. *The Suicidal Corporation.* New York: Touchstone Books, 1989.

Welling, Bruce. *Corporate Law in Canada: The Governing Principles.* 2nd ed. Ontario: Butterworths, 1991.

INDEX

Trager, Evan, 167
transcripts, court, 41-42
trial preparation, 77
Tuck, Dick, 194

unfair insurance practices acts, 21
Unum Life Insurance Company, 7
UnumProvident, 19, 25
US Supreme Court decisions. *See*
    legislation
USA Today, 184

verdicts, 114, 163-166, 166-170
voir dire questioning, 66. *See also*
    juries/jurors

Wall Street Journal, 19, 184
Wang, Christopher, 167
Watjen, Tom, 130, 189
Watterman, Frank, 162
Wexler, Bruce, 18, 19, 96, 1112
White, Tom, 175
witnesses, 80, 81-82
Wolfson, Alice, 19, 64, 82-83, 186
work-product privilege, 139
Wright, Rosemary, 177-178

ABOUT THE AUTHORS

R AY BOURHIS IS A PARTNER WITH THE BOURHIS LAW GROUP IN SAN Francisco. He is the founder of InsuranceConsumers.com and the author of numerous books and articles on long-term disability insurance law. He was appointed by the California Superior Court to oversee reforms in the California Department of Insurance and by Senator Barbara Boxer to serve on her Federal Judicial Selection Advisory Committee.

Ray is a graduate of the Ohio State University and the UC Berkeley School of Law. His cases have been profiled by *60 Minutes*, *Dateline,* the *Wall Street Journal, USA Today* and other national media. The father of four grown children, he lives in Belvedere and Santa Barbara, California.

∧ ∨ ∧ ∨ ∧

MATTHEW BOURHIS IS A PARTNER WITH THE BOURHIS LAW GROUP IN San Francisco specializing in long-term disability and bad-faith insurance matters. He also contributes pro bono insurance-related legal assistance to California disaster victims and to low-income individuals who have suffered catastrophic fire, flood, and earth movement losses.

Matthew earned his bachelor's degree from Boston University and his juris doctor from the UC Davis School of Law. In 2015, he served Judge Alfred Chiantelli at ADR Services in mediation matters. He went on to work with the California Supreme Court on habeas corpus petitions in death penalty cases and served in the chambers of Justice Martin J. Jenkins in the California Court of Appeal. He lives in San Francisco, California.